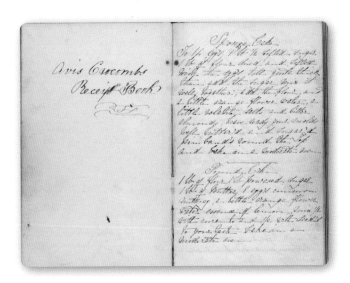

HOW TO COOK
THE VICTORIAN WAY
with MRS CROCOMBE

HOW TO COOK
THE VICTORIAN WAY
with MRS CROCOMBE

Annie Gray and Andrew Hann

ENGLISH HERITAGE

ENGLISH HERITAGE

EDITOR Katherine Davey
CONSULTANT EDITOR Rebecca Seal
DESIGNER Andrew Barron @ thextension
PRINCIPAL PHOTOGRAPHY Abi Bansal
HISTORICAL DEVELOPMENT CHEFS Miranda Godfrey and Ian Sutton
FOOD STYLIST Sophie Wright

PICTURE CREDITS
Portrait photographs on pages 146, 151 and 200 are courtesy of www.EliotsofPortEliot.com.
Photograph top right page 73 is courtesy of the collection of Stan and Sarah Casbolt.
All other photographs are copyright of Historic England.

1 3 5 7 9 10 8 6 4 2

First published in 2020 by English Heritage

British Library Cataloguing in Publication Data.
A catalogue record for this book is available from the British Library.

Printed in England by Page Bros, Norwich

ISBN 978-1-910907-42-9

END PAPERS Copies of the end papers in Avis Crocombe's manuscript.
TITLE PAGE The opening pages of Avis Crocombe's manuscript.
PAGE 2 Audley End kitchen.
FACING PAGE Kathy Hipperson as Avis Crocombe in the kitchen.

Contents

Mrs Crocombe:
My Great Great Aunt

by Bob Stride

To think I was going to throw this book in the bin. The original handwritten receipt book had first come to my attention in 1981, but the story really started with Avis Crocombe in the late 19th century.

Avis was cook to Lord and Lady Braybrooke at Audley End in the 1880s. She kept a notebook of recipes, which she had probably brought with her from her previous position of cook–housekeeper in Norfolk. In 1884 Avis married Benjamin Stride, a butler, whom she must have met in London when she was with the Braybrookes at their town house on Hanover Square. On her marriage she left service to become a lodging-house keeper in Marylebone in north London, taking her receipt book with her. Benjamin died in 1893 and Avis in 1927.

My grandfather, Daniel Stride, was one of Benjamin's nephews. In the early 1890s he joined the Metropolitan Police Force, and it's likely that as the only family member living in London, Daniel saw to the affairs of his uncle and step-aunt after their deaths, and so came into the possession of Avis' receipt book. When my grandfather died in 1949 he was living with his daughter, my aunt Elsie, in London. His possessions were left with her, including the book, which then went with Elsie when she married and moved to Staffordshire.

In 1981 my aunt Elsie moved into a care home. As the only young member of the family, I helped sort out her things and so acquired various family mementos, including the book, which I put away in a tea chest in the attic. It stayed there until 2009, when, clearing out the attic, my wife and I came across it again. We were on the point of putting it in the rubbish when, looking at the opening page with its

Bob Stride and Kathy Hipperson with the manuscript at Audley End in 2009.

pencil notes, written perhaps by my grandfather, we thought again. The notes told us that the book had been kept by Avis, who had worked at Langley Park in Norfolk and Audley End in Essex. We decided to contact Audley End to ask if they would be interested to see it. It was a surprise a few days later when there was a call from English Heritage to say that they would be very interested indeed.

Which is how we came to bring the book with us to Audley End when we visited that August. The most amazing thing was that just the previous year, the service wing had been completely refurbished with displays set to depict life at Audley in the 1880s, and English Heritage, knowing from its records that Avis had been cook at that time, had historical interpreters – among them Kathy Hipperson – already playing Avis and her colleagues during live events at the house.

Giving the manuscript to Audley End meant that the historical actors could prepare recipes Avis actually wrote in her book, rather than more general dishes from the Victorian era, as they had been doing. Since then the receipt book has featured in newspapers and magazines, as well as the BBC programme *Britain's Hidden Heritage*, while the numbers following the cooking videos on YouTube have escalated.

And now a book! – it's overwhelming.

Introduction

by Annie Gray

Welcome to the world of Avis Crocombe. This book wouldn't exist without the many millions of YouTube fans who watch and comment on English Heritage's *The Victorian Way* videos and whose enthusiasm really has shaped it.

I am a food historian, specialising in the years between 1650 and 1950, and I led the live interpretation team in the service wing at Audley End House from its launch in 2008 until 2013, also appearing in character as the first kitchen maid. I remain an adviser on the videos.

Avis Crocombe's original manuscript recipe book is a wonderful thing to work from: a slightly worn hardback, full of brief lists of ingredients and hastily copied out recipes from the course of her career, including her time as cook in the 1880s to Charles Neville, 5th Lord Braybrooke, and his wife, Florence, of Audley End House. It is a working cook's book, never intended for publication, and there are repetitions as well as omissions. Avis was probably filling in the gaps left by the printed books she had access to, as well as noting down anything particularly good and her employers' favourites. It is a rare historical treasure to work from, but isn't a fully formed recipe book (there are very few vegetable dishes – though this is unsurprising, given most Victorian vegetables were simply boiled and served with a buttery sauce – no fish dishes, and few for meat). However, someone must have very much liked ginger beer, for she wrote down three versions of that, along with three orange marmalades and three types of short-bread. Her book is one of sweet treats and endless biscuits.

Victorian food could be fantastic – I am a huge fan of Victorian cookery and share with Queen Victoria a love of ten-year-old mutton. We'd be selling it short if this book did not include recipes from the

 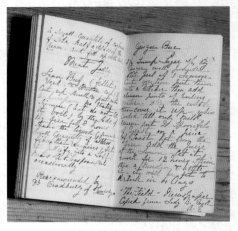

wider world of Victorian cuisine, from beyond Avis' collection, that she would almost certainly have cooked. This is, therefore, a collection of Victorian recipes, lightly modernised for the 21st-century kitchen (most people today probably don't have a roasting spit).

Mrs Crocombe's recipe book, which she kept over the course of her career.

It was an era of immense culinary innovation, when many of the dishes now regarded as part of the classic British repertoire were developed. The costumed team at Audley End were cooking Victorian recipes before Avis' manuscript was donated by Bob Stride, and the YouTube videos which emerged from their work also cover a broader range of dishes than Avis had collected. From the kitchen garden at Audley End, Avis would have had access to an enormous variety of fresh produce, and the wider estate provided both farmed meat and game. The Victorians regularly cooked with ingredients which have virtually disappeared today, and were ferocious fruit and vegetable breeders.

The recipes here remain resolutely Victorian in character, but I'd encourage you to experiment freely – after all, that's exactly what Avis would have done. Many are taken from her manuscript (we've selected the best … so you are spared the candied lettuce). Others are from books we know she had access to, or favourites of Kathy and the team in the kitchens of Audley End. A few were once based on a Victorian source but, through ten years of regular cooking at Audley, have evolved into distinct recipes of their own. We've included all the dishes featured on YouTube: enough to build a Victorian meal.

If that's not sufficient Avis, then at the back you will find a full transcription of her original book, with commentary (look out for the roasted swan). You'll also find a full bibliography, so you can immerse yourselves in Avis Crocombe's world even more.

Bringing Mrs Crocombe to Life

by Kathy Hipperson

I have been portraying Mrs Crocombe at Audley End House, where she lived and worked in the 1880s, since 2008. I am a historical interpreter and what I love about my job is that it gives visitors to Audley End the chance to see an extraordinary project – one wholly focused on recreating the kitchens, clothing and methods of one particular servant from history.

'Historical interpreter' is the term given to those who dress up in historically accurate costumes, play a specific character from history, and perform in the first person to educate and bring history to life for a modern audience. It is usually easier to portray kings and queens, or characters whose lives can be researched in detail, but it is more

difficult with lower-status characters, as less was written about them. Avis Crocombe is a prime example: a servant in Queen Victoria's time when servants were barely noticed, let alone recorded beyond the census. When Mrs Crocombe's great, great, step-nephew, Mr Stride, donated her hand-written recipe book it added an exciting layer to this unique experience for the visitor. And for me, seeing her handwriting for the first time, on pages she had touched, in a notebook she must have treasured, is something I will never forget.

What makes the interpretation at Audley End so wonderful is that I get to work in surroundings so appropriate to Mrs Crocombe, thanks to the pains-taking restoration of the kitchens by English Heritage. I wear clothing created by Past Pleasures Ltd based

on their detailed research of original items of costume, and I prepare recipes lovingly researched by Dr Annie Gray. In 2015 the first of the videos of Mrs Crocombe at work was posted onto English Heritage's YouTube channel, taking her and her recipes to a wider audience. Mrs Crocombe was unusual for her time, in that she was a female head cook working for a baron, when members of the aristocracy would usually have had a male cook. Bringing her to life has had a huge impact on my life. Not having been particularly interested in cooking before, or indeed in Victorian kitchens, I find that the project gives me a real appreciation of a working Victorian, a greater understanding of the science of cooking and the confidence to attempt recipes in front of an audience. (Although perhaps not sheep's brain croquettes, ever again!)

I hope this recipe book will bring as much joy to those who cook from it as I get from telling Mrs Crocombe's story.

FACING PAGE & ABOVE The cook's room, just off the kitchen at Audley End, where Avis Crocombe would have looked through her recipe books and planned her menus.

1

Audley End House

by Andrew Hann

Audley End was one of the greatest houses of Jacobean England and tells a story of favour and disgrace, wealth and poverty, and endless architectural change at the hands of a sequence of ambitious owners. It was originally built on the foundations of a Benedictine monastery, Walden Abbey, which had been founded in the mid 12th century. In 1538 the abbey was closed by King Henry VIII, during the Dissolution of the Monasteries. He gave the land and buildings to his Lord Chancellor, Thomas Audley, and made him the 1st Baron Audley of Walden.

Thomas pulled down much of the abbey and converted the rest into a grand residence, Audley Inn. His son-in-law and successor, Thomas Howard, 4th Duke of Norfolk, entertained Queen Elizabeth I here for a week in August 1571, but was executed for treason the following year after conspiring to marry the queen's rival, Mary, Queen of Scots.

The duke's second son, also Thomas, redeemed the family reputation, serving with distinction in the fleet that defeated the Spanish Armada. In 1603 he was made 1st Earl of Suffolk by the new king,

FACING PAGE
Audley End House today, from the west.

ABOVE Portrait of Thomas, Lord Audley, by a follower of Adriaen Thomas Key, 1569. Audley converted Walden Abbey into 'his chiefe and capital mansion house'.

James I, and appointed Lord Chamberlain of the Household, an important role in the royal court. In 1614 he was made Lord Treasurer (in charge of the finances of the kingdom), one of the most powerful positions in the country. The earl began rebuilding Audley Inn on a spectacular scale soon after he was given his title, in the hope that the king would visit him at his new house. It was a time when the royal court moved around the country during the spring and summer months, on what were known as royal progresses, inspecting the kingdom. To be chosen as a stopping-off point by the monarch was an honour, so leading courtiers tried to outdo one another in the magnificence of their country houses, hoping to attract a royal visit.

The first earl's newly built and renamed house – Audley End – was perhaps the greatest of these grand houses and was said to have cost £200,000 to build (about £50 million in today's money). However, the earl appears to have over-reached himself and when King James visited in 1614 he is said to have remarked that the house was too grand for a king, but might suit a Lord Treasurer. Two years later the earl was accused of embezzling funds from the Exchequer. He was found guilty but managed to avoid having his head cut off: instead he was heavily fined and retired in disgrace to Audley End.

The earl's fall from grace left his family with a huge house and huge debts. His grandson James, the 3rd Earl of Suffolk, who inherited Audley in 1640, had to sell off land elsewhere to raise £50,000 to pay creditors, and struggled to find the money to maintain the buildings and gardens. Handily, King Charles II was looking for a palace close to the racecourse at Newmarket. Charles agreed to buy Audley End for £50,000, with £20,000 left lying on mortgage.

The third earl was made keeper of his old house, now the new palace. The earliest detailed pictures of Audley date from this time: over 20 engravings by Henry Winstanley, the Clerk of Works at the palace. They show two courts, squares of buildings around open courtyards: an inner, or little, court beside a larger, outer court, like a squared-off figure of eight.

The inner court had symmetrical state apartments: for the queen on the north side and the king

Thomas Howard (1561–1626), 1st Earl of Suffolk, who rebuilt Audley Inn as the magnificent Audley End in the hope that the king would visit him.

A General Prospect of the Royal Palace of Audlyene.

H. Winstanley at Littlebury fecit.

on the south; the outer court to the west contained lodgings and offices. Further west was a vast walled garden, and the river Cam was straightened up, so that it flowed through the centre, parallel to the house.

Despite this magnificence, Charles II soon lost enthusiasm for Audley End. By 1670 he barely used it, and the house began falling into disrepair. In 1695 the 5th Earl of Suffolk, who, like the earlier earls, was keeper of the house, wrote to complain about it to the great architect Sir Christopher Wren, who was responsible for maintaining the king's buildings. 'Those last great windes has soe extramly shattered the chimneys of this house that it is dangerous to walke either in the courtyard or the garden, great stones falling from them daily.' So it is not surprising that in 1701, the new owner, King William III, decided to give the house back to the Howards. In return they had to cancel the outstanding mortgage of £20,000, still owed by the king.

Over the next 50 years the Howards drastically reduced the size of the house to make it more affordable to maintain; by 1725 little more than the inner court remained. Henry Howard, the 10th and last Earl of Suffolk, restored the family finances to some degree by marrying Sarah Inwen, the daughter of a rich London brewer, but he died in 1745 without an obvious heir, leading to divided ownership of the

One of the earliest drawings of Audley End, dating from about 1676, by Henry Winstanley. Only the middle range of these buildings (dividing the two open courts), and the two wings extending backwards from it, now remain.

estate and a protracted legal dispute during which the house was left empty and decaying.

The saviour of Audley End was Elizabeth, Countess of Portsmouth, one of the three beneficiaries of the estate. She bought the house and park in 1751 for £10,000 from one of the other beneficiaries and demolished the eastern long gallery range to produce a smaller, U-shaped house. She also restored the grounds, which were largely bare (the impoverished Howards had felled most of the trees for timber), creating a more informal setting for the house. She also had the kitchen garden moved behind the stable block, where it remains today.

The saviour of Audley End was Elizabeth, Countess of Portsmouth. She inherited part of the estate, and in 1751 bought the house and gardens, which she set about bringing up to date.

As the countess had no children, she chose as her heir her nephew John Griffin Whitwell, on condition that he change his surname to Griffin, her maiden name. Sir John Griffin Griffin, as he became, was a man of action. He'd enjoyed a distinguished military career during the Seven Years' War, but in 1760 he was wounded at the Battle of Kloster Campen and retired from active service. When, in 1762, he inherited Audley End, he immediately set about modernising it, employing the fashionable neoclassical architect Robert Adam and equally fashionable garden designer Lancelot 'Capability' Brown.

Sir John and Robert Adam created a new suite of reception rooms on the ground floor of the south wing, including a library. This magnificent room was decorated with classical friezes by the famous Italian artist Giovanni Battista Cipriani, and statues made with artificial Coade stone. They also built a stack of three galleries behind the hall and on the north side of the house, re-establishing a link between the north and south wings of the house, and built a new service wing, including the kitchen which was later to be Mrs Crocombe's realm.

Sir John was very keen on the new domestic technologies of his day, which were making country houses more comfortable and easier to run. He was quick to have them installed: a pumped water

Sir John Griffin Griffin inherited Audley End from his aunt the Countess of Portsmouth in 1762. He was very keen on the new domestic technologies of his day.

supply, service bells, a flushing water closet (toilet) in 1775 (a year before Joseph Bramah patented the device), and the new, bright, efficient Argand oil lamps soon after they were invented in 1780.

It was in the grounds, however, that he made the greatest changes. From the early 1760s he began to buy up plots of land to enlarge the park and in 1763 Capability Brown began work: getting rid of the last formal features and creating a newly fashionable, natural-looking, but idealised landscape of flowing lawns, winding water courses, and carefully positioned groups of trees and shrubs, which hid the service buildings from view. A number of cottages in Audley End village were bought and demolished so that workers' houses no longer interrupted the views and new garden buildings studded the landscape.

In 1784 Sir John was made 4th Baron Howard de Walden and immediately began yet another set of improvements. The saloon was redecorated to include full-length portraits of himself, his mother and all previous owners of Audley End, painted by the fashionable Italian artist Biagio Rebecca. Then the best bedroom suite was altered to form a new state apartment in time for an anticipated visit of George III, in 1786 – though sadly the king never came.

In 1788 Sir John was made 1st Baron Braybrooke. He had married twice, but had no children, so when he died in 1797 his chosen heir was Richard Neville, a descendant of the first husband of his aunt, Lady Portsmouth.

On becoming 3rd Baron Braybrooke in 1825 Richard and his wife, Jane, set about restoring the Jacobean character of the house. One of his guests described the third baron as 'rather a shy man in mixed company' but 'wondrous agreeable'.

Richard, now 2nd Baron Braybrooke, came to Audley End as a newly widowed, 47-year-old father of seven children. Audley was up to date but did, however, need a nursery, so Richard had one built on the second floor. He also had improved stoves installed to help heat the mansion. In 1819 the house finally received another royal visit: a daughter of George III, Princess Mary, visited with Prince William, Duke of Gloucester (both her husband and first cousin) and his sister Princess Sophia of Gloucester.

In 1820 the second baron retired to his ancestral estate, Billingbear, Berkshire, leaving Audley End to his eldest son, also Richard Neville, who'd recently married and started a family. On becoming 3rd Baron Braybrooke in 1825 he and his wife, Jane Cornwallis, set about making substantial alterations. Whereas Sir John had remodelled the house in what was then the fashionable neoclassical style, Richard – a scholar and antiquarian – wanted to restore its Jacobean character. He began the laborious process of removing the white paint on the staircases, panelling and carved screen of the hall, to reveal the original unpainted Jacobean wood. Working with the architect Henry Harrison, he saved the surviving Jacobean elements of the house and made sure any new work harmonised with them. He also moved the reception rooms back up to the first floor, where they had been when the house was first built. In the gardens they created a new parterre (a formal garden of paths and flower beds) to the east of the house.

Richard's successor in 1858 was his eldest son, Richard Cornwallis Neville. The fourth baron had been plagued by ill health and so could not join in with the usual activities for men of his time, but instead developed an interest in collecting and archaeology. He built up a

FACING PAGE
Charles, 5th Baron Braybrooke – Mrs Crocombe's employer – and his family at Audley End in about 1866–7. On his left is his wife, Florence, and at his feet their daughter, Augusta. Standing with her hand on his shoulder is Charles's niece Catherine, and at the far left her younger sister Mary; their mother is the woman seated to Charles's right. The other three women in the photo are probably Charles's sisters Mirabel, Louisa and Lucy, with the family chaplain, John Lane Oldham, the man in the hat.

large collection of fossils and stuffed birds which he displayed in cases on the lower and upper galleries and created a museum room to display antiquities and finds from his own excavations.

When he died at only 41 in 1862 he was succeeded by his brother Charles Neville, whose main interests were agriculture and cricket. Charles rebuilt the home farm, and used experimental methods to improve the milk yields of his Jersey cows. He also laid out a cricket pitch on the lawn in front of the house in 1842 (later moved to the other side of the river). It was Charles, the fifth baron, who was Lord Braybrooke when Avis Crocombe served as cook in the 1880s.

By then the house was much as we see it today – neither Charles nor later generations of the family made many changes. Only the Adam Rooms on the ground floor look different to the way they appeared in Avis' day, when they served as a bedroom suite: in the 1960s the Ministry of Works, the government department then responsible for buildings of national significance, restored these rooms to the way they would have looked in the late 18th century, a hundred years before Avis arrived at Audley End.

2

Cooking with Mrs Crocombe

by Annie Gray

THE RECIPES

This book is not an exhaustive list of every Victorian recipe, nor is it a full modernisation of Mrs Crocombe's scribbled notes, but it is somewhere in between. The recipes you will find in these pages are indicative of what Avis would have been cooking at Audley End and well over half of them are taken from her own recipe book. The others are from sources we know she had access to, or can reasonably surmise that she may have used.

We have used Avis' idiosyncratic spelling for the titles of her own recipes where it differs substantially from the usual form. Her minor misspellings we have corrected for ease of reading: for example Maitre dHotel is now Maître d'Hôtel.

The recipes are laid out in the same way as a Victorian meal, with sections on soups, fish, meat (more properly called 'savoury entrées'), vegetables, sweets ('sweet entremets' to a Victorian), and desserts and savouries, all of which would have formed the family dinner.

If you want to serve an upper-class Victorian meal in a style similar to that of the 5th Lord and Lady Braybrooke at Audley End, then your first course should include a soup, a fish dish and two entrées (from the meat section), laid out around a central floral arrangement. After you have finished that course, replace the dishes with something roasted (preferably game, also from the meat section), a vegetable dish and two sweets. Finally, replace these with four dishes from the dessert and savouries section. You should complete the meal with fresh fruit and end with coffee, tea or a glass of punch.

➡→

MEASUREMENTS AND INGREDIENTS

There are notes scattered throughout to explain Victorian habits and wording, but here are some notes on measurements and on commonly used ingredients, and the answers to some of the questions most frequently asked by our global YouTube audience.

Units The original recipes were all in Imperial pounds, ounces and pints (an Imperial pint being 20 fl oz, rather than the US 16 fl oz – blame the 1834 Weights and Measures Act). We have given metric and American cup equivalents. However, our advice would always be to buy some digital scales (which measure in both Imperial and metric measures) and not to use cups, which are very imprecise. Equally, we'd advise purchasing a digital probe thermometer for testing pies and meats. We promise that you'll never look back.

Whichever units you choose to use, stick with only those units in each recipe, and do not mix Imperial, metric and cup measurements within the same recipe.

The sizes of **teaspoons** and **tablespoons** differ marginally in Britain and the US. British spoons, based on the Imperial system, are slightly bigger than US spoons. As the difference is minimal, we have simply used 'teaspoon' and 'tablespoon'. If you are using a US spoon you could be very slightly generous in the spoonfuls, but for the purposes of the ingredients given in spoon measures, it won't really matter whether yours is an old Imperial or a US spoon.

A **pinch** is the amount you can take between your thumb and the first two fingers of your hand.

Eggs are assumed to be British medium. The original recipes in the back of the book list more eggs than we use in our modernised versions, because eggs were smaller in the past.

All **butter** is unsalted unless otherwise stated, but lightly salted is also fine to use.

Do adjust the **seasoning** to taste, and remember that even cakes usually need a pinch of salt to bring out the flavour.

You can use **black peppercorns** instead of white in those recipes that call for them, if you don't mind black specks in your sauce.

All **flour** is plain (all-purpose), unless otherwise stated.

Salt is normally sea salt, with a medium-sized crystal. This is known in the US as kosher salt. Avoid the fine-grained table salts: these usually contain additives which may throw the recipes off kilter (and make them too salty, where we give amounts in teaspoons). Of course, everyone has different tastes, so be guided by your own.

Milk is always whole.

Where **cream** is listed, you can use any type. However, if we specify double cream, it is what is known as heavy cream in the US. In Britain we also have whipping cream, slightly lower in fat and ideal for whipping. If in doubt, go for the most multi-purpose version you can find. In Victorian recipes you'll never go wrong with high-fat cream.

Baking powder is widely available as a ready-made mixture. If you cannot find any, just mix ½ tsp bicarbonate of soda (baking soda) with 1 tsp cream of tartar.

Gelatine is given in leaf form. If using powdered gelatine use 1 tbsp for every 3 leaves.

Suet is the hard fat that surrounds the kidneys of most animals. It is widely available in shops, online, or fresh from a good butcher.

Generally beef suet was used, but other types existed. We tend to use beef and cannot guarantee the results of using another type of fat. A vegetarian alternative is available.

Puff pastry should always be made with butter. It is easily available ready-made, at least in Britain, but do check the packet as some brands made with vegetable fats can be nasty. If you cannot get an all-butter puff, you may be better off choosing another recipe (or making your own puff pastry). In most cases you could use a basic butter shortcrust pastry instead.

Black treacle can be replaced by blackstrap molasses, though you can also buy treacle online.

We would always advocate using the best-quality **meat** possible. The Victorians did not routinely administer hormones or antibiotics to their cattle, nor did they practise battery farming. In Britain, there are various welfare marks which indicate well-cared-for animals, and we think that the organic standard is worth seeking out, both for ethical reasons and because the meat will taste better and be easier to handle. Wherever you live, it is worth making friends with a decent butcher.

Where we call for **stock**, we assume a good-quality, preferably home-made, vegetable or relevant meat stock (it is easy to make). If you choose to use stock cubes, be aware that they tend to be salty and can have a synthetic taint that will affect the taste. Mrs Crocombe would have had at least five stocks of various grades to choose from – some stocks were better than others, depending on what sort it was, how much meat went into it (rather than just bones) and whether or not the meat had been roasted first. Veal stock, for instance, was considered the best.

Where **wine** is needed, the Braybrookes would have used European wines, such as claret (red) and hock (white). Go for a medium-dry, fairly fruity red (Bordeaux or Côtes du Rhône style) or a light, fruity and medium white (Riesling style). Do not go near wines labelled as 'gutsy' or 'full-bodied'. Malbec or oak-aged wines should be avoided.

Alternatives Some of the ingredients are expensive – this is Victorian upper-class cookery, after all. However, you can swap a cheap fortified wine (such as port, sherry, vermouth or ginger wine) for almost all of the alcohol, or use unbranded versions. Quails' eggs are available pickled. Truffles are optional, and may be substituted with porcini mushrooms (for flavour) or pickled walnuts (for looks).

If you need to adapt a recipe for special dietary needs, do go ahead. We assume you have plenty of experience in doing so, and will know the best things to substitute. We would encourage you to experiment and adapt the recipes for your own needs and likes, just as Mrs Crocombe would have done. (However, we've tested them only as written, so we cannot give you advice on the potential results.)

Different countries have different regulations for food hygiene and safety. For example, in Britain our chickens are vaccinated against salmonella, whereas elsewhere they may not be. This means that raw eggs are low risk in Britain, but may be riskier elsewhere. Use your own judgement, especially if cooking for the elderly, infirm, very young or pregnant.

We have assumed access to certain modern conveniences, such as blenders and mixers. If you do not have them, all of the recipes are, of course, cookable without.

Have fun!

SOUP

RABBIT [OR CHICKEN] SOUP

Avis Crocombe, *unpublished manuscript* (no date)

SERVES 6–8

2 whole rabbits or 1 chicken, jointed

3 small onions, peeled

2 carrots, tops removed

2 celery sticks

2 bay leaves and 1 thyme sprig
(or a prepared bouquet garni)

2¼ litres/4 pt/2⅓ quarts water

2 egg yolks

115 ml/4 fl oz/½ cup double cream

salt and pepper, to taste

croutons, to serve

CROUTONS

Croutons were the usual accompaniment for soups in the Victorian era. Little pieces of fried or sometimes baked bread, they were cut into shapes and served in a separate bowl. Mrs Crocombe still uses the old-fashioned name, sippets, which dates back to the 16th century. Sippets were originally used as garnishes for all sorts of dishes, not just soup.

Every aristocratic dinner started with soup, generally a choice of two types: 'light' (clear) soup and 'dark' (thick) soup. Some writers suggested that light was most suitable for ladies and dark for gentlemen. Others noted that soups made with game or red meat were ideal for gentlemen, while ladies should opt for more delicate white meat and vegetables. The original recipe for this, in Avis Crocombe's manuscript, suggests that if it is intended for guests, then chicken, which was much more expensive than rabbit, is preferable. It can also be made with veal.

Put the rabbits or chicken in a large saucepan with the vegetables and herbs. There is no need to chop the vegetables, though you can halve them if they are too long to fit in the pan. Add the measured water and bring to the boil, skimming any scum which rises to the surface. Cook until the meat is tender (about 90 minutes).

Strain the broth through a colander into a bowl. Discard the herbs from the colander and pick the meat from the bones (discard the bones and skin). Chop the meat and vegetables roughly.

Return the cooked vegetables and meat to the broth, then blend until smooth. Return to the boil in a clean pan, then reduce the heat to just below a simmer. Add salt to taste and pepper if desired.

Whisk the egg yolks well with the cream in a bowl. Pour the egg yolk mixture into the hot soup, stirring well until it starts to thicken. Do not let it boil, or it will end up as scrambled eggs.

Turn off the heat and serve the soup in a warmed tureen, with croutons on the side.

For a slightly less bland alternative, set aside the rabbit fillets or chicken breasts when stripping the meat from the bones. Chop the meat into equal, neat squares. (Any trimmings can be added to the meat you strip from the bones.) The neat squares should be returned to the soup just before it goes into the tureen.

VEGETABLE SOUP

Maria Rundell, *A New System of Domestic Cookery* (1806)

SERVES 4–6

1 small onion

1 cucumber

1 lettuce (Little Gem, or similar tight-headed type)

55 g/2 oz/¼ cup butter

1¼ litres/2 pt/1⅓ quarts vegetable stock or water

115 g/4 oz/¾ cup peas

cayenne pepper, to taste

115 ml/4 fl oz/½ cup double cream (optional)

salt and pepper, to taste

croutons, to serve

Avis drew from a wide variety of sources to add to her handwritten book. She would certainly have been familiar with Maria Rundell's best-selling *A New System of Domestic Cookery*, as it was reprinted in both official and plagiarised forms for more than a hundred years. Originally written for Rundell's own family, it was full of practical advice and carefully tested recipes, which very much stood the test of time.

Peel and slice the onion and cucumber. Trim and shred the lettuce. In a large saucepan, melt the butter and add the onion. Cook over a low heat until translucent (about 20–30 minutes). Add the cucumber and lettuce and stir well. Cook for a further 10 minutes over a low heat, then add the stock or water. Increase the heat and bring to the boil, then reduce the heat to a simmer.

Simmer for 15 minutes, until the vegetables are tender. Add the peas and cook for a further 10 minutes, then blend until smooth. Return to a clean pan to heat through. Season to taste with salt and pepper, and add a little cayenne pepper for a truly Victorian hit. If you prefer soup creamy, add the cream and mix well.

Serve the soup in a warmed tureen, with croutons on the side.

....

PURÉEING

Mrs Crocombe would have puréed the vegetables not in a blender, but by pounding them in a mortar with a pestle, before forcibly pushing the mixture through a tammy (a strainer of cloth, usually made from coarse muslin). She may also have pushed the purée through a sieve.

....

SOUP *MAIGRE*

Avis Crocombe, *unpublished manuscript* (no date)

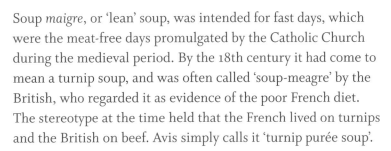

SERVES 6

5 turnips

5 celery sticks

2 onions

55 g/2 oz/¼ cup butter

2 bay leaves and 1 thyme sprig
(or a prepared bouquet garni)

1¼ litres/2 pt/1⅓ quarts
chicken stock

115 ml/4 fl oz/½ cup double cream

salt and pepper, to taste

croutons, to serve (optional)

....

ONIONS

Onions were associated with the poor,
as they were cheap and bulky, and led
to smelly breath and flatulence. They
were used very sparingly in dishes
intended for upper-class dinners.
One contemporary of Mrs Crocombe's
recorded a sign seen in a Cambridge
dining room, stating simply 'gentlemen
partial to spring onions (scallions)
are requested to use the table under
the far window'.

....

Soup *maigre*, or 'lean' soup, was intended for fast days, which were the meat-free days promulgated by the Catholic Church during the medieval period. By the 18th century it had come to mean a turnip soup, and was often called 'soup-meagre' by the British, who regarded it as evidence of the poor French diet. The stereotype at the time held that the French lived on turnips and the British on beef. Avis simply calls it 'turnip purée soup'.

Using a sharp knife or, better still, a food processor, mince all the vegetables. Melt the butter in a large saucepan over a medium heat and add the minced vegetables. Cook gently for 5–10 minutes until soft but not brown. Add the herbs and stock, bring to the boil, then reduce the heat to a low simmer.

Simmer for about 40 minutes, stirring occasionally. Remove from the heat and blend until smooth, then return to a clean pan to heat through, without allowing the soup to boil. Stir in the cream, mixing well, then season to taste.

Serve the soup in a warmed tureen, with croutons on the side if you want them.

RHUBARB SOUP

Anon, *Cassell's Dictionary of Cookery* (c.1875)

SERVES 4–6

1 small onion

255 g/9 oz/2½ cups rhubarb

170 g/6 oz/¾ cup tomatoes

2 rashers of streaky bacon

1 tbsp butter

1¼ litres/2 pt/1⅓ quarts beef stock

2 thin slices of white bread, crusts removed

salt and pepper, to taste

croutons, to serve

Typical of Victorian inventiveness, this soup is essentially a beef consommé given a boost by the sharpness of rhubarb. The rhubarb would have come, like most of the fruit and vegetables used at Audley End, from the kitchen garden. It would have been available to the kitchen as both forced (grown under a pot to exclude the light, making tender, pale stalks, ready early in the year) and unforced. Rhubarb works a little like lemon or tamarind (a flavour known to the Victorians, if seldom used as an ingredient). When choosing rhubarb, note that the redder the rhubarb, the more vibrant in colour the soup will be.

Roughly chop all the vegetables, keeping them separate, and chop the bacon into small pieces. Melt the butter in a large saucepan over a medium heat and add the bacon. Fry until just browning, then reduce the heat. Add the onion and cook until just coloured, about 20 minutes.

Add the rhubarb, tomatoes, stock and bread and bring to the boil. Simmer for about 25 minutes, until the vegetables are very tender.

Blend until smooth, then return to a clean pan to heat through, seasoning to taste.

Serve the soup in a warmed tureen, with croutons on the side.

The kitchen garden at Audley End.

MOCK TURTLE SOUP

Jules Gouffé (trans. Alphonse Gouffé), *The Royal Cookery Book* (1867)

SERVES 8–10

1 boned calf's head, including tongue

340 g/12 oz/1½ cups butter

2 kg/4 lb 8 oz veal and beef, diced

1 large onion, chopped

115 g/4 oz/1¼ cups button mushrooms, chopped

30 g/1 oz/⅔ cup parsley stalk, chopped

1 celery stick, chopped

170 g/6 oz/1⅓ cups flour

550 ml/18½ fl oz/2⅓ cups Madeira

2¼ litres/4 pt/2⅓ quarts beef or veal stock

1 basil sprig

1 lemon thyme sprig

1 marjoram sprig

2 bay leaves and 1 thyme sprig (or a prepared bouquet garni)

½ tsp cayenne pepper

570 ml/1 pt/2⅓ cups veal or chicken stock

2¼ litres/4 pt/2⅓ quarts strong beef stock or consommé

2 tbsp lemon juice (about 1 small lemon)

salt and white pepper, to taste

Turtle soup was one of the most prestigious dishes of the 18th century. It required live turtles, imported from the West Indies, and was often served in the shell or in lavish silver turtle-shaped tureens. By the early 19th century mock turtle soup, using a calf's head instead of a turtle, had developed as a cheaper and more readily available alternative. It caught on rapidly, and became one of the most quintessentially British dishes of the Victorian era, often elevated to a terrifying degree of complication, laden with garnishes, including brain quenelles (poached balls of seasoned ground meat or fish) and fried tongue. The French called it *soupe à la tortue Anglaise*, or 'turtle soup, English style'. It could be made as a thick or clear soup (see p29).

Start by preparing the boned calf's head. Blanch it in boiling water for 3 minutes, then remove. This gets rid of any impurities.

In a large saucepan, melt the butter and add the diced veal and beef. Fry until brown, then add the onion, mushrooms, parsley stalk and celery and fry until golden. Add the flour and stir so that it is well mixed in. Add two thirds of the Madeira and heat until it is reduced to half the original amount. Pour in the beef or veal stock, add the herbs and cayenne pepper, season to taste and bring to the boil. Add the head (you may need a little more water to cover it). Reduce the heat to a simmer. After 1½ hours, remove the tongue, leaving the rest to continue simmering for a further 1½ hours.

When the tongue is cool enough to handle, skin it and cut it into 2.5 cm/1 inch squares. When the pan has simmered for the full 3 hours, remove the calf's head from the pan, drain, then press it between 2 baking trays in the fridge, firmly weighted down. After at least 3 hours cut this, likewise, into 2.5 cm/1 inch squares. You can do all this the day before the soup is required.

THE MOCK TURTLE
Lewis Carroll's Alice in Wonderland *includes a character called the mock turtle, inspired by the soup. He is pictured as having the body and front flippers of a turtle, and the hind hooves, tail and head of a calf.*

To finish, strain the broth remaining in the pan through a fine strainer and discard the meat, vegetables and herb sprigs. Add the veal or chicken stock and simmer gently for 1 hour. It should be fairly thick and slightly gelatinous. Taste and adjust the seasoning.

When you are ready to serve, put the pieces of head into a clean saucepan, pour over the beef stock or consommé, bring to the boil and simmer for 20 minutes. Drain, discarding the stock, and put the pieces of head into a tureen. Pour the prepared soup over it, add the remaining third of the Madeira and the lemon juice and garnish with the pieces of tongue.

If you feel particularly ambitious, you could also make some brain quenelles, or fry some veal meat balls. Hard-boiled egg yolks were also sometimes used as a garnish, along with fried sippets (croutons).

This soup can also be made as a clear soup. To do so, omit the flour, allow the stock to cool after straining, then clarify it (see p160) before reheating it and pouring it over the head.

FISH

FRIED WHITEBAIT

Anon, *Cassell's Dictionary of Cookery* (c.1875)

SERVES 6–8 (AS A STARTER)

500 ml/18 fl oz/generous 2 cups fat (preferably lard or beef dripping), for frying (you may need more, depending on the fryer)

450 g/1 lb whitebait (or sprats)

55 g/2 oz/½ cup flour

cayenne pepper, to taste

salt, to taste

6–8 slices of thickly buttered brown bread, to serve

2 lemons, cut into wedges, to serve

....

DINNER TIME

When you ate dinner was a question of class – the working classes ate dinner at midday, and the upper classes in the evening. This came from the way timings for dinner changed up to the late 18th century. In the Tudor era, dinner was at 11am; by 1700 it was nearer 2pm, and by 1750 the fashionable classes were eating between 4pm and 5pm. As dinner got later for the wealthy, a new meal crept in; it was called various names, but 'luncheon' was finally settled on. In Avis' time the wealthy ate dinner after 8pm, but the working classes still ate theirs at 12.30pm – when the wealthy were having lunch. The confusion still reigns today.

....

There was a veritable craze for whitebait in Victorian England. Politicians and other (male) society figures would pour out of London and head down the Thames to Deptford and Blackwall, where local taverns served hot fried whitebait, eaten whole with vinegar, to the eager hordes. Debate raged as to what these tiny, tasty fish actually were, and it was not until the 20th century that they were identified as the spawn of a wide variety of other fish, predominantly herrings. The diner got, on average, 180 fish in an Imperial pound (just under half a kilogramme) of whitebait, which could include 20–30 species. Today in Britain whitebait is regarded as unsustainable, but you can use sprats instead.

Preheat the lard or dripping in a deep-fat fryer to 190°C/375°F (you can also use a deep saucepan on the hob). Toss the whitebait in the flour so that they are evenly coated. Plunge them into the hot fat and fry them for 3–4 minutes, shaking a couple of times, until golden brown and crispy.

Drain on kitchen paper to blot off excess fat, then give them a light coating of salt and cayenne pepper, shaking lightly to distribute.

Serve piping hot, with the thickly buttered brown bread and lemon wedges on the side.

OYSTER BOUCHÉES

Jules Gouffé (trans. Alphonse Gouffé), *The Royal Cookery Book* (1867)

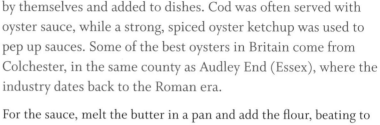

MAKES 12

12 oysters, shucked (retain any juices)

285 g/10 oz puff pastry

1 egg, whisked with a little water and a pinch of salt, to form an egg wash

chopped parsley leaves, to garnish

FOR THE SAUCE

1 tbsp butter, at room temperature, plus extra (optional), for the top

2 tbsp flour, plus extra for dusting

115 ml/4fl oz/½ cup hot chicken or veal stock

salt and white pepper, to taste

FOR THE FILLING

2 tbsp butter

115 g/4 oz/1½ cups assorted mushrooms, finely chopped

55 ml/2 fl oz/¼ cup white wine

55 ml/2 fl oz/¼ cup double cream

Oysters were tremendously popular in the Victorian era, both by themselves and added to dishes. Cod was often served with oyster sauce, while a strong, spiced oyster ketchup was used to pep up sauces. Some of the best oysters in Britain come from Colchester, in the same county as Audley End (Essex), where the industry dates back to the Roman era.

For the sauce, melt the butter in a pan and add the flour, beating to form a thick paste. Gradually add the stock, beating at each addition, to form a thick, silky sauce. Add the well-strained oyster juices, if any. Season to taste (white pepper keeps the sauce white, with no dark specks). Cover the surface with cling film (plastic wrap) or a little melted butter, to stop a skin forming.

For the filling, heat the butter in a saucepan until foaming and then add the mushrooms. Cook until they start to turn golden, then pour in the wine. Reduce by half and add the cream. Reduce again, until you have a thick sauce. Season to taste and add to the sauce.

Roll out the pastry on a flour-dusted surface to 3 mm/¹⁄₁₀ inch thick. Using a 6 cm/2½ inch fluted pastry cutter, cut 24 discs. Take 12 of these and cut a smaller disc from the centre, using a smaller fluted (or plain) cutter. The border should be about 0.5–1 cm/¼–½ inch thick. Brush the top of the first set of discs (without the hole) with egg wash and stick the second set on top. Brush with more egg wash. Chill for 1 hour.

Preheat the oven to 180°C/350°F. Bake the cases for 15–20 minutes until golden brown. Cool on a wire rack. Once cool, press the hole in the middle to enlarge the space; be careful not to pierce the base.

Reheat the sauce with the oysters. Cook for a scant 5 minutes, then spoon an oyster into each case and top with the sauce. Garnish with parsley and serve on a plate, with a doily to stop them sliding about.

TURBOT WITH LOBSTER SAUCE

Charles Elmé Francatelli, *The Modern Cook* (1846)

SERVES 6

1 whole turbot, 1.5–2kg (3 lb 5 oz–4 lb 8 oz)

2 lemons, plus lemon slices, to garnish

generous handful of salt

parsley sprigs, to garnish

FOR THE SAUCE

1 whole lobster, preferably with coral (roe)

juice of 1 lemon

140 g/5 oz/⅔ cup unsalted butter

2 tbsp salted butter

30 g/1 oz/¼ cup flour

370 ml/13 fl oz/1½ cups hot chicken or fish stock

55 ml/2 fl oz/¼ cup double cream

salt and white pepper, to taste

....

NOTE

Please ensure that any fish you use for this or any other dish is sustainable. The Marine Stewardship Council (MSC) site is a good guide, and currently rates farmed turbot as 'good', while wild turbot varies in rating, depending on how it is caught.

....

Turbot was, and remains, perhaps the most prestigious fish dish in the English repertoire. It was served boiled or baked, and was prepared in a fish kettle specifically designed for its distinctive diamond shape, called a *turbotière*. This recipe is also known as *turbot à l'Anglaise*, or 'turbot English fashion', denoting a simple preparation method, namely gentle poaching. The original recipe suggests serving the fish with a choice of sauces: for the YouTube video we chose a lobster sauce.

It is safest with this recipe to make the sauce in advance, so that you can give your full attention to the fish. Open the lobster and remove the tomalley (the liver: greenish in colour), along with the coral (pinkish when raw, red when cooked), if you are lucky enough to have some. Push both through a sieve, sprinkle with the lemon juice and mix well with the unsalted butter in a bowl. Roll into a sausage shape, wrap in baking parchment or cling film (plastic wrap) and chill until needed.

Now make a roux: melt the salted butter in a saucepan and beat in the flour until they form a soft paste. Pour in the hot stock gradually, beating well between additions, until you have a smooth, velvety sauce. This is known as sauce velouté. Whisk in the cream and keep the sauce hot, but not boiling.

Cut the chilled lobster butter into small slices and add them gradually to the sauce, beating well and heating through. After you have added half the butter, stop and taste – you may find that this is strong enough for you. If you do not use it all, the butter can be kept chilled for up to a week, or you can freeze it for future use for up to 3 months. Season with salt and white pepper to taste. Set aside until needed. A layer of cling film pressed directly onto the surface of the sauce will stop a skin from forming.

➡➔

Now cook the turbot. Start by trimming the fish (or ask the fishmonger to do this for you). Using a sturdy pair of kitchen scissors, cut out and remove the gills, cut off the tail, leaving about 2.5 cm/1 inch of stub, cut off the fins by the head and trim the long fins running around the fish. If the fish is ungutted, make sure to gut it as well. Rub it all over with the juice of 1 lemon.

Slice the remaining lemon and put the slices under the drainer of a turbot kettle. Place the fish on the drainer and lay it in the kettle. Pour over cold water to cover and add a generous handful of salt (some recipes rather poetically suggest that the water should be as salty as the sea). Place the kettle over a medium heat and bring to the boil, then reduce the heat right down and simmer very gently for about 20 minutes. Remember that the fish will continue to cook when it is removed from the heat.

Just before the turbot is ready, reheat the sauce, being careful not to let it boil. Slide the turbot onto a hot plate and cover it loosely with a clean cotton or linen napkin. Garnish with parsley sprigs and lemon slices and serve immediately, with the sauce on the side.

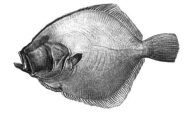

THE PRICE OF FISH
In the 1880s, turbot cost anything from 2s. 6d. to a whopping 15s., roughly the equivalent to 4 days' wages for Mrs Crocombe. By contrast flounders, regarded as a much inferior flat fish, were 2d. to 6d. each. Although it is now farmed, turbot remains expensive. But this sauce will accompany any white fish, so there is no need to panic if you don't have a turbot kettle to hand!

A COD'S HEAD AND SHOULDERS

Isabella Beeton, *The Book of Household Management* (1861)

SERVES 4

1 cod's head with about 8 cm/
2½ inches of shoulder

170 g/6 oz/⅔ cup sea salt

4 bay leaves and 2 thyme sprigs
(or 2 prepared bouquets garnis)

12 white peppercorns

200 ml/7 fl oz/scant 1 cup white wine

4 lemons

1 large bunch of watercress

16 quails' eggs, hard-boiled for
1 minute 45 seconds

1 tbsp grated horseradish

FOR THE SAUCE

18 oysters

140 ml/5 fl oz/⅔ cup cream

pinch of cayenne pepper

85 g/3 oz/⅓ cup butter

1 tbsp flour

225 ml/8 fl oz/1 cup hot fish stock

pinch of ground nutmeg

1 tsp white wine vinegar

salt and white pepper, to taste

A poached cod's head and shoulders was a very popular dish on both the 18th- and 19th-century dinner table. It was practical, as it used a cut which would otherwise be used for soup or stock, but which held quite a bit of flesh. It also had the advantage of having several types of texture and flavour: meaty tongue, delicate cheeks and, of course, the firm cod steaks themselves (the shoulders). It would have been cooked in a fish kettle, but the original recipe also advises that you can steam it, which is a slightly safer way to cook it, as over-boiling makes it fall apart. The accompaniment is another Victorian classic, oyster sauce, but you could also use melted butter sauce (see p79).

Rub the fish all over with the salt and leave in a covered plastic or earthenware bowl for 2 hours in the fridge. Do not use a metal bowl, as this will taint the fish. Rinse the cod and put it in a fish kettle or large pan with a wire rack or perforated tray at the bottom. Cover with water, add the herbs, peppercorns and wine and gradually bring to a simmer. Turn off the heat, cover and leave for 15 minutes.

Meanwhile, slice the lemons very thinly, wash the watercress and discard coarse stalks, and shell the eggs, halving them lengthways.

Make the sauce by shucking the oysters, retaining their juices. Strain the juices and poach the oysters in their juices in a small saucepan; this should take 2–3 minutes on a gentle heat. Remove the oysters to stop them cooking and add the cream and cayenne.

Melt the butter and flour in a separate pan, stirring, then pour in the stock gradually, stirring to give a thick, smooth sauce. Add the cream mixture and heat through, then taste and season. Just before serving, pop the oysters back into the sauce and add the nutmeg and vinegar.

Remove the cod from its poaching liquid and slice it onto an oval plate. Garnish it with the watercress, eggs topped with horseradish, and lemon slices. Serve the sauce on the side.

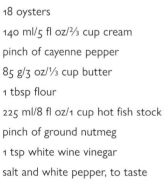

MEAT

QUAIL IN PASTRY

Charles Herman Senn, *The New Century Cookery Book* (1901)

SERVES 6 (AS PART OF A
VICTORIAN MEAL) OR 3 (AS
A STAND-ALONE MAIN COURSE)

2 whole truffles

70 ml/2½ fl oz/⅓ cup brandy

6 quails, boned except for the legs
(ask the butcher to do this for you)

1 chicken breast, chilled

½ tsp coarse sea salt

1 egg white, chilled

115 ml/4 fl oz/½ cup double cream,
chilled

85 g/3 oz/⅓ cup foie gras

200 g/7 oz puff pastry

flour, for dusting

100 g/3½ oz/6 rashers of streaky
bacon or lardo

6 vine leaves in brine

TO SERVE

large bunch of watercress

croustade of bread (optional)

....

EXPENSIVE INGREDIENTS
*Truffles were – and are – expensive,
which is why they were used so
liberally in recipes intended for the
wealthy. Mrs Crocombe's employer
was a baron. He was, we think, a
little down on his luck, given he
was employing a female cook rather
than a more prestigious (but more
expensive) male one.*

....

A classic example of late Victorian high-end cookery, this uses several techniques and is very time-consuming, but the result is excellent. It was developed as a restaurant dish, as the impetus in cookery passed from domestic chefs to restaurateurs. The end of the 19th century was the age of the French chef and restaurateur (Georges) Auguste Escoffier, and the rise of restaurants as places in which the rich could entertain as well as dine privately. Avis left Audley End in 1884 to work with her new husband, Benjamin Stride, in a small boarding house in London, where she almost certainly provided meals for the residents. Her joining the ranks of the capital's caterers was timely: the Savoy, London's first truly luxury hotel, the restaurant of which revolutionised eating out in Britain, opened in 1889, and by the end of the century a new age of eating out was in full force. If you prefer not to use foie gras, a rich liver pâté will work instead.

➤➤

Preheat the oven to 200°C/400°F. Slice the truffles into 6 rounds and steep them in the brandy in a small bowl. If you haven't managed to get the quails boned, remove the rib cage and backbone, leaving the legs intact. Flatten the quails out and chill.

Prepare a chicken mousse by chopping the breast into small pieces and blitzing in a food processor with the salt and egg white. Add the cream in a slow trickle until the mixture forms a thick paste. All the ingredients should be very cold, to stop the mousse from separating.

Shape the foie gras into a tight sausage shape and wrap it in baking parchment. Chill for at least 1 hour, then slice it into 6 equal parts. Roll the pastry out on a flour-dusted surface and cut it into 6 rectangles, each large enough to wrap a quail.

Fill each quail with 2–3 tbsp of chicken mousse. Top with a truffle slice and a piece of foie gras (you can reuse the truffle-flavoured brandy in any of the savoury recipes in this book which use brandy). Re-form each quail into its original shape and wrap with a piece of streaky bacon or lardo to hold it in place. Wrap the breast with a vine leaf and cross the legs over at the ankles.

Next fold each quail up neatly in a rectangle of puff pastry: place the quail on the rectangle at a diagonal. Fold over the corners at the top and bottom, then the other two corners and seal well. Leave the feet (assuming they are still on) sticking out. Place the quail parcels on a greased baking tray, with the pastry seams underneath.

Bake for 30–35 minutes until the pastry is golden brown. Serve on a bed of watercress and, for a full Victorian flourish, arrange them around a baked croustade of bread. A simple meat gravy makes a good accompaniment.

BREAD CROUSTADES
These were much used in Victorian cookery. At their simplest, they were a hollowed-out wedge of bread, used to give height to a dish and stop roast meats sliding off the plate. However, they could also be elaborate carved bread chalices, filled with cream and cascading with crayfish.

ROAST PHEASANT

Eliza Acton, *Modern Cookery for Private Families* (1845)

SERVES 2

2 tbsp butter

1 pheasant

1 thyme sprig

100 ml/3½ fl oz/generous ⅓ cup port

1 tsp arrowroot mixed with 1 tbsp cold water (optional)

1 slice of bread 2.5 cm/1 inch thick, crusts removed

salt and pepper, to taste

FOR THE BREAD SAUCE

85 g/3 oz/1 cup slightly stale breadcrumbs

240 ml/8½ fl oz/1 cup milk

¼ tsp salt

pinch of ground mace

pinch of cayenne pepper

2 tbsp butter

1 tbsp double cream

....

NOTE

When serving two pheasants it was customary to lard the breasts of one of them (for the technique, see p58 and the photo on p59). However, debate raged in the pages of cookery books as to whether this ruined the flavour.

....

No Victorian dinner was complete without at least one roast. Generally you could expect both roast 'butchers' meat' (farmed animals) and roast game. In the 18th century, when only two courses plus dessert were eaten, the second course would be centred on roast game, with vegetables and sweet dishes served simultaneously upon the table. The roast was usually plain, not even stuffed, with a simple gravy or bread sauce on the side, so that the distinct gaminess of the meat came through. Because game was served whole, it showcased the skill of the gun (the person who shot it) in not obliterating the head. It was perfectly possible for a dinner guest to be able to point at the pheasant or hare on the table and proclaim proudly that he or she was responsible for its fine shape and perfect presentation. At houses such as Audley End, roasts were always cooked on a spit in front of the open fire.

Preheat the oven to 200°C/400°F. Melt the butter in a saucepan and season with salt and pepper. Truss the pheasant. If you really wish to do it the Victorian way, this should be with the head tucked under the wing, with the beak laid straight along the breast, and the legs skewered straight without being crossed. If, however, you have bought the pheasant from a game dealer, you probably don't have the head and legs and will have to be dangerously modern.

Put the pheasant on a rack in a roasting tin and pour a little water around it. Tuck the thyme under the pheasant. Roast for 15 minutes, then reduce the oven temperature to 160°C/325°F and roast for a further 30 minutes. The internal temperature should be about 65°C/150°F – pheasant should be served slightly pink. Remove from the oven and leave to rest for 10 minutes while you make the gravy.

Add a cup of boiling water to the tin and use this to sluice out the juices. Strain them and, if you have a fat separator, use this to drain the stock from the fat. Otherwise, leave the liquid to settle in a jug for a few minutes and spoon off most of the fat. Pour the liquid into

....

ROASTING TO A TURN

'Roasting' originally referred to the process of cooking meat on a spit in front of a fire. Fully mechanised spits were invented in the 17th century, and in houses such as Audley End were absolutely obligatory. Audley had a smoke-jack, a mechanism consisting of a wheel like a windmill, fixed in the chimney and turned by rising hot air from the fire. The wheel was connected via a series of cogs to a chain which turned the spit. Other houses used weight-driven or clockwork spits. By the late 19th century, ovens were slowly replacing spits, although Audley retained its spit until the house passed into government ownership, after the Second World War.

....

SWANS

Mrs Crocombe's manuscript contains only one recipe for roast meat, and that is swan. Swan was very prestigious and was associated with Christmas time, when it was at its best. The would-be swan-eater could either buy or raise cygnets, to be fattened up over the autumn, or could buy the swan ready-fattened. There was a thriving swan trade in Norwich, 12 miles north-west of Langley Hall, where Avis worked in the 1870s. Her recipe is a slightly shortened version of that which was sent out with Norwich swans, and which was written in rhyme.

....

a small saucepan, add the port and boil fast to reduce. If it does not thicken up, use the arrowroot mixed with cold water to thicken it. Taste and adjust the seasoning.

To make the bread sauce, soak the breadcrumbs in the milk for 20 minutes. Put the mixture into a saucepan and bring to the boil. Add the salt and spices, turn off the heat, and add the cream and butter.

Make a small hollow in the slice of bread and put it on a plate. Remove the string or skewers from the pheasant and pop it on top. Garnish with the tail feathers, if you have them, and serve the gravy and bread sauce on the side.

PIGEON PIE

Developed by the team at Audley End, based loosely on Eliza Acton,
Modern Cookery for Private Families (1845)

SERVES 6–8 (MAKES A 21 CM/
8 INCH RAISED PIE)

FOR THE PASTRY

740 g/1 lb 10 oz/scant 6 cups flour

200 g/7 oz/generous ¾ cup butter,
chilled and diced, plus 2–3 tbsp for
the mould

200 g/7 oz/generous ¾ cup lard,
chilled and diced

3 tsp salt

3 eggs, lightly beaten

2–3 tbsp cold water

FOR THE FORCEMEAT (STUFFING)

600 g/1lb 3 oz/scant 3 cups
minced veal

140 g/5 oz/1⅔ cups fresh
breadcrumbs

200 g/7 oz/4–6 slices of cooked ham,
finely chopped

salt and pepper, to taste

....

FROM HEAD TO TAIL

*The Victorians had no squeamishness
about using every part of animals,
birds or fish. A good cook was able to
transform anything into a delicious
meal and was not put off by eyes,
legs or gaping mouths. Indeed, such
elements showed control of nature,
as well as proving that whatever was
being eaten was the genuine article.*

....

Raised pies were one of the more spectacular elements of the
Victorian table. Elaborate copper or tin moulds were used and
the tops ornamented with pastry decoration. Often, as here, the
pies were further decorated with bits of the bird. Pigeon pie had
the feet poking out, for instance, while pheasant pie used the
head, wings and tail on sticks. These bits could be gently baked
beforehand to retain their shape (and prevent raw meat leaking
onto the pie). By the late 19th century, the canny cook could
order bird parts from a taxidermist. If you don't have a suitable
pie mould, you can use a tall springform cake tin (often sold as
'panettone tins').

Mix all the pastry ingredients except the water in a blender or food
mixer. Add enough water to form a malleable dough. It's fine to
overwork it, as it needs to stand firm when released from the mould.
Chill for at least 2 hours, or overnight. Set aside a third for the
lid and decoration. Shape the rest into a rough cone and chill for
30 minutes.

For the forcemeat, mix all the ingredients and season well: if in
doubt, fry up a bit, taste and adjust the seasoning.

Prepare the mould by buttering it lavishly, ensuring you work the
butter into any design. Using your hands, press down the centre of
the pastry cone, forming a bowl. Shape it roughly, until slightly
smaller than the mould, but with high sides. Put it into the mould
and continue to work it, using your fingers to spread the pastry up
the sides until you have a 2.5 cm/1 inch overhang all the way round.
Ensure the pastry is of even thickness, without holes. This is the
Victorian way of lining a pie mould; you can roll it out, but ensure
that joins are well sealed, with at least 3 cm/over 1 inch overlap,
especially at the bottom.

45 g/1½ oz/½ cup mushrooms, sliced

1½ tbsp sliced truffles, or 2 truffles if whole (optional)

8 pigeon breasts

14 quails' eggs, hard-boiled for 1 minute 45 seconds (or use pickled quails' eggs)

pinch each of salt, ground cloves and ground mace

1 tbsp finely chopped parsley leaves

1 tbsp finely chopped sage leaves

1 tbsp brandy

1 tbsp port

1 egg

1 tbsp milk

3–4 pigeon feet and first part of the leg, toenails removed, scalded and, if large enough to do so, skinned (optional, unless you are Mrs Crocombe)

170 ml/6 fl oz/¾ cup chicken stock

3 leaves of gelatine

watercress, to garnish

pickles, to serve

....

NOTE

The meat may look a little pink when you serve it. Provided you gave it the full time in the oven, and preferably checked the internal temperature with a probe thermometer, all is well. The nitrites in bacon tend to tint things pink.

....

Line the pastry with about two thirds of the forcemeat, using a little water to smooth it out. Layer in evenly half the filling ingredients, starting with the mushrooms and truffles (if using), then the pigeon, and lastly the eggs, which may need holding in place with a little forcemeat. Add the salt, spices and herbs. Layer in the remaining filling ingredients and sprinkle with the brandy and port. Top with the remaining forcemeat. Poke your finger down the centre to form a hole through the forcemeat into the pie to allow stock to seep in. Chill.

GAME

Pigeon was widely eaten in the Victorian era. Unlike most game birds, pigeons could be shot throughout the year. They were not the feral pigeons so common in urban areas today, but wild wood pigeons, which are lean with delicious dark meat. They were, of course, free. You could substitute any other game bird or, for a lighter pie, chicken or turkey. Game was a very important element of the Victorian dinner. It had long been associated with the rich, whose right to manage and shoot game had, since medieval times, been enshrined in law. Game was generally cooked and served with heads and legs still on, and some of the first cookery book illustrations showed how to truss for roasting and how to carve.

Roll out a third of the remaining pastry. Whisk the egg, milk and salt to make a wash. Brush the overhanging pastry edges with egg wash and attach the lid firmly. Crimp the edges with your fingers or a pie crimper and cut off any overhanging bits, or you won't be able to remove the mould.

Make a hole in the middle of the pie and fix a 'chimney' round it with a small wall of pastry – it needs to stay open and be tall enough to retain any rising juices during baking. To be properly Victorian put 3–4 pigeon feet into the hole, which will keep it open and show diners what is in the pie.

Roll out the remaining pastry and pastry trimmings thinly and cut out shapes with a cutter. The Victorians favoured floral and leaf shapes. Fix them to the pie using the egg wash.

Heat the chicken stock while you soak the gelatine leaves in a bowl of water for 5 minutes. Remove the gelatine from the water, squeeze out the liquid, then whisk the softened gelatine into the stock. Pour half the stock through the pie chimney, reserving the rest. Egg wash the pie all over and chill for at least 1 hour (or overnight).

Preheat the oven to 150°C/300°F and cook for about 3 hours. Check the internal temperature with a probe thermometer, if you have one (it should reach at least 75°C/165°F). Remove from the oven.

You can serve this pie hot, in which case demould quickly and plate. However, it is better cold, in which case leave it to cool overnight, then reheat the reserved stock and pour it into the chimney of the cold pie. Chill for at least 2 hours before serving, to allow the stock to set. To demould a chilled pie, either pop it in a hot oven for a couple of minutes, or use a cook's blow torch around the mould. This melts the butter and allows the mould to slip off easily. Garnish with watercress and serve with pickles.

MARIONADE OF CHICKEN

Avis Crocombe, *unpublished manuscript* (no date)

SERVES 4

1 whole chicken, jointed into 8, or 4 chicken legs (attached thighs and drumsticks)

finely grated zest and juice of 1 lemon

2 bay leaves

pinch of ground allspice

3 cloves

225 g/8 oz/1¾ cups flour

225 ml/8 fl oz/1 cup sparkling water

oil, to deep-fry

salt and pepper, to taste

lemon wedges, to serve

This is one of the sparser recipes in Avis' manuscript, but it is nevertheless very good. The marionade is essentially a marinade for chicken, which is then battered and deep-fried. It would have been an excellent way to moisten and tenderise elderly birds that had finished laying. 'Chicken' was distinguished from 'fowl' in the Victorian era, the former being the young version of the latter. Recipes for 'fowl' tended to be longer-cooked, involving stewing or spicing to suit older, darker meat, whereas 'chicken' lent itself to more delicate preparations. Chicken was seen as the more digestible meat, particularly suited to children and the sick. Avis may well have intended her original recipe to use the remains of a roast fowl, as many other recipes for fried chicken use a cold roast bird. The recipe works well with a chicken gravy, which would also be appropriately Victorian.

Place the chicken pieces in a large bowl and cover with cold water. Add the lemon zest and juice, the bay leaves and spices and leave to soak for 3–4 hours.

Make a batter by whisking 170 g/6 oz/1⅓ cups of the flour in a bowl with the sparkling water until smooth. Put the remaining flour on a deep plate, or in a food-safe bag. Remove the chicken from the water and pat dry with kitchen paper. Dust the pieces with the flour and season with salt and pepper.

Heat the oil in a deep-fat fryer to 175°C/345°F (you can also use a deep saucepan on the hob). Dip the flour-dusted chicken pieces into the batter mix and deep-fry them until they are golden brown and crispy. Check the internal temperature with a probe thermometer, if you have one (it should be at least 75°C/165°F). Briefly drain on a rack or kitchen paper and serve with lemon wedges.

MUTTON CUTLETS WITH SAUCE PIQUANTE

Avis Crocombe, *unpublished manuscript* (no date); the sauce from
Anne Eliza Griffiths, *Cre-Fydd's Family Fare* (1864)

SERVES 4–6

1 rack of mutton, or 12 cutlets

1 onion

1 carrot, peeled

2 bay leaves and 1 thyme sprig
(or a prepared bouquet garni)

225 ml/8 fl oz/1 cup hot lamb stock

salt and pepper, to taste

minced parsley leaves, to garnish

mashed potato, to serve (optional)

FOR THE SAUCE (OPTIONAL)

340 g/12 oz/3¾ cups whole
mushrooms

340 g/12 oz/3 cups walnuts

340 g/12 oz/1¼ cups salt

1 tsp mustard seeds

¼ tsp ground mace

4 cloves

8 allspice berries

1 tbsp black peppercorns

1 tbsp peeled and grated fresh ginger

½ tsp cayenne pepper

1 shallot

6 garlic cloves, whole

140 ml/5 fl oz/⅔ cup port

85 ml/3 fl oz/⅓ cup soy sauce

85 ml/3 fl oz/⅓ cup red wine

Mutton was immensely popular in the 19th century. It is the meat of sheep of more than two years old, and it was thought to improve with age. Queen Victoria enjoyed mutton when it reached about ten years old. Lamb was eaten as well, but was seasonal, being at its best in the spring. (Some lambs, however, were specially reared for the Christmas market.) Mutton is a rich meat, full of flavour, and works well with spice. Avis Crocombe does not specify which sauce to serve with her cutlet recipe, but this piquante sauce was a popular choice. It also goes well with game. Note that the sauce given here takes a long time to make (and benefits from keeping): a basic gravy or an accompaniment of redcurrant or cranberry jelly is also fine.

If you plan to make the sauce, start with that. Be warned! It takes a week to make and is best after 3 months. Put the mushrooms and walnuts in a non-metal container with the salt, cover and put into the fridge for a week. Stir each day, gently bruising the mushrooms.

At the end of the week, wash off the salt and separate the walnuts and mushrooms into 2 saucepans. Cover both with cold water. Bring to the boil, skimming off any residue until no more rises to the surface and the water is clear. Strain, reserving the boiling liquid. Discard the mushrooms and walnuts.

Measure out 1¼ litres/2 pt/5 cups of the boiling liquid, put it into a clean saucepan and add all the spices, the shallot and the garlic. Boil for 20 minutes. Pour into a bowl and cool. Add the port, soy sauce and red wine and decant into sterilised bottles (see p231). This can be used immediately, but is best kept for 3 months to mature first. Once opened, keep in the fridge and use within a week.

If you have decided to serve the cutlets plain, or with redcurrant or cranberry jelly, skip the above stages and go straight to the cutlets.

➡

It's often suggested that Victorian food would have been served lukewarm, as it was such a long way from the kitchen to the dining room. This is untrue. Cooks were sacked for serving cold food. It may be a long way from the kitchen of a house such as Audley End to its dining room, compared to our own homes, and it seems all the longer when we walk slowly around the house, admiring the paintings and exciting taxidermy. But footmen were paid more the taller they were, and a 6ft-tall footman, walking at pace, could whisk food from kitchen to dining room very quickly indeed. Add in hot plates and copious food covers and it's safe to say that the food would have been eaten at the perfect temperature. After all, while no one wants to eat tepid food, they don't want to burn their mouths either.

If using a whole rack, cut and trim the cutlets. Slice the onion and carrot and place them in a saucepan. Nestle the herbs among them. Season the cutlets and put them on top, pouring over the hot stock.

Bring to the boil, then reduce the heat to a low simmer. Cover with a disc of baking parchment and then the lid. Simmer for 90 minutes.

When cooked, remove from the pan with a slotted spoon and strain the stock. Put the cutlets onto a tray, cover with another tray and weight down to flatten them. Chill for at least 2–3 hours (you can leave them overnight). Reduce the stock until it is thick and coats the back of a spoon when stirred. If you have made the sauce piquante, add 70 ml/2½ fl oz/⅓ cup of it to the stock at this point, then reduce again until it is thick and unctuous.

Trim off any excess fat and ensure the cutlets have what the Victorians would have called a 'nice' shape. Place in a pan with enough reduced stock to reach halfway up their sides and heat through, turning 3–4 times. Serve the cutlets piled up on a plate, garnished with parsley, with the rest of the sauce piquante on the side. You could also serve them with a border of mashed potato.

BREAST OF MUTTON

Avis Crocombe, *unpublished manuscript* (no date)

SERVES 4–6

1 breast of mutton or lamb

1 carrot

1 onion

2 celery sticks

2 bay leaves and 1 thyme sprig
(or a prepared bouquet garni)

1 tbsp English mustard (optional)

200 g/7 oz/generous 1½ cups flour

1 egg

240 ml/8½ fl oz/1 cup milk

240 g/8½ oz/3 cups breadcrumbs

55 ml/2 fl oz/¼ cup clarified butter,
for frying (see method, right)

salt and pepper, to taste

FOR THE SAUCE

1 tbsp arrowroot mixed with
1 tbsp water

1 tbsp capers, roughly chopped

juice of 1 lemon

A variation on classic mutton with caper sauce, this very moreish dish also works with lamb or beef. Slow-cooked recipes such as this were very useful in the Victorian kitchen, as the meat could be tucked away at the back of the stove while other things were prepared. The poaching could be done the day before, especially when, as here, the meat is chilled and shaped before recooking. With only four people cooking for about 30 diners, four times a day, the kitchens at Audley End had to be brutally efficient.

Place the mutton breast in a large pot with the vegetables and herbs. Cover with water. Bring to the boil, skim any scum off the surface and reduce the heat to its lowest. Cook for 3 hours, until the breast is very tender, topping up with water if required to just cover.

Carefully remove the meat, reserving the cooking liquid. Cool the meat enough to handle, then slide out the bones. Put it on a baking tray, with another tray on top, and weight the upper tray down to flatten the mutton. Put it in the fridge for at least 4 hours (it can easily be left overnight). Once cold and flat, trim off any excess fat.

For the sauce, remove 570 ml/1 pt/2⅓ cups of the braising liquid and remove the fat, either with a fat separator or by chilling and then spooning off the now hard fat. Strain. When you are ready to serve, reheat this stock and add the arrowroot and water mixture. Stir until thick, then add the capers and lemon juice and season to taste.

Cut the mutton into bite-sized pieces and toss with the mustard, if using. Season with salt and pepper and dust with flour. Whisk the egg and milk together and coat the floured mutton pieces with this mixture, then toss them in breadcrumbs until well coated.

To clarify butter, melt it in a saucepan over a gentle heat, then remove from the heat and leave to settle. Pour off the clear melted butter, discarding the whitish solids. Fry the mutton in the clarified butter until crisp and golden. Serve with the sauce on the side.

LARDED SWEETBREADS

Charles Elmé Francatelli, *The Modern Cook* (1846)

SERVES 6

6 veal sweetbreads

450 g/1 lb lardo or fat bacon, in a piece

zest of 3 lemons, cut off without pith

55 g/2 oz/¼ cup butter

6 bread rolls

570 ml/1 pt/2⅓ cups hot veal stock

2 tsp mushroom ketchup (optional)

juice of ½ lemon

FOR THE PEA PURÉE

1 shallot, finely chopped

2 tbsp butter

255 g/9 oz/1½ cups peas (frozen are ideal)

1 mint sprig

140 ml/5 fl oz/⅔ cup hot vegetable stock

salt and pepper, to taste

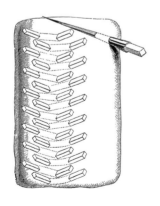

Francatelli was – briefly – Queen Victoria's cook, before being dismissed. His book *The Modern Cook* went through many editions, all promoted with the line that he had been chief cook to Her Majesty. Many of its recipes are on the queen's menus at Buckingham Palace, Windsor and elsewhere. Larded sweetbreads were served at the banquet given by Victoria's mother, the Duchess of Kent, after Victoria's marriage to Prince Albert in 1840. Sweetbreads are the thymus glands of calves, or occasionally lambs. They are subtle and creamy, and well worth getting hold of.

Chill the sweetbreads in a bowl of iced water for at least 2 hours to draw out any blood and firm up any fat. Bring a saucepan of water to the boil and blanch them for 3 minutes. Remove and allow to cool enough to handle. Trim off any excess fat or sinew, then chill.

Cut the lardo or bacon into strips about 5 cm/2 inches long and thin enough to fit into a larding needle. Put into the freezer for at least 30 minutes. Cut the lemon zest into strips of the same length, being careful not to include too much pith.

Using a larding needle, lard the sweetbreads with alternate rows of lardo and lemon zest (see photo on p59). It's best to leave the lardo in the freezer, taking out only small quantities at a time. If you don't have a larding needle, skip this stage and simply add the strips to the braising liquid. Return the sweetbreads to the fridge.

Preheat the oven to 160°C/325°F. Melt the butter. Carefully trim the crusts off the rolls and form them into squat towers, roughly oval-shaped, about 5–10 cm/2–4 inches high. Scoop out a small hollow from the top: this acts to stabilise the sweetbread, absorb the cooking juices and hold everything in place. Brush all over with melted butter. Bake for 15 minutes until golden. These will be the stands for the sweetbreads.

Make the pea purée: cook the shallot in the butter for 15 minutes until translucent but not browned. Add the peas, mint and stock and simmer for 6–8 minutes. Remove the mint and puree the rest in a blender until smooth. Taste, then season. Set aside until needed.

Increase the oven temperature to 200°C/400°F. Lay the sweetbreads in a baking dish. Pour the hot veal stock around them, cover with foil and braise in the oven for 25 minutes. Remove to a hot plate and keep warm while you prepare the sauce and finish the dish.

Strain the braising liquid into a pan and add the mushroom ketchup, if using. Bring to a fast boil and reduce by half. Reheat the pea purée.

To serve, put the bread stands on a plate, place a sweetbread on top of each, pour the pea purée around the bases and serve the reduced sauce in a sauceboat.

LARDING NEEDLES

Mrs Crocombe's kitchen would have been well stocked with all sorts of specialist tools which we've largely forgotten today. Larding needles were long needles with a fluted end, used for threading strips of fat bacon, lemon or cucumber (among other things) through the flesh of a joint. Larding not only looked pretty, but unlike barding (which meant simply wrapping bacon round a joint), it stopped the fat from falling off whatever it was intended to baste. This was particularly important in roasting, which at the time was always done using a rotary spit in front of a fire. If you decide to buy a larding needle for this recipe, avoid the hinged variety, which will tear the delicate sweetbread.

DEVONSHIRE SQUAB PIE

Frederick Bishop, *The Illustrated London Cookery Book* (1852)

SERVES 4–6

1 onion

2 eating apples, ideally Cox

1 tbsp vegetable oil

12 boneless mutton neck cutlets

butter, for the dish

55 ml/2 fl oz/¼ cup meat stock

310 g/11 oz puff pastry

flour, for dusting

salt and pepper, to taste

FOR THE EGG WASH

1 egg

1 tbsp milk

pinch of salt

....

COOKERS AND EATERS

Britain is the only country to distinguish firmly between culinary (cooking) and dessert (eating) apples. Prior to the mid 19th century most apples were dual usage, but the Victorians were avid fruit and vegetable breeders, and with about 3,000 varieties available by the end of the century, they were keen to differentiate between the cookers and the eaters.

....

A squab is a young pigeon, but for some unknown reason 'squab pie' is made of mutton and apples. It's usually associated with Devon, Avis Crocombe's home county, although there are a few recipes for a Kentish version. Both Kent and Devon were known for their apple orchards, mainly grown for cider production. Devonshire apple varieties included the wonderfully named Slack Ma Girdle, Fair Maid of Devon and Tremlett's Bitter. The pie works best with old heritage apples, but a Cox will be fine. If you cannot get mutton, hogget or even lamb will do.

Preheat the oven to 200°C/400°F. Slice the onion as finely as possible. Peel and core the apples and cut into slices of 0.5–1 cm/ ¼–½ inch. Heat the oil in a frying pan set over a high heat and fry the mutton cutlets until browned.

Butter an ovenproof pie dish, including the rim. Layer in the onion, apples and mutton, seasoning as you go (mutton generally requires lots of pepper). Pour in the stock and cover the dish tightly with foil, or put a lid on it. Braise in the oven for 90 minutes until tender. Remove and allow to cool. You can do all this the day before serving, in which case chill it, then return it to room temperature before covering with pastry, and increase the oven time by 10–15 minutes.

Roll out the pastry on a flour-dusted surface. If you have a pie funnel, put this in the centre of the pie dish. Fold the pastry over the dish, carefully sticking it to the funnel, if using. If you don't have a pie funnel, you will need to make an air hole in the lid, or cut a few slashes in it, to let out the steam as it heats. Decorate with pastry leaves and other designs. Mix the egg, milk and salt to make an egg wash and brush it over the pastry.

Return the pie to the oven for 25–30 minutes, until the pastry is puffed and golden and the filling is piping hot. Serve hot.

GALANTINE OF TURKEY

Loosely based on Richard Dolby, *The Cook's Dictionary* (1830)

SERVES 6–8

1 small turkey, about 4.5 kg/10 lb, galantine boned (see method, right)

FOR THE FORCEMEAT (STUFFING)

170 g/6 oz/2 cups mushrooms, finely chopped

½ tbsp butter

small bunch of parsley, leaves minced

200 g/7 oz/1 cup minced veal or pork

200 g/7 oz/1 cup minced fatty bacon; or 100 g/3½ oz/½ cup bacon plus 100 g/3½ oz/scant 1 cup suet

generous pinch each of ground mace, cloves, coriander, allspice and nutmeg

1 small apple, chopped

55 g/2 oz/½ cup pistachios

2 tbsp ground almonds

1 egg, lightly beaten

455 g/1 lb/about ¼ of a calf's tongue, sliced

2 truffles, sliced (optional)

6 rashers of streaky bacon

salt and pepper, to taste

FOR THE STOCK

split calf's foot (optional)

2 carrots

2 onions, halved

1 tsp black peppercorns, 3 blades of mace and 6 cloves

4 bay leaves and 2 thyme sprigs (or 2 prepared bouquets garnis)

2¾ litres/5 pt/3 quarts chicken stock or water

240 ml/8½ fl oz/1 cup brandy

Turkey had a long association with Christmas by the 1880s. It was first introduced to Britain from the Americas in the 16th century and, as a large and impressive bird, quickly became used for banquets. By the Victorian era, it was so popular as a Christmas feasting bird that flocks were driven from Norfolk to London every autumn, their feet covered in tar to protect them on the roads, to be fattened up ready for December. It was not the only meat dish on the table though, and the wealthy always served roast beef. Smaller or poorer families tended to favour geese or chicken, instead of the expensive turkey. This recipe is a very useful way to serve turkey, as it can be cut straight through with no bones. Often served cold, it is ideal for the sideboard, or as a picnic dish. This is the Audley riff on a basic, flexible recipe.

Ask the butcher to 'galantine bone' the turkey: cut it along the spine and remove all bones, but leave the skin intact. Flatten it out and remove any hard ligaments or remaining bits of cartilage.

Fry the mushrooms in the butter in a frying pan until they yield their water. Cool. Mix in a bowl with the parsley, minced veal and bacon (or bacon and suet). Add the spices, apple, nuts and egg, season generously and mix well to form a sausagemeat.

Lay the turkey out on a board and even out the meat. Usually the mini fillets will be separate, and can be laid in to cover any gaps. To get it very even, you can lay cling film (plastic wrap) on top and give it a firm roll with a rolling pin, then remove the film.

Now cover the meat with a layer of tongue, truffles and streaky bacon. On top of this, spread an even layer of forcemeat. Carefully re-form the turkey around the stuffing. You may need to tie it with string. Roll it tightly in a clean cloth and tie this well with string or cloth tape. You can put a layer of baking parchment round the turkey first, which makes it easier to remove the cloth afterwards.

FOR THE CHAUDFROID SAUCE

770 ml/1⅓ pt/3¼ cups double cream

1 litre/1¾ pt/4 cups strained stock from boiling the turkey

85 ml/3 fl oz/⅓ cup white wine

2 tbsp softened butter

30 g/1 oz/¼ cup flour

18 leaves of gelatine

TO FINISH

2 leaves of gelatine

various vegetables and edible flowers, thinly sliced and cut into shapes
or
hatelet skewers threaded with pickled mushrooms, truffles and cockscombs

....

MAYONNAISE

In the YouTube video, Mrs Crocombe covers her turkey with a mayonnaise sauce thickened with gelatine. This is a good shortcut, as mayonnaise can be made a day in advance. To make mayonnaise take 1 egg yolk, 1 tsp mustard, a good pinch of salt and 200 ml/7 fl oz/1 cup flavourless vegetable oil or lightly flavoured olive oil. Mix all but the oil together, then drizzle the oil into the mixture very slowly, mixing fast, until very stiff (careful not to let it split). Finish with a splash of tarragon vinegar, then stir in a plain gelatine mixture: 3 leaves of softened gelatine melted in 2–3 tbsp hot water and allowed to cool to room temperature.

....

Make the stock. Put the calf's foot, if using (it adds texture), in a very large stockpot with the vegetables, spices and herbs, and stock or water. Add the brandy. Bring to the boil, then lower in the turkey. Put the lid on and reduce the heat to a simmer. Cook on the hob until the turkey is piping hot. The best way to check this is with a probe thermometer. It should take about 3 hours. (Do not be alarmed if the stuffing is pink in places when served, as the bacon tends to colour it.)

Remove the turkey from the stock, put it on a baking tray, place another tray on top and weight it down gently – too much and it risks splitting. Chill overnight. Strain the stock, allow to cool, then remove the fat with a spoon.

The next day, remove the cloth from the turkey and put it on a wire rack.

For the sauce, boil the cream and the measured stock together, add the wine and a pinch of salt and remove from the heat.

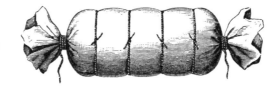

Mix the softened butter and flour together to form a paste (*beurre manié*). In small pinches, drop it into the cream mixture, stirring continuously with a whisk to prevent lumps. Bring to the boil, then simmer for 3–4 minutes. It should coat the back of a spoon.

Soak the gelatine leaves in a small bowl of water for 5 minutes. Remove the gelatine from the water and squeeze out the liquid, then whisk the softened gelatine into the sauce until it is thoroughly dissolved. Cool to room temperature. It should be thick, but still pourable.

To finish the turkey, pour some of the sauce over the bird on its rack, spreading gently with a brush if necessary to cover. Chill for 20–30 minutes, then repeat. (You may need to gently warm the sauce just to keep it at pouring consistency.) You are aiming for a pale cream, very smooth and even coating.

Heat 2–3 tbsp water and add the gelatine, whisking until it dissolves completely. Cool to room temperature.

Decorate the turkey with thinly sliced vegetables or edible flowers, dipped briefly into the gelatine so that they have a nice shine. Alternatively, if you happen to have some Victorian hatelet skewers handy, you could thread them with pickled mushrooms, truffles and cockscombs and stick them in the top – you could even do both.

The best way to serve the galantine is as slices cut straight through, but any scraps could be used for sandwiches, or made into a curry (see p170).

HATELET SKEWERS
Hatelet (or atlet) skewers were ornate silver skewers used for decoration, topped with elaborate designs: a family crest, game, fish or other motifs. For savoury dishes they were threaded with delicacies like crayfish, truffles and cockscombs, then stuck into a pie or roast. For sweet dishes, marzipan or jelly versions were used. The name comes from the French for 'little spear'.

FILLET OF BEEF PARISIAN WITH MAÎTRE D'HÔTEL BUTTER

Avis Crocombe, *unpublished manuscript* (no date)

SERVES 2

115 g/4 oz/½ cup butter, softened

finely grated zest and juice of 1 lemon

1 tbsp minced parsley leaves

3 medium-sized potatoes, peeled

2 tbsp clarified butter (see p57), for frying

2 fillet steaks

1–2 tsp olive oil

salt and pepper, to taste

A classic example of a very English dish given an air of sophistication with a French name and some snazzy garnishing. Beef was regarded as very English indeed, to the extent that roast beef and Englishness were seen as synonymous by the 18th century. Indeed, roast beef and plum pudding were used as symbols of Englishness by satirists such as Thomas Rowlandson and James Gillray in drawing a contrast between the doughty, rather solid English farmers and the bandy-legged, underfed types from across the Channel. The lack of elegance inherent in both dishes was the cause of some tension. On the one hand, lack of pretension was a good thing, and the idea of the plain-talking Englishman celebrated. On the other, it was rather embarrassing for the British middle and upper classes to be associated with quite such a level of plebeianism. After all, the French were still setting fashion, especially in food, well into the 20th century.

Make the maître d'hôtel butter by beating the butter with the zest and juice of the lemon, together with the parsley and seasoning to taste. Form the mixture into a cylinder, wrap in baking parchment or cling film (plastic wrap) and chill.

Boil the potatoes whole until tender, then drain. Cool enough to handle and slice into rounds of equal thickness, just under 1 cm/ ½ inch. Fry them in the clarified butter until they are light brown and crispy but not broken apart. Keep hot.

Put the steaks between 2 pieces of baking parchment or cling film and beat them lightly with a rolling pin to ensure that they are the same thickness all the way through. Brush with oil and season on both sides with salt and pepper. Grill (broil) under a hot grill, turning 2–3 times, until they are done to your liking (everyone is different).

Serve the steaks with the potatoes around them. Just before serving, put a slice of the butter on top of each steak so that it will melt onto it, forming a sauce.

....

À LA FRANÇAISE

French was often used in naming recipes, as it was considered more upmarket and fashionable in culinary terms. Even if a dish was very English, it was given a French name; the vast majority of upper-class menus were written in French. Worried middle-class hostesses could even buy books teaching them French names for dishes, and how to lay out a menu in the French fashion.

....

3

Mrs Crocombe's Domain

by Andrew Hann

Audley End's service wing in the 1880s was relatively small compared with the vast service ranges of many 19th-century country houses, like Wrest Park or Waddesdon Manor. And unlike these monsters it wasn't planned and built in one go, but developed over time. It's on the north side of the house, hidden from the view of those approaching the main entrance by the magnificent 'cloud' hedge.

Originally, the great Jacobean kitchen stood here but this kitchen was pulled down in about 1710 when the family, short of money, began to reduce the size of the house and moved the kitchens to the northern pavilion of the outer court, linked to the main house by an underground tunnel. This proved impractical, so when Sir John Griffin Griffin inherited the estate in 1762 he had a new kitchen built in its old position, and a separate brewhouse and dairy. Later he added a small courtyard of offices east of the kitchen and then, in about 1780, a laundry between the kitchen and the brewhouse/dairy, linking them together. This was now the service wing.

On 4 September 1881 a serious fire broke out in the kitchen. It was first spotted in the north-east corner of the roof near to one of the boilers. It was put out, thanks to the prompt action of the estate staff,

FACING PAGE
Audley End
kitchen, with the
scullery beyond.

Fire buckets hanging in the Bucket Hall, as it is known, beside the great hall at Audley End.

but the kitchen, larders and the kitchen maids' dormitory above were gutted. The refurbishment of the kitchen seems not to have been finished until the summer of 1882, so for several months Avis and her team had to cope with a makeshift kitchen in the brushing room (now the visitors' lavatories), which must have been a challenge.

A corridor separates the kitchen block from the rest of the house, sensible given the ever-present danger of fire. At the house end of this corridor are the bell lobby, servants' hall, housekeeper's room, butler's pantry, stillroom and a staircase down to the cellars. The kitchen is at the other end of the corridor, through a heavy wooden door. To the side of this door is a hatch where the butler and footmen would have collected dishes of prepared food to take to the family in the house. The kitchen was the heart of the service wing. In 1881 it had a staff of four, but at busy times of year country houses usually got daily help from the local village.

THE KITCHEN

In the 1880s the kitchen was the domain of Avis and her team: the kitchen maids Mary Ann Bulmer and Sylvia Wise, and the scullery maid, Annie Chase. Other servants would only have been allowed to enter the kitchen with the cook's permission, and house servants, in particular, rarely ventured over the threshold.

The kitchen has a high ceiling to allow heat to escape, and large windows to provide lots of light. The floor is stone-flagged. Along the wall opposite the windows are cooking ranges set in arches: at the centre is the coal-fuelled roasting range. To its right is the main range, a large cast-iron range probably put in in 1882, after the fire. It has three ovens, a charcoal-fuelled stove for boiling vegetables, making sauces and grilling (broiling) meat and fish, and hobs, including a hotplate (used to keep dishes warm). To the left of the roasting range is a pastry oven, used for baking pies, pastries and bread; finally, to its left is another, smaller range, earlier in date than the main one.

The kitchen table in the centre of the room was where most of the work took place. But not all the action happened in the kitchen itself. Through a door to the right of the cooking ranges is the small pastry

FACING PAGE
FROM TOP LEFT
The main cooking range of about 1882; the dry laundry; the pastry room next to the kitchen, which provided a clean space, away from the heat and bustle of the kitchen.

room where pies and other pastries were made and stored. It was designed as a clean space, away from the heat and dirt of the main kitchen, useful not only for pastry and confectionery, but also for storing small kitchen items which would get lost in the large drawers and hurly burly next door.

Avis also had her own cook's room, which is the little room in the north-west corner of the kitchen. It would have been built when the house employed a male chef, who, for reasons of prestige and practicality, needed his own room to work and sleep. Avis could sit at her desk to read recipe books, prepare menus, deal with correspondence and do the accounts. It must also have provided a pleasant escape from the noise and heat of the kitchen.

Beyond the cook's room was the scullery, its north wall lined with two wooden-framed, lead-lined sinks and fitted with work surfaces. Here vegetables would have been washed, fish gutted, and meat and game prepared. Plates, dishes and cooking utensils were also washed in here by the scullery maid, Annie. A smaller scullery through a doorway to the east contained copper boilers, large enough to boil very big joints of meat, as well as stock and soups, necessary both for feeding the servants and for catering for very large parties.

On the other side of the main scullery were two larders: a wet larder for storing raw meat and fish, fruit, and vegetables, well ventilated by tall louvred windows; and a dry larder for storing cooked, pickled and bottled foods, which had to be kept cool.

THE SERVICE YARD

Outside in the service yard there were two game larders. Both remain in place today. Throughout the autumn and winter they would have been filled with venison, hares, rabbits and game birds destined for the table. Lord Braybrooke kept pheasants and partridges on the estate, and held regular shooting parties. In fact, there was a much larger game larder down at the stable block where game destined for sale to commercial dealers was stored. During the winter of 1882–3 one dealer, Edward Howard, bought £530-worth of game from Lord Braybrooke (more than £60,000 in today's money).

Back in the house, on the east side, is another important room: the butler's pantry. Here the house silverware was stored and cleaned, and the butler, William Lincoln, prepared drinks to be taken up to the dining room. He had responsibility for managing the wine and beer cellars. The cellar books kept by one of William Lincoln's predecessors, in the 1860s, show 70–100 bottles of sherry consumed each month, some for cooking, as well as port, Madeira, claret, champagne and hock. On the opposite side, to the west, is the housekeeper's room, and adjacent to that the stillroom, where cakes, preserves and home-made drinks were prepared.

RIGHT The coachman in full livery with two horses outside the stables in the mid 19th century.

LEFT Samuel Barker, one of the Audley End gamekeepers in the 1880s, with his black Labrador. He was reputed to be merciless towards poachers.

BELOW The Audley End gardeners in front of the stables in about 1905. Head gardener James Vert is seated at the centre, wearing a bowler hat.

THE SERVANTS

Most of the servants ate in the servants' hall, now the public restaurant. (This room had served as the kitchen before Sir John Griffin Griffin built the current kitchen block in 1763.) The upper servants, including Mrs Crocombe if she wasn't on duty, dined in the housekeeper's room, or in the butler's pantry. Daily records of the numbers dining in the house from 1877 show on average 20 people in the servants' hall and 7 in the housekeeper's room. So, 27 servants, while the numbers eating in the dining room were only two, three or four, unless the family had guests. Some of the outdoor servants would have eaten close to their workplace, like the garden apprentices and journeymen gardeners whose meals were prepared by a bothy woman in the kitchen garden. The bothy was behind the greenhouse, part of a range of lean-to buildings which included the head gardener's office, a tool shed, a mushroom house, a potting shed and accommodation for the unmarried garden staff.

THE DAIRY, LAUNDRY AND BEYOND

At the far end of the service wing was a block containing the dairy, brewhouse and old bakehouse, which had been converted to a gun room by the 1880s. The dairymaid, Fanny Cowley, had a relatively comfortable, albeit solitary, working life. Alongside the dairy room, where milk was settled in pans to extract the cream, and the dairy scullery, where Fanny churned butter, she had her own sitting room with a fireplace. It's likely that she slept in a room over the dairy.

Since the early 19th century the Nevilles had kept a pedigree herd of Alderney cattle, which produced a creamy milk that was excellent for butter making. The dairy registers kept by Lord Braybrooke's land steward, William Hosley, show that the dairy produced over 3,700 quarts (over 4,200 litres or 1,100 US gallons) of cream and 4,000 lb (over 1,800 kg) of butter from September 1881 to August 1882. The two were very interested in the scientific analysis of milk yields, collecting detailed information about the quantity and quality of milk produced by each cow and how this varied over the course of the year and according to their diet. In 1882 their dairy registers received a special award from the British Dairy Farmers' Association (now the Royal Association of British Dairy Farmers).

The dairy room at Audley End.

The final area of the service wing was the laundry. Here the laundry maids Sarah Barrance and Ellen Findell toiled to complete the weekly washing cycle. Every weekend the dirty laundry would arrive from the house, or by train if the family was in London. It was sorted and left to soak overnight in a solution of soda and hot or cold water. On Monday washing began: items were rubbed, rinsed and wrung to remove any dirt. Coarser whites were boiled in the laundry copper to sterilise them, though not to remove stains. Once the washing was done it was put through a wringer to remove excess moisture, then dried outside on the drying green hidden from the house by the cloud hedge. It was then brought into the dry laundry and sorted according to the method of finish needed. Sheets, towels, table linen, pinafores and stockings could be damped, folded and put through a mangle for basic pressing. Delicate clothing needed ironing, using a flat iron heated on a stove. Shirt collars and fronts had to be starched. Everything was then hung up to air on hanging drying racks. It would usually all be finished by Friday night, leaving Saturday for cleaning the laundry, distributing clean clothes, and collecting and sorting more dirty ones. Then the whole cycle began again.

From the 1880s the service wing remained in use and little changed until the Second World War. After the war Audley End was taken into State care and the service wing used for staff accommodation and workshops. It's only more recently, with growing interest in life below stairs, that the importance of the service buildings has been recognised. In the 1990s the kitchen, dry laundry and dairy were opened to the public, and then in 2008 the whole service wing was opened after painstaking research and conservation work to restore it to its appearance in the 1880s.

The stable block at Audley End; these buildings have been used as stables since about 1610.

VEGETABLES

ARTICHOKES AND SPROUTS

Alexis Soyer, *The Modern Housewife* (1849)

SERVES 4–6

12 Jerusalem artichokes (sunchokes), roughly the same size

1½ tbsp salt

2 tbsp butter

1 onion, roughly sliced

12 Brussels sprouts, roughly the same size

mashed potato or boiled rice, to serve

maître d'hôtel butter (see p66), to serve

....

ALEXIS SOYER

Alexis Soyer was one of the best-known chefs of the Victorian period. He was the chef at the Reform Club, London, where he had an excellent reputation, but he was also a campaigner who got involved with some of the most pressing issues of his day. He worked on soups to alleviate the horrific situation of the Irish (who were starving in the wake of the potato famine of the 1840s), and he also went out to the Crimea during the war of the 1850s. There, his pioneering work on military cooking technology, and insistence on better hygiene in the hospital kitchens, helped to save many lives and improve military catering beyond all measure. The stove he designed remained in use for well over 100 years.

....

One of the more remarkable things about Victorian vegetable cookery is that it does not shy away from produce with apparently undesirable effects. Mention either Jerusalem artichokes or Brussels sprouts to a Brit, and they will invariably wince and mention flatulence. Trapped wind is especially painful in a corset. Yet both vegetables were enjoyed widely in the 19th century, especially at Christmas, when they are most in season. This recipe, from Victorian celebrity chef and all-round good guy Alexis Soyer, takes it to the extreme, combining both in one dish. The book it is taken from is one of the most enjoyably odd of the era, as it is written – by a French chef – in the form of letters between two fictional Englishwomen.

Peel the artichokes and, using a paring knife, shape them gently into a pear shape. Cut the bases so that they are flat enough to stand up. Put 1¾ litres/3 pt/1¾ quarts of water into a pan with the salt, butter and onion. Bring it to the boil, add the artichokes and cook them whole until tender (15–20 minutes). Drain, then discard the onion.

Trim the outer leaves from the Brussels sprouts and score lightly across the base of the stalk. Bring a pan of salted water to the boil and cook them for no more than 5 minutes. Remove from the heat and drain.

To serve, make a border of mashed potato or rice and lay out the artichokes, points upwards. Put a sprout between each one, to resemble a chessboard. Serve the maître d'hôtel butter on the side.

TOMATA SAUCE

Avis Crocombe, *unpublished manuscript* (no date); from Richard Dolby,
The Cook's Dictionary (1830)

MAKES ABOUT 485 ML/17 FL OZ/
2 CUPS

680 g/1½ lb/20–25 ripe tomatoes

1 tbsp olive oil

a little sugar, if needed

PER 455 G/1 LB OF PULP

1¼ litres/2 pt/1⅓ quarts chilli vinegar

generous pinch of ground cloves

1 tbsp minced garlic

1 tbsp minced shallot

juice of 3 lemons

salt and pepper, to taste

....

NOTE

*If you do not have any chilli vinegar,
you can make your own by gently
heating 1¼ litres/2 pt/1¼ quarts of
distilled vinegar with 20 red chillies,
roughly chopped – pick them to suit
your tolerance for heat. Leave to cool
for 24 hours, then strain.*

....

Tomatoes originated in the Andes of South America and
were brought to Europe in the 16th century. They were slow to
catch on as an edible fruit, as they were initially thought to be
poisonous. However, by the end of the 17th century, recipes were
starting to appear for them, initially in Italy and slowly spreading
outwards. By the late 18th century they had been fully accepted,
though were more usually cooked than eaten raw. They were
valued for their acidity and savoury flavour, which we would
now call umami. Tomato sauces such as this were generally
served with meat and fish, although the combination of tomato
sauce and pasta was also known. This recipe is actually for what
was more commonly known as tomato ketchup, though it bears
little resemblance to the condiment sold under that name today.
An alternative name for the tomato was the rather charming
'love apple'. This sauce is excellent with almond and potato
pudding (see p80).

Preheat the oven to 180°C/350°F. Slice the tomatoes in half, drizzle
with the olive oil and bake until tender. If the tomatoes aren't very
flavourful, sprinkle a tiny bit of sugar on them first.

Put the tomatoes in a blender and purée. Weigh the purée, and,
to every 455 g/1 lb, add the vinegar, cloves, garlic and shallot in the
correct ratios, with salt and pepper to taste. Put the mixture in a
heavy-based pan and bring to the boil. Simmer to reduce, until the
mixture has the consistency of thick cream.

Add the lemon juice, again in the correct ratio, taste and adjust the
seasoning if required. The sauce can be kept for several days in a
fridge, to be reheated when needed.

SEA KALE WITH MELTED BUTTER SAUCE

Alexis Soyer, *The Modern Housewife* (1849); sauce from Isabella Beeton, *The Book of Household Management* (1861)

SERVES 4

24 sticks of sea kale, about 21 cm/ 8 inches in length

FOR THE SAUCE

55 g/2 oz/¼ cup butter, plus 2 tbsp to finish

1 tbsp flour

285 ml/½ pt/1¼ cups hot water

scant 1 tsp salt

scant pinch of nutmeg

1 tbsp malt vinegar

pepper, to taste

BUTTER SAUCE

'Serve with melted butter' is a common suggestion in old recipe books – it refers to melted butter sauce, not just plain butter. This was the standard sauce for all vegetables, as well as being popular with fish.

The Victorians ate a much wider variety of fruit and vegetables than we do. Houses such as Audley End had kitchen gardens and orchards, staffed by a team of highly skilled gardeners. It was a mark of wealth to showcase unusual produce, which was hard to grow out of season (forced if early, retarded if late) or very rare. Sea kale is abundant along the coastlines of Britain, where it grows wild, but in a domesticated context is now very rare. In Avis' time it was grown under large forcing pots, similarly to rhubarb, so the stalks were long, thin, pale and very tender. You could also make this recipe with celery, parsnips cut into batons or any other delicately flavoured vegetable.

To make the sauce, melt the butter in a saucepan with the flour to form a roux. Gradually add the measured hot water, stirring at each addition, to form a smooth sauce. Allow to boil, mixing, until it thickens. Add the salt and a good pinch of pepper, plus the nutmeg and vinegar. Remove from the heat and stir in the 2 tbsp of butter to finish. Set aside while you cook the sea kale.

Wash the sea kale, trim the stalks to equal lengths and tie them together in a bundle with some string. Put them in a saucepan of boiling water and cook for 3–4 minutes. Drain.

Put the sea kale on a warmed serving plate, untie or cut the string, and remove it carefully. Ideally, the stalks should be served in a triangular stack. Serve hot, with the sauce on the side or poured over, as you prefer.

ALMOND AND POTATO PUDDING

Avis Crocombe, *unpublished manuscript* (no date); from Anne Eliza Griffiths, *Cre-Fydd's Family Fare* (1864)

SERVES 6–8 (FILLS A 850 ML/ 1½ PT/3½ CUP MOULD)

170 g/6 oz/½ cup cooked mashed potato (without skin)

115 g/4 oz/generous 1 cup ground almonds

285 ml/½ pt/1¼ cups milk

finely grated zest and juice of 1 lemon

115 g/4 oz/½ cup butter, plus extra for the mould

pinch of ground nutmeg

5 eggs, separated

¼ tsp cream of tartar or squeeze of lemon juice (optional)

salt

chopped almonds, to decorate

lemon slices, to serve (optional)

Almond and potato pudding is a recipe which appears in different forms in a number of books of Avis' time. However, it is also one of the few recipes in her manuscript which we know she copied word-for-word from elsewhere. Her source was a book first published in 1864, Anne Eliza Griffiths' *Cre-Fydd's Family Fare*, explicitly aimed at 'the moderate and economical, yet reasonably luxurious, housekeeper'. Avis dated the copying of this recipe to 20 May 1875. Given this date, Avis was probably working at Langley Hall in Norfolk at the time, where she was the cook–housekeeper to a baronet, exactly the kind of household which would want to balance luxury and (limited) economy.

If you do not have any cold mashed potato to hand, start by peeling, dicing and mashing some potatoes and allowing them to cool.

Put the ground almonds in a saucepan with the milk, lemon zest and juice, and butter. Warm until the butter is melted and the milk is blood-warm, and mix well. Remove from the heat and stir in the mash. Add the nutmeg and a good pinch of salt, together with the egg yolks. Mix well and set aside. Preheat the oven to 180°C/350°F.

Whisk the egg whites to stiff peaks (the cream of tartar or a squeeze of lemon juice will help). Fold the eggs gently into the potato mix.

Butter an 850 ml/1½ pt/3½ cups mould or 900 g/2 lb loaf tin and pour in the mixture. Give it a couple of gentle taps to settle it.

Bake in the oven for 1 hour until light brown and set through. Invert onto a wire cooling rack, demould, decorate the top with chopped almonds and serve hot, surrounded by lemon slices (optional). You can also leave it to cool in the mould for 1 hour before turning it out, slicing it, sprinkling it with a little flour and frying it in a little butter.

SWEETS

PUDDING À LA VICTORIA

Avis Crocombe, *unpublished manuscript* (no date)

SERVES 4–6 (FILLS A 570 ML/
1 PT/2⅓ CUP ROUND, STRAIGHT-
SIDED CHARLOTTE MOULD)

250 g/½ lb leftover sponge cake

2 tbsp butter, softened, plus extra
for the mould

1 egg, plus 1 egg yolk

170 ml/6 fl oz/¾ cup milk

pinch of ground nutmeg

1 tbsp caster sugar

30 g/1 oz/⅓ cup preserved cherries
(see note, below)

30 g/1 oz/¼ cup candied citron or
lemon peel

150 g/5½ oz perfectly ripe plums,
preferably Victoria
(about 3 plums)

15 g/½ oz/¼ cup flaked almonds

finely grated zest and juice of 1 lemon

NOTE

*It is vital that the fruit used here is of
the best possible quality, preferably
from a local market or a handy friend's
garden. Likewise the cherries need to
have bags of flavour – do not use glacé
cherries or those in insipid syrup, but
look for morello cherries in brandy
or similar.*

Another recipe ostensibly named for the queen, this may well actually take its name from the plums it is based on. The variety 'Victoria' is ideal for this recipe, as it is an excellent cooking plum. Bred in the 1840s, it is one of the most popular plum varieties in Britain, because it not only cooks up well (if picked slightly under-ripe), but is delicious as an eating plum. It is aptly named, for Queen Victoria loved fruit and was an enthusiastic, knowledgeable kitchen garden visitor, often touring the gardens and orchards of houses she stayed at when a princess and a queen, and spending time with the royal gardeners before every state banquet. This pudding also works well with greengages.

Cut the sponge cake into even, thin slices. Spread each with a thin layer of softened butter.

Combine the egg and egg yolk, milk, nutmeg and sugar in a bowl and whisk well.

Chop the cherries, mince the candied citron peel, and stone and slice the plums.

Butter the mould and line the base with a disc of baking parchment. Put in a layer of cake, butter side uppermost. Now add a sprinkling of cherries, peel, almonds, plums, lemon zest and juice, then another layer of cake. Continue until you have three-quarters filled the mould, ending with a layer of cake, this time butter-side down. Press down firmly.

Trickle in the egg mixture, allowing it to settle between additions. Stand for 2–3 hours in the fridge so that the mixture is absorbed.

Preheat the oven to 160°C/325°F and set a deep baking tray in it, filled halfway with water. This will be the bain-marie. Cover the top of the pudding with a layer of foil, and place in the bain-marie. Cook for 45 minutes until it is just set. Allow to cool for 15 minutes before turning out and serving (it will otherwise collapse). It can also be served cold.

GÂTEAU DE POMMES

Avis Crocombe, *unpublished manuscript* (no date); from Eliza Acton,
Modern Cookery for Private Families (1845)

SERVES 8–10 (FILLS A 1¼ LITRE/
2 PT/1⅓ QUART MOULD OR DISH)

285 ml/½ pt/1¼ cups water

455 g/1 lb/2¼ cups sugar

900 g/2 lb peeled, cored and
roughly chopped apples
(about 8 medium apples)

finely grated zest and juice of
2 lemons

1–2 tsp butter, for the mould

TO SERVE

2–3 tbsp flaked almonds

custard (see p113), to serve

apple slices, to serve

....

NOTE

*The best apples to use here are older,
dual-use varieties such as James
Grieve, Pippins and Cox. The original
recipe calls for Nonesuches, which are
still grown in the kitchen garden
(below) at Audley End. Don't use
Bramleys or you'll be stirring the
mixture for weeks. If its too sloppy
reboil it for another 15 minutes or so
until it stiffens up and then remould.*

....

This is one of the few recipes in Avis' manuscript book for which
a definite source is identifiable. She copied it from Eliza Acton's
best-selling *Modern Cookery for Private Families*, which was one
of the rare books of the time not mainly plagiarised from other
sources. Acton was the first recipe writer to give a separate list
of ingredients, at the bottom of each recipe, which was the
giveaway in identifying this and three other recipes taken from
the same book. Gâteau de pommes is a more elegant name, in
Acton's slightly dubious French, for plain old apple cheese,
under which name variations of the recipe had appeared in the
18th century. It is quite different to modern notions of cream-
and-pastry based gâteaux. Mrs Crocombe included two versions
of this in her manuscript. It can also be made with quinces,
damsons or any other fruit with lots of pectin.

Make a syrup by boiling the measured water and sugar together
in a preserving pan. Add the chopped apples and lemon juice and
simmer until the apples fall apart. Increase the heat and boil the
mixture, stirring constantly until it thickens, dries out and turns a
golden brown – about 20 minutes. It should have the consistency
of very thick jam. Add the lemon zest and allow to cool.

Butter the ceramic mould or pudding dish – quite intricate moulds
can be used as the mixture will set hard and will happily take quite
complicated designs. When the apple mixture is completely cool,
pour it into the mould, smooth off the top, and put it in the fridge
to chill overnight. It can, at this point, be left for up to a week,
although do cover it with a larger upturned bowl, if leaving.

When you are ready to turn it out of the mould, ease a knife into
the middle and prise it out of the mould. It should come out easily.
Decorate it with spikes of flaked almonds, pour custard around
the base and serve with apple slices. It is eaten like a jelly.

TRIFLE

Theodore Garrett (ed.), *The Encyclopaedia of Practical Cookery* (c.1891)

SERVES 6–8

FOR THE CUSTARD

170 ml/6 fl oz/¾ cup double cream

170 ml/6 fl oz/¾ cup milk

2 vanilla pods, split

4 egg yolks

55 g/2 oz/¼ cup caster sugar

6 leaves gelatine (or 2 tbsp powdered gelatine), soaked in cold water

100 g/3½ oz/1 cup ground almonds

FOR THE TRIFLE

100 g/3½ oz leftover sponge cake (any of the sponge recipes in this book will do, though the Savoy cake is particularly good, see p187)

55 ml/2 fl oz/¼ cup brandy

100 ml/3½ fl oz/generous ⅓ cup jam (jelly), such as strawberry, raspberry or peach

85 g/3 oz/½ cup crystallised ginger, cubed

100 g/3½ oz ratafia biscuits or macaroons (for Mrs Crocombe's take, see Mackronis p126)

115 ml/4 fl oz/½ cup sherry, port or another fortified spirit

570 ml/1 pt/2⅓ cups whipping cream

1 tbsp icing sugar (confectioner's sugar)

A trifle is a thing of no consequence, and how it also came to be the name of one of Britain's most beloved dishes is the cause of some debate. Early trifles were more like fools (puréed fruit mixed with sweetened cream), and it took about 250 years for them to develop into the layered mixture of cake, fruit, custard and cream that usually forms the basis of the modern dish. The late 19th century was a sort of heyday for them, and Avis Crocombe would certainly have had a few variations in her repertoire. Like so many very common dishes though, she did not write one into her manuscript book: it would have been so familiar to her that she would not have needed a recipe. The amounts are thoroughly flexible, as are the contents. In the spirit of the time, we'd encourage you to play around with substitutes in this loose recipe, to make your own version. The key, as with so many Victorian recipes, is not to skimp on the alcohol.

Start by making the custard. Put the cream, milk and vanilla in a saucepan and heat without boiling, to infuse the vanilla, for about 5 minutes. Remove the pods (you can rinse and dry them and pop them in a jar of sugar to make vanilla sugar). Whisk the egg yolks and sugar together and pour the hot milk over the mixture, whisking as you do. Return the mixture to the pan and cook gently until it thickens. Do not let it boil, or it will curdle. Add the softened gelatine and ground almonds and allow to cool to room temperature.

Cut the cake into even slices. Dice any of the fruit for decorating which needs it (see overleaf), and ensure all the ingredients are within reach (your fingers are about to get very sticky!).

½ tbsp flaked almonds

15 g/½ oz/3–4 long strips of candied angelica

fresh or candied cherries or other fruit

fresh or candied edible flowers

....

SAVOURY TRIFLE

The American TV series Friends *once featured an accidental savoury trifle. They did exist in reality: one recipe book gave both a lobster and a veal version. Bread replaced the cake, with the result more of a fried bread chalice filled with a seasoned mixture than the usual sweet layered delight.*

....

NOTE

Yes, there is a lot of alcohol in this. It was not intended as nursery food: children generally only joined their parents at small family dinners until they reached their late teens. Victorian sweets do often include alcohol, especially brandy. Trifle is eaten by being spooned out into individual bowls, with the server making sure to dig deep through all the layers. (To make this vegetarian, thicken the custard with cornflour/corn starch instead of gelatine.)

....

Now you can build the trifle, which should be presented in a glass bowl. Start with a layer of cake slices, then pour over the brandy. Spread with the jam. Add the crystallised ginger, then a layer of the biscuits. Pour the sherry or port over this and put the bowl in the fridge to rest for 10 minutes.

Remove the bowl of trifle from the fridge and pour over the custard, smoothing it out as you go. Return this to the fridge until just set (15–20 minutes, or up to 30 minutes before serving). Whip the whipping cream and icing sugar to piping consistency and transfer to a piping bag fitted with a wide fluted nozzle. Pipe the cream on generously, piling it to form a peak.

Decorate with artfully arranged almonds, angelica, candied fruit and flowers. The Victorians favoured symmetrical arrangements, with lots of colour.

CHOCOLATE PUDDING

Avis Crocombe, *unpublished manuscript* (no date)

225 g/8 oz/1⅓ cups chocolate
(about 70% cocoa solids)

285 ml/½ pt/1¼ cups milk

140 g/5 oz/⅔ cups butter, plus extra
for the mould

140 g/5 oz/1¼ cups fine breadcrumbs
(preferably fresh)

4 eggs, separated

115 g/4 oz/½ cup caster sugar, plus
extra for the mould

285 ml/½ pt/generous 1 cup cream,
to serve

....

CHOCOLATE

*Chocolate was introduced to Britain in
the mid 17th century as a drink, bought
in a block of what we would now call
cocoa liquor (100% cocoa solids). It
was often spiced with chilli or spices,
and flavoured with orange flower water
or jasmine. It was drunk with milk,
sometimes thickened with ground
almonds. Recipes for cooking with
chocolate appeared in the 18th century,
including sorbet, blancmange, and
delicate pastry and molten chocolate
entremets. Drinking cocoa appeared in
the 1830s, and was very popular. But it
was not until the Swiss developed what
we would recognise as milk chocolate,
designed for eating, that chocolate
started to become ubiquitous.*

....

One of the later recipes in the manuscript book, this is not in
Avis' handwriting. It is possibly Edwardian, but is more likely to
be a 1920s recipe, added when Avis was elderly or had handed
her book down to the next generation. Similar recipes can be
found in books of about this time, when eating chocolate was
established enough to have crept into the culinary repertoire,
and cheap enough to form the basis of mid-range puddings of
this type. It is an excellent recipe, and can easily be given a more
modern twist, if desired, with the addition of sweet spices such
as cinnamon or ginger, or hot spices such as chilli – all of which
were common when chocolate was still predominantly a drink,
in the 17th and 18th centuries.

Melt the chocolate with the milk and butter in a bain-marie (or a
bowl placed over a saucepan of hot water; don't let the base touch
the water). Mix, add the breadcrumbs and remove from the heat.

Whisk the egg yolks and caster sugar together until paler and
increased in volume, then fold into the chocolate mixture. Whisk
the whites in a clean bowl until they form stiff peaks. Fold them
gently into the chocolate mixture.

Butter the pudding basin or plain mould, then roll around a little
sugar, tapping to remove excess. Pour in the mixture and smooth
the top. Cover with baking parchment, cut to fit, and then foil or a
pudding cloth, remembering to make a pleat in the foil or cloth so
that the pudding can rise.

Steam for 60 minutes, then turn out and serve hot, with cream.

The original recipe suggests that the pudding is also nice cold, cut
into slices, as indeed it is. You can also make it in individual moulds,
in which case reduce the steaming time to 20–30 minutes.

SOUFFLÉ LORD CURZON

Avis Crocombe, *unpublished manuscript* (no date)

SERVES 8

6 eggs, separated

200 g/7 oz/scant 1 cup caster sugar, plus extra for the moulds

finely grated zest of 1 orange

finely grated zest of 1 lemon

¼ tsp cream of tartar (optional)

45 g/1½ oz/⅓ cup cornflour (corn starch), sifted

butter, for the moulds

This recipe is one of a series with names attached to them, and given its position in the manuscript, it must have been written down by Avis in the mid 1870s. There was no Lord Curzon at the time, but the likely person referred to is Alfred Nathaniel Holden Curzon, 8th Baronet and 4th Baron Scarsdale, whose family name was Curzon but whose title was Lord Scarsdale. His lands were in Derbyshire, where he was the rector of Kedleston. Avis' employers may have known him and dined with him, or hosted him in their turn, or perhaps she may have got the recipe from one of his cooks or maids. Soufflés date from the 18th century and were notorious for their difficulty.

Preheat the oven to 180°C/350°F.

Whisk the yolks, sugar (reserving 1 tbsp) and zests together in a bowl until light and pale. In a separate bowl, whisk the egg whites together with the remaining 1 tbsp sugar and cream of tartar, if using, until the mixture reaches soft peaks.

Combine this meringue mixture and the yolk mixture, gently folding them together (do not mix vigorously, or beat) along with the sifted cornflour. Butter eight 70 g/2½ oz ramekins, then spoon in some sugar and roll them around, tapping out the excess, to line the moulds. Spoon in the soufflé mixture.

Bake for 20 minutes until the soufflés have risen and are just set. Serve immediately.

SWISS PUDDING

Avis Crocombe, *unpublished manuscript* (no date)

SERVES 6–8 (FILLS A 1 LITRE/
1¾ PT/4 CUP OVENPROOF
SAUCEPAN OR DEEP TATIN TIN)

FOR THE CARAMEL

55 g/2 oz/¼ cup sugar

1 tbsp water

FOR THE PUDDING

2 eggs, plus 6 egg yolks

55 g/2 oz/¼ cup caster sugar

570 ml/1 pt/2⅓ cups milk

1 tbsp chopped candied peel

2 tbsp sweet sherry

2 tbsp water

finely grated zest and juice of 1 lemon

This is what would now be called a crème caramel. Why Avis' version is called a 'Swiss Pudding' is unclear: the recipe was already in circulation as *crème au caramel* (in modern French it is usually called *crème renversée au caramel*, because it is turned upside down) but, as was common in Victorian Britain, the same recipe often existed under several different names. Large crèmes like this can be problematic to cook through without burning, so the oven-based bain-marie is vital. Audley End's version would have sat on the stovetop; indeed there is still one in situ today.

Preheat the oven to 180°C/350°F and set a deep roasting tray in it, filled halfway with water. This will be the bain-marie.

For the caramel, put the sugar in the ovenproof saucepan or deep Tatin tin and moisten it with the measured water. Boil without stirring until a caramel forms. Once you have a golden colour, very carefully swirl the caramel around the pan or tin to cover the sides, then immediately remove from the heat.

Now make the pudding. Whisk the eggs and yolks in a bowl. Place them in a heavy-based saucepan with the sugar and milk and gently heat, stirring continuously to form a thick custard. Do not let it boil or it will curdle. Remove from the heat and stir in the candied peel.

Spoon this mixture into the caramel-lined pan or tin. Cover with foil and make a small hole in the middle to allow the steam out. Place the pan or tin into the bain-marie and cook for about 60 minutes. It should be set firm, but have a slight wobble. Allow to cool.

Mix the sherry, measured water, zest and juice in a saucepan and boil rapidly to form a syrup. Slide a plate over the pudding tin and invert carefully (best to do this over a bowl to catch any caramel, which you can then add to the sherry sauce). Just before serving, pour the sauce over the pudding, or serve it on the side if you prefer.

LA CRÈME AU NESSELRODE

Avis Crocombe, *unpublished manuscript* (no date); from Eliza Acton,
Modern Cookery for Private Families (1845)

SERVES 6–8 (FILLS AN 850 ML/
1½ PT/3½ CUP MOULD)

vegetable shortening, for the mould

100 ml/3½ fl oz/generous
⅓ cup water

200 g/7 oz/scant 1 cup caster sugar

200 g/7 oz/1¾ cup cooked chestnuts

3 tbsp Madeira, plus 1 tbsp for the
whipped cream (optional)

570 ml/1 pt/2⅓ cups double cream

1 vanilla pod, split

zest of 1 lemon, cut off without pith

9 leaves of gelatine, soaked in
cold water

55 g/2 oz/⅓ cup dried cherries,
chopped

55 g/2 oz/⅓ cup candied peel,
chopped

Nesselrode cream started life as 'Nesselrode pudding', which
was named for the diplomat Count Karl von Nesselrode, and
reputedly created for him by Antonin Carême, one of the most
influential figures of French cuisine. Carême worked briefly
for the Prince Regent (later George IV) in 1816, before leaving
under a cloud and escaping with a sigh of relief back to France.

Start by greasing the mould. Avis would have used a large copper
or ceramic culinary mould, but you can also use individual moulds.
If you are using a metal mould, there is no need to grease it.

Boil the measured water in a saucepan with half the caster sugar.
Reduce by a third. Add the chestnuts and Madeira, if using, and
simmer for 5 minutes. Remove from the heat and allow to cool a
little. Strain the chestnuts, reserving the syrup. Purée the chestnuts
in a blender, using a little of the syrup, if necessary, to obtain a
smooth paste. Cool thoroughly.

Put half the cream in a pan with most of the remaining caster sugar,
reserving 1 heaped tbsp, and add the vanilla pod and lemon zest.
Bring to a low simmer. Add the softened gelatine and mix. Simmer
for 5 minutes to infuse the flavours, then strain into a jug. Whip the
remaining cream with the 1 tbsp Madeira, if using, and the reserved
1 heaped tbsp of sugar, until you obtain soft peaks.

Put the chestnut purée into a cold bowl, add the infused cream
mixture and mix well. Fold in the whipped cream and finally the
dried cherries and peel.

Pour the mixture into the mould and set in the fridge for at least
6 hours before turning out. If you have used a metal mould, dip the
base into hot water quickly to help to release it, or use a cook's blow
torch to warm the outside.

A GERTRUDE À LA CRÈME

Avis Crocombe, *unpublished manuscript* (no date); from Eliza Acton,
Modern Cookery for Private Families (1845)

SERVES 6–8 (MAKES 1 X 15 CM/
6 INCH CAKE)

1 slightly stale sponge cake, approx
15 cm/6 inches across (see p175)

1½ tbsp each raspberry, cherry,
apricot, greengage and strawberry
jam (jelly), or any others you like

4 egg whites

170 g/6 oz/¾ cup caster sugar

¼ tsp cream of tartar

green food colouring powder

red food colouring powder

100 g/3½ oz/½ cup white marzipan
(almond paste)

1 tbsp icing sugar (confectioner's
sugar), plus extra for dusting

350 ml/12 oz/1½ cups whipping cream

FOR THE SUGAR SYRUP

1½ tbsp water

1½ tbsp sugar

TO DECORATE

edible flowers (optional)

Another recipe from Eliza Acton, the most reliable of Victorian cooks. This is a good way to use a whole, slightly stale sponge cake. Stale cakes are not something modern households usually have to deal with, but they were not uncommon in large houses such as Audley End: ovens took a while to come to temperature, and could be fickle, while unexpected guests might well descend, wanting tea and cake, so it was a wise precaution to have a few extra cakes in hand (and recipes which would make use of the leftovers). Waste was very much frowned upon, and while the Braybrookes' meals may seem extravagant, they were carefully planned so that very little food was thrown out. Gertrude must be a mistaken corruption (which appears in Acton's original and was copied by Avis) of the French *guirlande*, meaning 'garland', which is what this sweet is supposed to resemble.

Slice the cake horizontally into 6 discs (or fewer, if necessary). With a 5 cm/2 inch round cutter, remove the centre of each disc (if you have a deep enough cutter, you can do this before you slice it), so that when you reassemble the cake it has one deep hole in the middle. The discards can be eaten or used for trifle (see p87).

Spread each cake slice with a different thin layer of jam and rebuild the cake, carefully lining up the slices. It is helpful if the top layer is less full of jam than the rest. Preheat the oven to 140°C/275°F.

Whisk the egg whites with the sugar and cream of tartar to make a thick meringue (the consistency should be somewhere between meringue and royal icing); at this point you can add a little powdered food colouring, if desired. The original recipe suggests green or rose are appropriate colours, but you can also leave it white. Using a palette knife, spread the meringue over the whole surface of the cake, including the sides of the central hole.

Bake the cake for 50–60 minutes until the meringue is hardened but not brown. Remove and allow to cool.

Make a sugar syrup by boiling the measured water and sugar in a saucepan until the sugar has dissolved. Leave to cool.

Colour about two thirds of the marzipan green and the rest red. Roll out the green marzipan on an icing sugar-dusted surface to 3–4 mm/¹⁄₈ inch thick and cut out to form leaves, marking them lightly to form veins. Stick these to the cake with a little sugar syrup. With the red marzipan, make berries or other leaves. The decoration should resemble a leafy garland, so arranging it to look like sprays around the cake is the aim.

Just before serving, whip the cream and icing sugar together to form stiff peaks, and fill an icing bag fitted with a star nozzle. Pipe the cream into the central hole in the *guirlande*, top with edible flowers, if using, and serve.

APPLES AND CREAM
IN A MOULD

Avis Crocombe, *unpublished manuscript* (no date)

SERVES 8–10 (FILLS A 1¼ LITRE/
2 PT/1⅓ CUP MOULD)

10 leaves of gelatine

485 ml/17 fl oz/2 cups double cream

finely grated zest of 1 lemon

2 tbsp caster sugar

55 ml/2 fl oz/¼ cup amaretto liqueur

500 g/17 oz/2 cups apple purée
(applesauce), sweetened to taste
(or see note below to make
your own)

vegetable shortening, for the mould
(optional)

2 litres/3½ pt/generous 2 quarts ice
cubes, for setting (optional)

edible rose petals, to serve (optional)

....

NOTE

*The original recipe calls for apples
'as for a charlotte'. You can easily
make your own apple purée by peeling,
coring and dicing 4–5 large eating or
dual-purpose apples, and stewing them
in a saucepan with 4–5 tbsp of water
and a small knob of butter. You can
also microwave them. Once done, mash
or blend them and taste, adding sugar
if required (how much will depend on
personal preference, as well as the
variety of apple).*

....

Moulded foods were extremely popular at the Victorian table, and Mrs Crocombe included a number of recipes which lent themselves to being moulded. Moulds were available in a bewildering variety of sizes, shapes and materials, and used for frozen, chilled, baked and boiled dishes. In the 21st century, when the range of moulded foods has dwindled to jelly and the occasional blancmange, it's hard to fully appreciate why kitchens such as that at Audley End had such a wide variety of culinary moulds, or to realise how elegant the results could look when presented. This relatively simple recipe can be made in any mould – copper, ceramic, or the more modern plastic or glass – but do remember to grease it first. To achieve an even more striking look, angle the mould slightly for each successive layer, which gives a series of asymmetric lines (see photo opposite).

Divide the gelatine equally between 2 bowls, and soak in cold water to soften it. Mix the cream, lemon zest, sugar and amaretto together in a saucepan and bring to a very low simmer. Add half the gelatine and stir well to dissolve. Remove from the heat and allow to cool to room temperature.

Heat the apple purée in another saucepan and add the remaining gelatine to this. Again, stir to mix, remove from the heat and cool to room temperature.

Prepare the mould. If it is very plain (for example a charlotte mould or loaf tin), you can line it with cling film (plastic wrap). However, for anything more complicated, it is best to use a little vegetable shortening to grease it.

The Victorian way to make a layered cream was to set the mould in a bowl of ice (cover the ice with a tea towel first, to stop the cubes leaping around when you are repositioning the mould). It's a good method to use, as it means you don't need to constantly open the fridge and can angle the mould easily to create diagonal lines if you want to. However, if you don't have any ice to hand you can just put the mould in the fridge.

Pour a 2.5 cm/1 inch-thick layer of the cream mixture into the bottom of the mould. Leave to set lightly, about 20–30 minutes. Then add a layer of the apple purée, of a similar thickness. Leave to set for 20–30 minutes. Repeat until the mould is full and you have used up both mixtures, making sure that the top layer sets level. Leave for at least 1 hour, preferably 4–6, before demoulding.

To demould, run a knife gently around the very edge of the set cream, about 3 mm/⅛ inch down. Place a plate on the mould, then swiftly invert it onto the plate. Shake hard and the cream should slide out. It is then best left for at least 30 minutes before serving, so that the gelatine can soften slightly. Scatter with edible rose petals to serve, if you like.

ICE SUPPLY

Like Audley End (right), most country houses had an ice house – a large, deep well, topped with a brick structure to keep air out. Ice was stored for years, very slowly melting into the ground through a drain at the bottom. The ice often came from lakes and ponds which froze solid most years (this was well before climate change). Ice was also shipped from the US and Canada, to be stored and sold. When the Braybrookes were at their London residence, they would have bought ice from a commercial dealer such as Carlo Gatti, who had a huge ice house near what is now Kings Cross (you can still visit it, as it is now the London Canal Museum).

CITRON PUDDING

Anon, unpublished manuscript found in the Audley End archive, *c.1830*

SERVES 8–10

butter, for the dish

455 g/1 lb puff pastry

flour, for dusting

30 g/1 oz/¼ cup candied citron peel

2 tbsp candied lemon peel

2 tbsp candied orange peel

6 egg yolks, plus 2 egg whites

115 g/4 oz/½ cup caster sugar

225 g/8 oz/1 cup clarified butter (see p57), warm

whipped cream, to serve

Other than the recipes identified as having been written down during Avis Crocombe's time at Audley End, this is the only recipe attached to the house. It probably dates to 1853–6, before Mrs Crocombe's time, as it was found tucked within the pages of a supply ledger of that date. Citrus fruit of all types would have been grown at Audley End. The house did not have an orangerie – a dedicated citrus-growing greenhouse – but its many glasshouses would have enabled the gardeners to produce citrus anyway. Citron itself is one of the five citrus varieties from which all the others are derived, and was quite possibly the first citrus to reach Western Europe. (The other four are the pomelo, mandarin, papeda and kumquat.) Inedible raw, it is a large, often uneven-skinned yellow fruit with more rind and pith than interior, and is invariably used for its peel, which still forms the basis of a lot of the mix in mixed candied peel. It is worth trying to source large chunks of the peel for this recipe.

Butter a 28 cm/11 inch baking dish or flan tin. Roll out the pastry on a flour-dusted surface to about 3 mm/⅛ inch thick and use it to line the dish, trimming the edges. Preheat the oven to 175°C/345°F.

Finely slice the candied peels into julienne. Whisk the egg yolks and whites together with the sugar in a large bowl with electric beaters. Gradually drizzle in the warm clarified butter, beating on a medium setting, until all is well mixed and forms a smooth emulsion.

Layer the julienned peel into the pastry-lined dish, then add the egg mixture. Bake for 45 minutes until the custard is set but still wobbly and the top is a light brown. If the top starts to rise, reduce the oven temperature, as this means the custard is overcooking. If necessary, remove it from the oven and stand the dish or tin in cool water for a few minutes to stop the cooking.

Serve with whipped cream. This pudding is best served on the day it is made, otherwise the pastry will turn soggy.

CUSTARD PUDDING (VERY GOOD)

Avis Crocombe, *unpublished manuscript* (no date)

SERVES 8–10 (FILLS A 1¼ LITRE/
2 PT/1⅓ CUP MOULD)

5 egg yolks

100 g/3½ oz/½ cup sugar

850 ml/1½ pt/3½ cups single cream

1 tsp orange flower water, or
a few drops of extract

2 tbsp brandy

6 leaves of gelatine, soaked in
cold water

vegetable shortening, for the mould
(if using ceramic or glass)

wine sauce, to serve (optional,
see p105)

strained jam (jelly) or fruit coulis,
to serve (optional)

One of the few recipes in the manuscript to have further annotation, this pudding has 'very good' written next to it, and has therefore always been known as 'custard pudding very good' to the team at Audley End. It is essentially a set custard, with the addition of a gelling agent (originally isinglass), to ensure that it will take the form of a mould and can be demoulded easily. The original calls for 'sugar to taste', and it is worth considering what you plan to serve with it: a very sweet sauce will require less sugar in the pudding itself, and of course individual tastes differ. If you are a nervous custard maker, add 1 tbsp of cornflour (corn starch) or custard powder to the cold milk, which will help to thicken and stabilise the mixture.

Whisk the egg yolks and sugar together in a saucepan, add the cream, then heat gently, stirring constantly, until it thickens. Do not let it boil, or the custard will curdle. Remove from the heat, then add the orange flower water and brandy. Stir in the softened gelatine, mix until dissolved, then strain through a fine sieve. Leave to cool to room temperature.

If using a ceramic or glass mould, grease it well. Pour in the custard. Chill in a fridge overnight, or for at least 6 hours. Turn out and serve with wine sauce on the side. You could also serve it with strained jam or a fruit coulis, if you prefer.

FIG PUDDING

Avis Crocombe, *unpublished manuscript* (no date)

SERVES 4–6 (FILLS A 570 ML/
1 PT/2⅓ CUP PUDDING BASIN
OR OTHER MOULD)

85 g/3 oz/scant ½ cup chopped fresh
figs, or 155 g/5½ oz/1 cup chopped
dried figs with 1 tbsp of milk

85 g/3 oz/1 cup breadcrumbs

85 g/3 oz/⅓ cup caster sugar

pinch each of ground cinnamon
and nutmeg

3 tbsp brandy

¼ tsp bicarbonate of soda

85 g/3 oz/⅔ cup suet

vegetable shortening, for the mould

wine sauce (see p105), cream or
custard (see p113), to serve (optional)

Another of Avis' many recipes for steamed suet pudding, this is a classic of the mid-Victorian era. Figs would have been among the many fruits grown in the kitchen garden at Audley End, so were readily available fresh, although the pudding also works with dried fruit. The original recipe does not specify which she used. Like many such pudding recipes, it is very versatile and the same basic concept can be used for other sweet fruit, fresh or dried. It is not to be confused with figgy pudding, as celebrated in the carol 'We wish you a merry Christmas' – that one was just another variant on the theme of plum pudding (see p109).

Mix all the ingredients except the suet in a large bowl. Stir in the suet, being careful not to overwork the mixture, or the pudding won't be so light.

Grease the mould. If the top is flat, a small piece of greased baking parchment cut to fit will aid demoulding later. Put the mixture into the mould and cover with a piece of greased baking parchment, again cut to fit. Cover with a prepared pudding cloth or foil, ensuring you make a pleat in it to allow the pudding to rise.

Steam the pudding in a steamer, or in a saucepan of water (the water should come about three-quarters of the way up the basin), over a low heat, for 3 hours.

Remove from the steamer, allow to cool for 10 minutes, then carefully turn out of the mould. Serve with wine sauce, cream or custard.

SWISS BASKETS

Avis Crocombe, *unpublished manuscript* (no date)

SERVES 6

FOR THE CASTLE PUDDINGS

200 g/7 oz/generous ¾ cup butter, plus extra for the moulds

200 g/7 oz/scant 1 cup caster sugar, plus extra for the moulds

200 g/7 oz/generous 1½ cups flour, plus extra for the moulds

finely grated zest of 2 lemons

4 eggs

TO TRANSFORM THEM INTO SWISS BASKETS

2 tbsp redcurrant jelly, pushed through a sieve to remove any bits

115 g/4 oz/1 cup very finely chopped or crushed pistachio nuts

115 ml/4 fl oz/½ cup whipping cream

6 candied cherries

15 g/½ oz/6 long stalks of candied angelica

These fun little puddings are another example of Victorian efficiency, as well as of the rise of rather kitsch presentation in the late 19th century. They are based on castle puddings, a recipe for which Avis wrote into her manuscript, but take them to a whole new level. As with the many recipes based on sponge cake, they are intended for the cook who habitually doubles up on his or her baking, in order to have cakes ready-made for a later date. The idea of leftovers, as something to be used up and rather inferior, is a 20th-century one. For the Victorians, 'cold meats' or the remains of a dinner were an intrinsic part of meal planning and welcomed for making life easier. The castle puddings can be served plain if you prefer, with a lemon curd or syrup, wine sauce (see p105) or clotted cream.

First make the castle puddings. Preheat the oven to 180°C/350°F. Butter 6 dariole moulds, or high-sided cupcake moulds. Sprinkle these lightly with a little caster sugar and flour, rolling and tapping to remove the excess. Cream the butter and sugar until pale and light, adding the lemon zest gradually during this process. Then add the eggs one at a time, mixing between each addition. Fold in the flour and mix together.

Divide the batter between the moulds, filling them about two thirds full. Place them in a baking tray filled with hot water to reach about halfway up each mould. Cover each mould with a disc of baking parchment, cut to fit (this will keep the moisture in, stop the cakes sticking to the foil and help them to stay flat). Now cover the whole tin with foil and bake for 50 minutes, or until a skewer comes out clean. Cool in the moulds for 10–15 minutes before turning out.

LEFTOVERS

The remains of meals eaten upstairs were reused in a number of ways. Meat could be made into rissoles, fritters and the very Victorian 'hash', curries or toad-in-the-hole. Vegetables might find their way into curries or garnishes. Genuine leftovers usually went to supplement the servants' diet. Upper servants, such as Mrs Crocombe, ate some meals separately to lower servants, and regarded the best bits of what was left as their prerogative. Anything remaining would go to the local poor, with scraps fed to pigs.

Trim the tops of the castle puddings so that they are flat. Turn them over and use an apple corer to remove the centres, creating a vertical hole. If the puddings were made in cupcake moulds, you may need to widen the hole proportionately (you can eat the trimmings or turn them into trifle, see p87). Turn them the right way up again.

Warm the redcurrant jelly slightly on the hob or in a microwave, and use a pastry brush to brush the sides and top of the cakes with liquid jelly. Spread the pistachio nuts on a plate and coat the outsides of the cakes by rolling the cakes in the nuts. Whip the cream to stiff peaks, fill an icing bag with a plain or fluted nozzle, and pipe the cream into the central holes until they are just full and the cream is poking out slightly.

Pop a cherry on top of each creamy peak. Steam the angelica briefly to soften it, and use to form handles over the baskets.

WINE SAUCE

Avis Crocombe, *unpublished manuscript* (no date); from Eliza Acton,
Modern Cookery for Private Families (1845)

MAKES ABOUT 285 ML/½ PT/
GENEROUS 1 CUP SAUCE

VARIATION 1

200 ml/7 fl oz/scant 1 cup water

100 g/3½ oz/scant ½ cup caster sugar

100 g/3½ oz/⅓ cup apricot jam (jelly),
pushed through a sieve to remove
the lumps

juice of 1 lemon

55 ml/2 fl oz/¼ cup sweet sherry
or port

VARIATION 2

55 g/2 oz/¼ cup butter

1 tsp flour

200 ml/7 fl oz/scant 1 cup water

100 g/3½ oz/scant ½ cup caster sugar

zest of 1 orange, cut off without pith,
plus 2 tsp orange juice

100 ml/4 fl oz/½ cup fortified wine,
such as Madeira or sweet sherry

Wine sauce was a standard Victorian accompaniment for sweets, especially puddings. The first of these recipes occurs late in Mrs Crocombe's manuscript, but she recommends it to go with several of her earlier recipes, including college puddings, sponge cake pudding, custard pudding and castle puddings (see p248, p163, p100 and p103). There were many variations on this theme, and the second of those given here is an earlier version, from Eliza Acton, from whose *Modern Cookery for Private Families* Avis copied a number of recipes. The use of flour to thicken the sauce is characteristic of the earlier era: by the 1890s sauces had become a little less rich. However, both work very well. Ginger wine can be used instead of the fortified wines in both cases, if you are looking for a budget option.

For the first variation, heat the measured water and sugar in a saucepan to form a syrup. Add the jam, lemon juice, and sherry or port and bring to the boil. Reduce by one-quarter. Serve.

OR

For the second variation, mash the butter and flour together and chill. Boil the measured water, sugar and orange zest together in a saucepan for 10–15 minutes to form a syrup. Add the chilled butter and flour mix, orange juice and wine and return to the boil, whisking until thick and lump-free. You can also use port, in which case the original recipe recommends using lemon zest and juice instead of orange, and adding a pinch of nutmeg.

MARBLED EGGS

Louis-Eustache Ude, *The French Cook* (1813), with Audley End tweaks

FILLS 10 EGGS (DEPENDING ON SIZE)

1 litre/1¾ pt/4 cups double cream

3 tbsp sugar

12 leaves of gelatine, soaked in cold water

½ tsp vanilla extract

3 tbsp chopped chocolate (100% cocoa solids, or as dark as you can get it)

10 eggs

crushed ice, to set

a little flour and water, to make a paste to seal the holes in the eggs

TO SERVE

multiple egg cups
or
ring of transparent white wine jelly with candied peel strips set within it to resemble a nest
or
sponge cake made in a ring mould, piped with royal icing

The idea for this layered cream comes from the 19th-century chef Louis-Eustache Ude. Ude had started his career in the kitchens of Versailles, France, eventually moving to Britain. He worked for a number of notable households before heading up the catering at Crockford's, one of London's leading gentlemen's clubs, in 1827. He began on the then-enormous salary of £1,200 a year, and apparently left ten years later because he considered he ought to be paid £4,000 – more than 13 times the salary of Queen Victoria's chief cook. Ude's best-known book, *The French Cook*, contains a number of superb recipes, including many for jellies and set creams, which were popular as sweet entremets. The idea of setting jellies in eggs is slightly later. This adaptation is a dish that the team at Audley End make regularly.

Heat the cream in a saucepan to just below boiling. Add the sugar and heat to dissolve. Mix in the softened gelatine until completely incorporated. Pour half the cream mixture into a jug and add the vanilla extract. Add the chocolate to the other cream mixture on the hob and whisk it over a very low heat until it has melted. Pour this into a separate jug. Allow both mixes to cool to room temperature.

Blow the eggs. To do so, pierce a hole in the top and bottom of an egg with a pin, enlarge the hole in the base to about 3 mm/⅛ inch and that in the top to about 7 mm/¼ inch. Break up the contents inside the egg with a needle or skewer. Hold the egg over a bowl, place your mouth firmly round the hole in the top of the egg, forming a good seal. Blow the contents of the egg into the bowl. They will be lightly beaten, perfect for scrambled eggs, omelettes or cakes. (You may need to strain out stray bits of shell first.) Repeat to blow all the eggs.

Put the crushed ice in a bowl and cover it with a clean tea towel. Use the flour and water paste to cover the bottom small holes of the hollowed eggs. Stand the eggs upright in the ice. Pour a few tbsp of the vanilla mixture into the eggs, using a small funnel or a piping nozzle. Allow this layer to set for about 10–15 minutes on the ice, then add a few tablespoons of the chocolate mixture. Keep building up the layers of cream until the eggs have been filled. Chill in the ice or in a fridge for 2–3 hours.

Once the eggs have set firmly you can begin to remove the shells. One of the easiest ways to do this is by sliding a teaspoon between the shell and the set cream. It's useful to keep a small bowl of cold water and a cloth ready to wipe your fingers between eggs, so as not to smudge colours.

The most straightforward way to serve the eggs is in egg cups. However, you could make a nest from a clear white wine jelly set in a ring mould with strips of candied peel arranged within it to resemble a nest. Or, for an Audley End flourish, you could make a sponge cake ring intricately piped with white royal icing and place the eggs inside, just like Mrs Crocombe did.

....

JELLIES AND GELATINE

Gelatine was invented in the US and was available in packet form from the mid 19th century. It is a gelling agent extracted from animal tissues such as hooves and skin. Packet gelatine was not in widespread use until the end of that century, and Mrs Crocombe would have extracted jelly herself – by making boiled calf's foot jelly. The resulting liquor was then flavoured (usually with white wine and sugar) before setting. Creams such as this one were set with isinglass, made from the swim bladder of a sturgeon.

....

CHRISTMAS PUDDING

Eliza Acton, *Modern Cookery for Private Families* (1845)

SERVES 8–10 (FILLS A 1¼ LITRE/
2 PT/1⅓ QUART MOULD)

170 g/6 oz/1 cup raisins

170 g/6 oz/¾ cup currants

1 tbsp candied peel

115 g/4 oz/1 cup peeled and chopped
eating apple (about 1 large apple)

85 g/3 oz/⅔ cup flour, plus more
(optional) for the muslin

85 g/3 oz/1 cup breadcrumbs

170 g/6 oz/scant 1½ cups suet

140 g/5 oz/⅔ cup sugar (white
or brown)

½ tsp mixed ground nutmeg and
mace, or mixed spice (pumpkin spice)

3 eggs, lightly beaten

115 ml/4 fl oz/½ cup brandy,
plus 55 ml/2 fl oz/¼ cup, to serve

butter, for the mould

salt

....

NOTE

*Mrs Crocombe would have used her
hands to mix this Christmas pudding,
as with any other heavy dough. Fingers
are much more practical than a
wooden spoon, which tends to end in
blisters. In some kitchens hands would
be more hygienic, as badly cared-for
wooden implements can split and
harbour bacteria.*

....

Christmas pudding has its origins in the late medieval plum pottage – a rich, spiced mix of dried fruit, beef and gravy. 'Plum' was just a generic term for any dried fruit (although, confusingly, 'sugarplums' meant sugared almonds). Plum pottage was sufficiently expensive to become associated with feasting, especially in the winter, as the ingredients did not rely upon fresh produce. By the 18th century the pottage had become a pudding, with the addition of suet and breadcrumbs, boiled in a cloth or sometimes a mould. The patriotic dishes of Britain became roast beef and plum pudding (served, and eaten, together). The pudding can be made several days or even several months in advance, if desired. Modern puddings are often aged for months, but there is no need for that with older recipes.

Mix all the ingredients together well, apart from the brandy to serve, adding a pinch of salt. Do not overwork: mix quickly so that the suet does not get warm and sticky, but remains in pieces. Butter the mould and put in the mixture. If you are using a patterned mould, make sure to butter all the corners or the pudding will stick.

➤➔

Cut a piece of baking parchment to fit the top and butter it before placing it on the pudding. Now cover this either with a piece of wetted, floured butter muslin or a pudding cloth and tie it firmly in place with string. If you don't have a cloth, you can use foil. Whichever you use, make a pleat across the middle when you put it in place, to allow the pudding to rise when it cooks without straining against the cloth or foil.

Lower the pudding carefully into a large saucepan of boiling water, ensuring that the water comes to about 2.5 cm/1 inch below the top of the bowl. Allow the water to return to a full boil, then reduce the heat so it is at a rolling boil, but not bubbling so vigorously that it splashes over the top too much.

Boil for 4 hours, keeping an eye on the water level and topping up with boiling water as necessary – if the water gets too low the pudding won't cook properly.

After 4 hours, remove the pudding from the water. The Victorians would have demoulded it and served it straight away, but at this stage you can leave it to cool and then store it somewhere cool and dry until needed (it can be stored for at least a year), in its mould or wrapped in baking parchment or in a sealed container. When required, simply pop it back in the mould, cover it with a fresh layer of buttered parchment and muslin or foil and boil for another hour to heat through.

When the pudding is hot, stick a holly sprig in the top and, just before serving, heat the remaining brandy in a small saucepan. Pour it over the pudding and carefully set fire to it. Enter the dining room bearing the flaming pudding, to wild applause.

....

SWEETS, PUDDINGS AND DESSERT
'Pudding' in Britain today tends to mean what in the 1920s and 1930s was called a 'sweet', and in the 19th century a 'sweet entremet': it's a generic term for the sweet course at the end of the meal (confusingly, sometimes also called dessert). However, 'pudding' is also a type of dish, and this is the way it would have been understood by Mrs Crocombe. 'Pudding' could be savoury or sweet, boiled, baked, steamed or frozen. It was usually made in a pudding basin or complicated mould, but – even more confusingly – early puddings were boiled in cloths or stomachs (usually those of pigs or sheep; like black pudding, sausages can be puddings, and haggis is definitely a pudding). Clear?!
....

A MERINGUE OF ANY KIND OF FRUIT

Avis Crocombe, *unpublished manuscript* (no date)

SERVES 8

8 ripe pears suitable for cooking, such as Conference, William or Warden

1 vanilla pod

juice of ½ lemon

FOR THE CUSTARD

70 g/2½ oz/generous ½ cup cornflour (corn starch)

310 ml/11 fl oz/1⅓ cups milk

310 ml/11 fl oz/1⅓ cups double cream

6 egg yolks

130 g/4½ oz/generous ½ cup caster sugar

FOR THE MERINGUE

4 egg whites

200 g/7 oz/scant 1 cup caster sugar

TO DECORATE

fresh fruit (redcurrants, raspberries, sliced strawberries), edible flowers or mint sprigs (optional)

This recipe was written towards the end of Avis' manuscript, after her marriage, from the era when she was running a boarding house with her new husband, Benjamin Stride. It is less time-consuming to construct than many of her early recipes, but is nevertheless characteristically brilliant. It is reminiscent of other classic sweets, including Eton mess and pavlova, but is more elegantly presented. You can use any fruit as long as it will cook without falling apart. We've used pears, but strawberries, plums or peaches would all be excellent. It is served in its baking dish, so choose an attractive – but ovenproof – one.

First, make the custard: mix the cornflour with a small amount of the milk until it forms a loose paste. Combine the cornflour paste with the cream, egg yolks, all but ½ tbsp of the caster sugar and the rest of the milk in a heavy-based saucepan. Heat slowly, whisking continuously as the liquid starts to thicken. Do not allow it to boil or the eggs will scramble and the custard will split. Once thick, remove from the heat and sprinkle the remaining ½ tbsp of sugar over the top, to stop a skin forming. Preheat the oven to 200°C/400°F.

Peel, quarter and core the pears. Put them in a saucepan and just cover them with water. Add the vanilla pod and lemon juice, put the lid on (or, if you do not have a lid, place a disc of baking parchment on top) and cook until the pears are just cooked through. Be careful not to overcook them. Remove with a slotted spoon and drain.

Whisk the egg whites until soft peaks form, then add the caster sugar and whisk until the volume has doubled and the meringue is shiny. Spoon into a piping bag fitted with a star nozzle.

Put a third of the custard into the chosen ovenproof dish followed by half the pears, then another third of the custard, the final half of the pears and – finally – the remaining custard. Pipe the meringue on top. Bake for 8 minutes, until the top is golden brown and crisp. Garnish with fresh fruit, flowers or mint, if desired.

PANCAKES

Maria Rundell, *A New System of Domestic Cookery* (1806)

MAKES 8

1 egg, plus 3 egg yolks

200 ml/7 fl oz/scant 1 cup
double cream

1 tbsp white wine or orange flower
water (or a few drops of extract)

115 g/4 oz/scant 1 cup flour

1 tbsp butter, melted, plus 1 tbsp
butter, at room temperature

TO SERVE

85 g/3 oz/¼ cup apricot jam (jelly)

1¾ tbsp icing sugar
(confectioner's sugar)

....

FLIPPING AND FILLING
*Successful pancake flipping requires
a bit of practice. The trick is to flip
up and away, moving the pan to catch
the pancake as it drops back to earth.
You need a steady hand. However,
ultimately it is easier than using a
spatula. It is also very impressive.
The classic filling for pancakes in
Britain is lemon and sugar: serve the
pancakes as a simple stack, with
strained lemon juice in a small jug
and a sugar shaker to the side.*

....

Pancakes are one of the most ancient of foods, and appear across the world. At their most basic the Western European pancake is a mixture of flour, water or milk, and egg, but even within that there are variations. Maria Rundell, the author of the book from which this is taken, suggested that if eggs were hard to come by you could use 'clean snow' instead (actual snow, which apparently helps to aerate the mixture; we haven't tested this, however). Rundell was one of the most popular authors of the 19th century, with official and unofficial editions of her book, including a plagiarised edition, published after her death. It includes 'New England Pancakes', which are very thin (like the recipe here), and far from the more common thicker, fluffy American- and Canadian-style pancakes often eaten at breakfast today.

Whisk together the egg, egg yolks, cream, and wine or orange flower water. Gradually whisk in the flour and finally the melted butter, making sure there are no lumps. (You can also use a blender.) The batter benefits from 30 minutes of resting, and can be left for a couple of hours in the fridge at this point.

Heat a small amount of the remaining butter on a medium heat in a frying pan, spreading it out with a heatproof brush or spatula. Put a ladleful of batter into the pan, swirling it around to form an even pancake. Cook for 1–2 minutes until the top is just cooked through and then turn over using a spatula, or flip it if you are confident. Cook the other side for 1–2 minutes, then slide the pancake onto a hot plate. Keep warm while you repeat to cook all 8 or so pancakes (the final number will depend on the size of the pan).

Spread each pancake with apricot jam and roll up. Pile them into a pyramid, dust with icing sugar and serve on a hot plate.

BROWN BREAD PUDDING

Avis Crocombe, *unpublished manuscript* (no date)

SERVES 6–8 (FILLS AN 850 ML/
1½ PT/3½ CUP MOULD, OR CAN
BE MADE AS INDIVIDUAL PUDDINGS
IN 140 ML/¼ PT/⅔ CUP MOULDS)

115 g/4 oz/½ cup butter at room
temperature, plus extra for
the mould(s)

a little flour, for the mould(s)

3 tbsp caster sugar

1 tbsp black treacle

85 g/3 oz/¼ cup apricot jam (jelly)

3 eggs, separated

¼ tsp cream of tartar, or a squeeze
of lemon juice (optional)

225 g/8 oz/2⅔ cups brown
breadcrumbs

100 g/3½ oz/⅓ cup chopped
mixed peel

100 ml/3½ fl oz/scant ½ cup sherry

....

PUDDING CLOTHS

*Victorian puddings were often made in
cloths, or in a basin or mould covered
with a cloth. To prepare a pudding
cloth – which should be made of butter
muslin, undyed cotton or, better still,
linen cloth – wet the cloth, wring it out
and dust a layer of flour upon it. Shake
off the excess. Pleat the middle so that
you have a flap of about 2.5 cm/1 inch
and lay this flat to one side. Put the
cloth on top of the pudding basin,
smoothing it down, and then tie string
very firmly around the rim to hold it in
place. The pleat allows the pudding to
expand as it cooks.*

....

Bread was ubiquitous on the Victorian table, whether rich or poor, so inevitably that meant a lot of stale bread. Waste was frowned upon, however, and consequently there was a wide range of recipes designed to make use of bread, whether in the form of crumbs, slices or chunks. This pudding uses brown bread, traditionally associated with the poor, but which became slightly more popular at the end of the 19th century as manufacturers promoted it on health grounds. It is prevented from being a plain or lower-class recipe by the usual Victorian additions of candied fruit and alcohol. Queen Victoria's one-time chef Charles Elmé Francatelli published a version that included cherries macerated in brandy and named it for Prince Albert's natal province, Saxe-Coburg-Gotha.

Butter the mould, or individual moulds or muffin moulds, and dust with a little flour.

Beat the butter until soft and fluffy. Add 2 tbsp of the sugar and all the treacle and jam. Beat for 5 minutes until lightly foamy. Add the egg yolks and beat again.

In a separate bowl, whisk the egg whites (the cream of tartar or lemon juice will help them rise). Add the remaining 1 tbsp of sugar and whisk to form soft peaks.

Fold the breadcrumbs, mixed peel and sherry into the egg yolk mixture. Then fold in the egg white mixture and combine gently. Spoon the mixture into the mould(s) and cover the top(s) with a disc of buttered baking parchment and then either pleated foil or a pleated pudding cloth. Steam over boiling water for 30 minutes for small moulds, or 60 minutes for a large pudding. Allow to sit for 5 minutes before serving.

Serve with wine sauce (see p105).

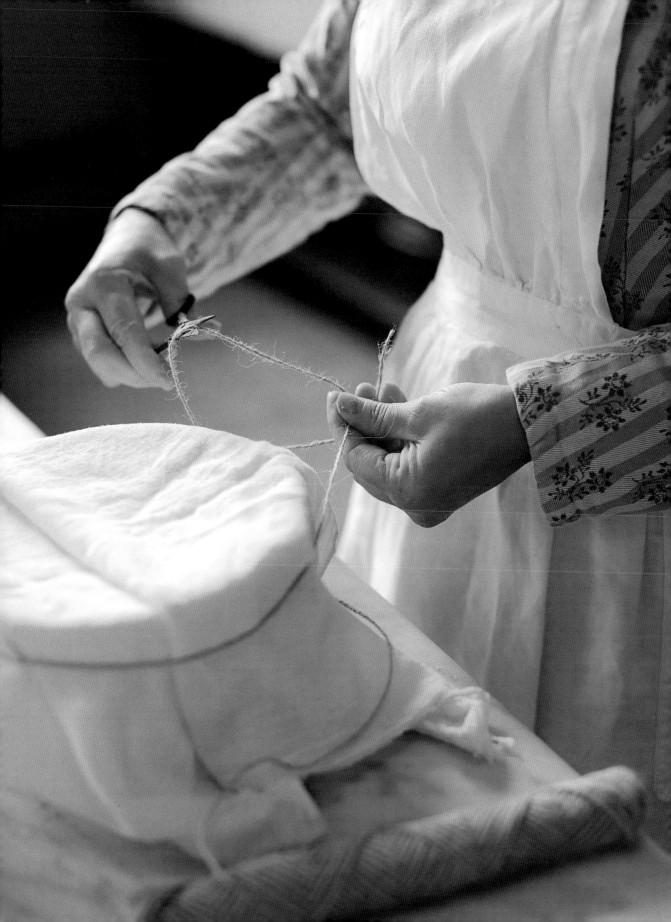

APPLE HEDGEHOG

Multiple sources, including Eliza Acton and Richard Dolby

SERVES 8–10

170 g/6 oz/¾ cup caster sugar

570 ml/1 pt/2⅓ cups water and
55 ml/2 fl oz/¼ cup water, separated

8 eating apples

4 apricots

1 tbsp apricot jam (jelly)

55 g/2 oz/¼ cup thick apple purée
(applesauce) (see note on p97)

FOR THE MERINGUE

3 egg whites

¼ tsp cream of tartar, or a squeeze
of lemon juice (optional)

200 g/7 oz/1 cup caster sugar

55 g/2 oz/½ cup flaked almonds

2 currants and 1 piece of candied
cherry (optional, if you want to give
the hedgehog a face)

Fantastical food dates back to the Romans. Medieval cooks delighted in creating food which looked like one thing but was made of another, most famously the mythical 'cockentrice': half a pig sewed to half a turkey or goose, then roasted and decorated. Hedgehogs were a common source of inspiration, due to their alien appearance and the fact that they were rarely eaten outside times of famine. An almond paste hedgehog recipe was in circulation in the 18th century, and in the 19th this version appeared. Most recipes simply prick the dome with almonds: the face is an old-fashioned addition which goes down very well with visitors to Audley End.

Make a syrup by boiling the sugar and 570 ml/1 pt/2⅓ cups of water together in a saucepan until it starts to thicken. Peel and core the apples without splitting them and gently poach them in the syrup, covered with a disc of baking parchment, until just cooked through. Be careful not to overcook. Remove and drain.

Stone and chop the apricots (there is no need to peel them). Put them in another saucepan with the jam and 55 ml/2 fl oz/¼ cup of water until the apricots break down and thicken. You will need to stir continuously to stop the mixture burning.

Fill the apples with the apricot mix. Line a 1¼ litre/2 pt/5 cup bowl with cling film (plastic wrap) and arrange the apples in it, fixing them in place with the apple purée. Cover and chill.

Preheat the oven to 200°C/400°F. Whisk the egg whites – the cream of tartar or lemon juice help the process – and gradually add the sugar while whisking to form thick, glossy, stiff peaks. Remove the apples from the fridge and turn out very carefully onto a large plate. Fill a piping bag fitted with a round nozzle and pipe the meringue over the apples. Use the flaked almonds to make hedgehog quills. It is up to you whether you want to give the hedgehog a face.

Bake for 8–10 minutes until the almonds are golden brown.

LEMON CHEESE CAKES

Avis Crocombe, *unpublished manuscript* (no date)

SERVES 6

3 egg yolks, plus 2 egg whites

225 g/8 oz/generous 1 cup
caster sugar

55 g/2 oz/¼ cup softened butter

finely grated zest and juice of
2 small lemons

1 tsp clear honey

12 ratafia or amaretti biscuits,
or amount to taste

Definitely not cheese cakes in the modern sense of the word, this is a very simple recipe which could be served either as a sweet or as a dessert. It is effectively a lemon curd, thickened with almond-flavoured biscuit crumbs, and can be served, as here, in glasses, or used as a filling for a blind-baked pastry case. (If using pastry, either a rough puff or all-butter puff works well.) This recipe can also be made with oranges. It is called a 'cheese' simply because it is a thick mixture, in the same way that the gâteau de pommes (see p84) is known as an apple cheese.

Cream the egg yolks, whites and sugar in a bowl, by beating very well until paler and increased in volume. Add the butter, lemon zest and juice. Put everything into a heatproof bowl over simmering water (a bain-marie), making sure the base of the bowl does not touch the water, and cook, stirring, until the mixture thickens. Add the honey.

Crush the biscuits into crumbs and add them as well (you can add more or less, according to taste). Serve hot, or better still, chilled, in glasses or small bowls.

....

COPPER BOWLS
Mrs Crocombe would have used a copper bowl to whisk her eggs. These were used because the copper reacts with a protein in the egg white which helped to stabilise the beaten whites in the same way a pinch of acid does. You can help the foam along when making meringue by adding a pinch of cream of tartar or a squeeze of lemon juice.

....

FASHIONABLE APPLE DUMPLINGS

Eliza Acton, *Modern Cookery for Private Families* (1845)

MAKES 6 (YOU WILL NEED
6 KNITTED DUMPLING CLOTHS OR
PUDDING/DISH CLOTHS)

225 g/8 oz/1¾ cups flour

85 g/3 oz/⅔ cup suet

½ tsp salt

6 eating apples, of roughly equal size
(older varieties are, as with every
recipe in this book, better – Cox and
Pippins are good)

6 tbsp orange or lemon marmalade
(see p231 for Mrs Crocombe's recipe)

85 g/3 oz/⅓ cup butter, for the cloths

wine sauce, to serve (optional,
see p105)

Dumplings, along with pancakes (see p114), are another food ubiquitous across time and cultures. In Britain they probably started life as balls of leftover bread dough, which were then boiled alongside the meat or vegetables. However, they rapidly evolved into a wide variety of types, both sweet and savoury, and by the 19th century the cook could choose to boil, steam or deep-fry his or her dumplings. They could be a plain side dish (especially common with stews), or a more elaborate item to be served in its own right. They were especially popular in cold, wet climates such as that of Britain, with the county of Norfolk, where Avis Crocombe worked in the 1870s, becoming particularly renowned for them. The phrase 'Norfolk dumpling' was used to describe people from Norfolk, often in a rather derogatory sense, although it could also be interpreted as referring to their sturdiness and uncomplicated natures.

Make the suet crust by combining the flour, suet, salt and a trickle of water, working fast so that the suet does not melt (you can do this in a food processor or blender). Add just enough cold water to make a stiff, not sticky, pastry. You do not need to let it rest, but if you are making the dumplings in several batches, it will sit happily in a fridge for up to 1 day. Divide it into 6 equal balls and roll them out into circles each large enough to fully envelope an apple.

Peel the apples and core them without splitting them. Trim the bases so that they are flat. Fill each hole from the core with 1 tbsp of the marmalade. Wrap each apple up in a suet crust disc, making sure that there are no gaps and that the covering is very even. Trim off any excess.

Melt the butter and, for each dumpling, use a pastry brush to brush it all over a clean knitted pudding cloth. Make sure you get the butter into all the crevices. Wrap the dumpling in the cloth tightly, tying it firmly at the top with string. Repeat for each dumpling.

You can cook these in standard pudding cloths, but they won't be as pretty. If you decide to knit or crochet your own cloth, a standard stocking stitch will be fine, but you can play with patterns to suit your taste. Make sure you use 100% cotton (preferably dishcloth yarn, which is Aran weight) – not man-made fibres, which will stretch and ruin the dumplings.

Lower the cloth-wrapped dumplings into a large saucepan of boiling water. Depending on the size of the pan, and how many cloths you have, you may need to do this in 2 batches. Keep the water at a rolling boil, or the crust will become soggy. Boil for 45 minutes, then fish the dumplings out using a fork through the top of the cloth, above the string. Being careful not to burn your fingers, remove them from the cloths and serve on a cloth doily, which will catch any moisture and stop them sliding around.

These are intended to be served boiled, but also work baked. You can also choose to boil and then bake them, which gives you a dumpling that is beautifully crispy outside and fluffy within. They are good on their own, but even better with wine sauce.

DESSERT AND SAVOURIES

RAMEKINS

Avis Crocombe, *unpublished manuscript* (no date)

SERVES 4

butter or neutral oil, for the moulds

55 g/2 oz/½ cup grated sharp Cheddar cheese

55 g/2 oz/¾ cup breadcrumbs

3 eggs, lightly beaten

generous pinch of cayenne pepper

115 ml/4 fl oz/½ cup cream

2 tsp English mustard

A classic cheese dish, related to the more common rarebit, which retained its popularity for about 350 years but has since disappeared. Ramekins originated in the 17th century, with recipes published by the French chef François-Pierre La Varenne for *ramequins* of cheese and also of meat or other titbits. By the early 19th century ramekins were ubiquitous in books as a quick savoury or supper dish, and by the end of the century it was possible to buy little ceramic dishes specifically designed for cooking them. The word ramekin came to mean both the recipe and the dishes, and even today that second meaning survives. Avis' manuscript suggests cooking them in paper cases, but they are better done – naturally – in actual ramekin dishes.

Preheat the oven to 200°C/400°F. Put a deep baking tray or roasting tin in the oven, half-filled with water. This will be the bain-marie.

Butter or oil 4 individual moulds or ramekins. In a large bowl, mix all the ingredients together. Fill the moulds three-quarters full with the cheese mixture. Place them into the bain-marie.

Cook for 20 minutes, until set but still bouncy. Serve immediately, either in their dishes or turned out, as you prefer.

....

DESSERT AND SAVOURIES

Savouries emerged in the late Victorian period as an alternative or addition to the dessert course. Dessert dishes were small, with refreshing flavours intended to cleanse the palate and aid digestion. Savouries – based on strong flavours such as chilli, smoked fish, cheese, offal and salt – added a zingier element. They were seen as rather masculine, and ideal for the pause after dinner during which the sexes parted, the men remaining in the dining room to drink (and use the chamber pot).

....

MACKRONIS [MACAROONS]

Avis Crocombe, *unpublished manuscript* (no date)

MAKES 35

85 g/3 oz/generous ¾ cup ground almonds

2 tbsp butter, softened

140 g/5 oz/⅔ cup caster sugar

1 large egg white

55 g/2 oz/scant ¼ cup mashed potato (skinless), chilled

35 whole almonds

....

MACAROONS AND *MACARONS*
There are macaroons, and macarons. *Macaroons are what we have here – Avis' Mackronis. A macaron, however, has come to mean a pastel-coloured double biscuit, sandwiched together with chocolate ganache or fruit paste. Although there were recipes for sandwich meringues in the early 19th century, meringue-based modern macarons are different: delicate little confections which emerged from the Parisian confectionery scene in the mid 1980s. They have since almost completely eclipsed their plainer cousin, the macaroon.*

....

This is one of the odder recipes in Avis' manuscript. Macaroons were, at this point, biscuits made of egg white, sugar and ground almonds, with various flavourings from lemon zest to chocolate. They were sometimes baked on wafer paper and topped with slivered or blanched almonds. Easy to make, they were also fairly cheap to buy, so very popular for dessert. They dated back to at least the 17th century, and although various myths surrounded their invention, by the 1880s they were ubiquitous across Europe. This version, which uses potatoes, is not at all common, though it does work.

Combine the ground almonds, butter and sugar in a food mixer (or by hand) until well mixed. Add the egg white and continue to mix. Mix in the chilled mashed potato. Transfer the mixture to a piping bag fitted with a wide nozzle.

Line a large baking sheet or 2 with baking parchment or a silicon mat and pipe on 35 small blobs of mixture. Leave space between each blob so that the mixture can spread out in the oven. Top each with a whole almond and chill for at least 30 minutes.

Preheat the oven to 180°C/350°F. Cook the mackronis straight from the fridge for 18–20 minutes, until golden brown. Cool before serving.

WINDSOR SANDWICHES

Avis Crocombe, *unpublished manuscript* (no date)

SERVES 6–8 (MAKES 18–24)

100 g/3½ oz/4–6 slices of cooked tongue

100 g/3½ oz/1 scant cup grated Parmesan, plus more to coat

2 tbsp butter

¼ tsp cayenne pepper, or to taste

12 slices of good-quality bread, crusts removed

2 tbsp flour

55 g/2 oz/¼ cup clarified butter (see p57), for frying

....

ROYAL RECIPES

The Victorians were very fond of naming recipes for the royal family or their palaces. There doesn't seem to be any obvious link between Windsor and these tongue-and-cheese sandwiches, and other recipes for 'Windsor sandwiches' are not the same.

....

If you are making the galantine of turkey (see p62), this recipe is ideal for using up trimmings from the tongue.

Put the tongue, Parmesan, butter and cayenne into a blender and blend into a stiff paste. If you do not have a blender, you can pound the ingredients in a mortar with a pestle. Divide the paste in half.

Put half of the paste between 2 sheets of baking parchment and roll out to a rectangle of about 36 × 12 cm (14 × 4¾ inches). Cut the rectangle into 3 pieces, to fit on 3 slices of bread. Repeat for the other half of the paste. Put the remaining 6 slices of bread on top of the pasted slices and press firmly.

Cut the large sandwiches into bite-sized pieces. You can leave them as squares, or use a shaped cutter, such as a leaf. Put the flour on a shallow dish and dust the sandwiches with flour. Melt half the clarified butter in a non-stick pan and fry each sandwich on both sides until golden brown. Drain on kitchen paper.

Dust the sandwiches generously on both sides with grated Parmesan, pressing lightly to help it stick. Melt the rest of the butter and fry the sandwiches again until the Parmesan is golden. Serve very hot.

CHEESE SEFTONS

Avis Crocombe, *unpublished manuscript* (no date)

MAKES 4 RINGS AND
20–22 STRAWS

FOR THE BASIC PUFF PASTRY

225 g/8 oz/1¾ cups flour, plus extra
for dusting

100 g/3½ oz/scant ½ cup butter,
chilled, plus extra for the baking
parchment

FOR THE CHEESE PASTE

115 g/4 oz/generous 1 cup grated
Cheshire cheese

55 g/2 oz/½ cup flour

55 g/2 oz/¼ cup butter

pinch of cayenne pepper

....

CHESHIRE CHEESE

*Cheshire is a British cheese made with
cows' milk. It is pale, crumbly, quite
sharp and very good for cooking.
You could use virtually any hard,
sharpish cheese – a good Cheddar
might be too strong, but it depends on
personal taste. Goats' or sheeps' cheese
will work nicely, too.*

....

This recipe is a good example of the challenge involved in interpreting historic recipes, especially those not intended for publication. Avis simply jotted down a list of ingredients and some working notes. If you make the mix as she wrote it and cook it up, you simply get a tray of (very nice) melted cheese. There are other recipes for Seftons around, including Louis-Eustache Ude's original in the 1829 edition of *The French Cook* – it was named for his employer, the Earl of Sefton – and which use leftover puff pastry. Ude's method is the one used by the team at Audley End, but for an alternative, see the commentary on Avis Crocombe's manuscript on p259.

Start by making the basic puff pastry: mix the flour with enough cold water to form a very rough, fairly stiff dough. Now roll it into a rectangle on a flour-dusted surface and mark it lightly with your fingers into thirds, widthways. Take slices of chilled butter (a third to a half of the whole amount), work them briefly between your fingers and lay them in the middle third of the pastry. The butter doesn't have to completely cover the strip, but try not to leave big gaps. Allow 1 cm/½ inch without butter at the top and bottom.

'Book fold' in the sides: first one, then the other. Give it a good roll with a rolling pin and turn it all through 90 degrees. Roll out again to form a rectangle and repeat as above. If it is a hot day, you may need to chill the pastry for 15–20 minutes between turns. Put in 2–3 layers of butter. Finally, give it another book fold and roll without any additional butter. Chill for at least 1 hour.

You can also buy ready-made puff pastry, in which case you can skip the above stages.

➡→

Mrs Crocombe uses a lot of cayenne. It was widely used, along with mace, nutmeg, black and white pepper, ginger, cinnamon and cloves. The British were nervous of highly spiced foods, having neither the palate nor the cultural inclination. Earlier in the 19th century it was held that highly spiced foods led to sexual incontinence; it was also thought to be prudent to keep young children well away from them.

Mix the cheese, flour, butter and cayenne and form the resulting paste into a block. Chill for 20 minutes. Roll out the puff pastry on a flour-dusted surface to form a rectangle, and mark it lightly with your fingers into thirds.

Cut thin slices from half the chilled cheese mix and lay them on the middle third, again leaving a gap of 1 cm/½ inch at the top and bottom. 'Book fold' the sides, as on the previous page, roll lightly, turn through 90 degrees, roll out into a rectangle, and repeat. Repeat one last time without the cheese mixture, then chill for at least 1 hour. Preheat the oven to 200°C/400°F.

Roll the pastry out to about 1.5 cm/½ inch thick. Cut it into neat, even and equal length straws, about 15 × 1.5 cm/6 × ½ inches, but leave enough pastry to make 4 rings using 2 round cutters. One of the cutters should be about 5 cm/2 inches in diameter (for the outside of the rings), and the other about 4 cm/1½ inches (for the inside of rings). Cut out the 4 rings.

Place the rings and straws onto a baking sheet lined with lightly buttered parchment and bake for about 10 minutes, until light golden in colour, puffed up, cooked and crispy all the way through.

Thread the straws through the rings (like a napkin through a ring) and arrange the bundles on a plate to serve. They are best served hot from the oven, but can be reheated, ensuring that they are hot all the way through.

BEIGNETS À LA ROYALE

Avis Crocombe, *unpublished manuscript* (no date)

MAKES 6

FOR THE BEIGNETS

115 g/4 oz/1 cup grated Parmesan

1 egg, plus 3 egg yolks

285 ml/½ pt/1¼ cups milk

½–1 tsp English mustard

1 tbsp cream

¼ tsp salt

pinch of cayenne pepper

butter, for the moulds

TO COAT

30 g/1 oz/¼ cup flour

1 egg, lightly beaten

30 g/1 oz/⅓ cup finely grated breadcrumbs

TO COOK

2–3 tbsp neutral oil or clarified butter (see p57), for frying

minced parsley leaves, to garnish

Beignet means 'doughnut' in French, but these are far from the pastry-based, deep-fried confection we associate with the word today. This was one of the recipes that took a great deal of development work and experimentation; the original text acts as a reminder that Avis wrote her recipes down very much for herself, as an aide-memoire, not as a book intended to be used by or cooked from by other people. These beignets are essentially savoury custards, just cooked through and then shallow-fried to crisp. They require careful handling and should be served immediately: a real test for a would-be Victorian chef.

Preheat the oven to 200°C/400°F and put a deep baking tray or roasting tin in the oven, half-filled with water. This will be the bain-marie.

Mix all the ingredients for the beignets together in a blender. The mixture should be the consistency of thick cream. Butter 6 dariole moulds (you can also use small but deep muffin tins). Put a small disc of buttered baking parchment in the base of each mould. Distribute the mixture between the moulds.

Stand the filled moulds in the bain-marie and cover the whole lot with a large sheet (or sheets) of foil. Steam in the oven for 20 minutes until just cooked through and still wobbly. Allow to cool in the moulds, then turn out.

To coat and finish the beignets, pour the flour, egg and breadcrumbs into individual bowls. Place a frying pan over a medium heat and add the oil or butter. Gently coat each beignet first with flour, then with egg, then with breadcrumbs (be careful as they are delicate).

Shallow-fry the beignets in the oil or butter for 2–3 minutes, until crisp and golden brown, turning gently once or twice. Drain on kitchen paper and serve hot, garnished with parsley.

CUCUMBER CREAM ICE

Agnes Marshall, *The Book of Ices* (1885)

SERVES 6–8
(MAKES 850 ML/1½ PT/3½ CUPS)

1 large cucumber

230 g/8 oz/generous 1 cup caster sugar

285 ml/½ pt/1¼ cups water

3 tbsp ginger wine, or
2 tbsp ginger brandy

juice of 2 lemons

green food colouring

570 ml/1 pt/2⅓ cups whipping or double cream

blackcurrants and their leaves, and fern sprigs, to garnish (optional)

....

MAKING ICES

To make iced desserts, Mrs Crocombe would have used a sorbetière and bucket, or a hand-cranked freezing pail. Both methods relied on ice and salt, packed around a pewter freezing pot. The salt lowered the temperature of the ice, reducing its melting point. It could easily get to below -20°C/-5°F, colder than most modern freezers. You can still make it this way: use a plastic bowl of crushed ice and lots of salt, with a metal-lidded coffee caddy as the freezing pail. You can also put the mixture straight into the freezer, giving it a good stir every 10–15 minutes. Stir it very well and frequently, scraping the solids off the sides and back into the mixture. The best ice cream has very small ice crystals, which you achieve only with enthusiastic churning.

....

Victorian dessert tables invariably included ices. There were three main types: cream ice (ice cream), water ice (modern-day sorbet) and sorbet (water ice with the addition of quite a lot of liqueur or hard spirits). They were often served in elaborate moulds, with water ice in particular lending itself to very intricate designs. Much use was made of food colouring to achieve a really spectacular result. After all, the main meal was over: dessert was intended as a digestive aid, not a belly filler. Agnes Marshall, from whose book this recipe is taken, was a Victorian powerhouse who wrote a number of cookery books, of which the best are her two books on ices. She also ran a cookery school, went on lecture tours and sold a range of ice-cream making equipment for which she held patents.

Peel the cucumber, halve it lengthways and scoop out the seeds with a teaspoon (discard them). Chop it into chunks and put it in a saucepan with half the sugar and all the measured water. Bring to the boil, then reduce the heat to a simmer, cover and cook until tender (about 15 minutes).

Put the mixture in a blender and purée. Add the ginger wine or brandy, the lemon juice and a little green colouring – you want it to be pleasantly green, rather than scarily fluorescent. Chill.

Whip the cream and remaining sugar in a large bowl to form soft peaks. Fold in the chilled cucumber mix. Put this mixture into an ice-cream maker and churn until it is stiff. If you want to mould it, spoon it into a plain mould and freeze until you are ready to turn it out. The Victorians would have garnished it with spun sugar, small frozen water ices in complicated moulds, chilled fruits in syrup, or a maidenhair fern sprig. We have added blackcurrants and their leaves; feel free to do the same.

CROUSTADE AU PARMESAN

Avis Crocombe, *unpublished manuscript* (no date)

MAKES 30

55 g/2 oz/¼ cup softened butter

115 g/4 oz/1 cup grated Parmesan

1 small egg, separated

55 ml/2 fl oz/¼ cup double cream

1 tsp minced herbs, such as rosemary (optional)

30 bread discs, each 4–6 cm/ 1½–2½ inches

3 tbsp butter, for frying

salt and pepper, to taste

A delicate riff on the theme of cheese on toast, these croustades (another fashionably French term) are related to the perennially popular rarebits that emerged from Britain in the 17th century. A rarebit is basically cheese on toast, often with the addition of a spicy catsup, such as mushroom or anchovy (or Worcestershire sauce), or alcohol such as wine or beer. They were originally called 'rabbits' and there were many regional variants, although today only the Welsh version remains popular. For the Braybrookes' table, a rabbit would have been far too plebeian, hence this recipe, which uses cream and Parmesan rather than beer and Cheddar, and is served on bite-size pieces of toasted bread. It is very important to chill the croustades well before cooking, or the cheese will slide off the bread and cement itself to the oven.

Blend the softened butter and half the Parmesan in a blender. Mix in the egg yolk, salt and pepper. In a separate bowl, whisk together the egg white and cream until light and billowing. Fold into the blended mixture, along with the herbs, if using, then fold in the remaining cheese.

Fry the bread discs in the butter until golden. Drain on kitchen paper. Now spoon the cheese mixture onto each piece of bread, creating a domed effect. Place on a baking parchment-lined baking sheet or sheets and chill for at least 1 hour. (You can leave them for several hours with no ill effect.)

Heat the grill (broiler) and grill (broil) the croustades for 1–2 minutes until browned.

WATER ICE MADE FROM JAM

Agnes Marshall, *The Book of Ices* (1885)

SERVES 6–8 (MAKES 850 ML/
1½ PT/3½ CUPS)

225 ml/8 fl oz/¾ cup of jam (jelly)
or marmalade

juice of 1 small lemon

570 ml/1 pt/2⅓ cups of water

food colouring, as appropriate
to the jam

oranges or lemons, or candied orange
and lemon peel, to garnish

This is the simplest ice recipe around. You can use any type of jam, jelly or preserve, depending on your preference. Our YouTube version uses marmalade (see p231), but it also works with Mrs Crocombe's rhubarb jam (see p222). It's a good example of a water ice (made just with water, and without alcohol). If you want to have a go at moulding an iced dessert, then this is the recipe to use. Unlike cream ices, which are softer, water ices will happily mould into very intricate shapes, once churned – just don't do it before churning, or you'll end up with an ice lolly (popsicle). Specialist moulds were widely available, made in pewter, and every country house would have had a wide range of them – large, small and everything in between. You can convert this into a cream ice by substituting cream for the water.

Mix the first 3 ingredients together in a saucepan, heating gently to help the jam or marmalade dissolve. Add food colouring to taste. Cool, then chill in the fridge.

Put into an ice-cream maker and churn until it is stiff. (Then turn it into a mould, if you like, and freeze until needed.)

....

FOOD COLOURING
Food colouring was very popular in the past. Until the last quarter of the 19th century it was extracted from natural sources: spinach for green, sandalwood for yellow, beet for pinkish-purple. These were pounded in a mortar with a pestle before being squeezed in a cloth to extract the colour. By 1881, however, artificial dyes had been developed and were enthusiastically seized upon by the cookery authors of the day. There was no food-safe blue, however: that had to wait until the 1930s.

....

ALMOND FAGGOTS

Avis Crocombe, *unpublished manuscript* (no date)

MAKES 20–22

2 egg whites

¼ tsp cream of tartar, or a squeeze of lemon juice (optional)

115 g/4 oz/½ cup caster sugar

225 g/8 oz/2½ cups flaked almonds

1–2 large sheets of rice paper

A faggot simply meant a bundle of wood. These delicate little meringues are called faggots because the almonds sticking out of them look like bundles of wood. Until the mid 19th century it was still fairly common for houses and bakeries to use faggot ovens, brick beehive ovens heated by packing them with bundles of wood, which were then lit. When the fire died down, the oven was swept clean and the heat retained in the bricks would – in theory – be enough to bake with. Cooks had various ways to test the temperature, from throwing in a handful of flour and seeing how quickly it burnt, to having a brick built into the oven which changed colour depending on the heat. Avis Crocombe would probably have been familiar with such ovens, although the families she worked for once she started cooking for the aristocracy probably had coal-fired cast-iron ranges, such as the one that can still be seen at Audley End.

Preheat the oven to 110°C/225°F. Make a meringue by whisking the egg whites in a large bowl with the cream of tartar or lemon juice, if using, until they start to froth. Add the caster sugar in 3 stages, whisking between each and continuing to whisk at medium speed, until you have stiff peaks. The mixture should be thick and glossy.

Carefully fold in the flaked almonds.

Put the rice paper sheet(s) onto a baking tray. Using 2 spoons, form the meringue mix into pyramids on the rice paper sheet(s).

Bake for 80–100 minutes, depending on whether you prefer softer or harder meringues.

ORANGE WAFERS

Avis Crocombe, *unpublished manuscript* (no date)

MAKES 24

6 ripe eating oranges

540 g/1 lb 3 oz/scant 2½ cups caster sugar

neutral oil, for the baking sheet (optional)

This is not a traditional wafer, which was made out of batter, poured into a wafering iron and heated over a fire. Instead, this is what would now be called fruit leather. It is one of many recipes for preserving fruit in Mrs Crocombe's book, indicating the importance of making the most of seasonal produce. She worked as cook–housekeeper for a family called the Proctor-Beauchamps in 1871 and, as the housekeeper's role included preserving, this recipe almost certainly dates from that time. It is one of a small section of preserving recipes grouped together in the book. Oranges were usually labelled as one of two varieties – Seville, which were bitter and used for marmalade, and China, which were the sweet eating oranges we enjoy as fresh fruit today.

Wash the oranges and cut them in half. Place in a large saucepan with enough water to cover them. Cover with a disc of baking parchment and a lid and bring to the boil. Reduce the heat and simmer for 75 minutes or until the oranges are very tender. Drain off the liquid, reserving 200 ml/7 fl oz/scant 1 cup. Add the reserved liquid to the orange halves and put in a blender to purée thoroughly. It is best to push the orange purée through a drum sieve afterwards, to ensure it is very smooth. Preheat the oven to its lowest setting.

Put the orange purée in a saucepan and reheat. Add the caster sugar and mix thoroughly until the sugar has dissolved. Now spread the mixture out on a silicon baking sheet or lightly oiled baking parchment, to no more than 5 mm/¼ inch thick, the thinner the better. Put it in the just-warm oven overnight, to let it dry out. Mrs Crocombe's instructions suggest drying it out over 'some days'. In practice she may well have used a pastry oven.

To serve, cut the wafers into rectangles of 20 × 10 cm/8 × 4 inches and roll up lightly, piling the rolls in a pyramid. You can also cut rounds out, using any scraps to garnish other dishes.

....

SEASONAL EATING

The rich did their best to ignore the seasons, although did acknowledge that many fruits and vegetables were at their best when eaten during their normal growing or harvesting season. The dessert table always included fresh fruit, served at the perfect time. However, much was also cooked. It was a mark of wealth to be able to serve fruit and vegetables early or late, and gardeners were ingenious in devising ways to ripen produce early or keep it for a long time. Kitchen gardens such as that at Audley End made full use of heated walls and glasshouses to produce fruits such as pineapples and citrus, hard to grow in Britain.

....

4

Victorian Food and Kitchens

....

by Annie Gray

LIFE IN THE KITCHEN

The Victorian period was one of immense technological and social change. In 1837, when Queen Victoria came to the throne, Britain was an agrarian nation, with the majority of its population living in the countryside, working on farms or in associated occupations. In 1851, the census revealed that the British had become the world's first urbanised nation, with over 50% of its population living and working in towns and cities. By 1901, when Queen Victoria died, electricity, motor cars and telephones were creeping into the lives of many. Only the rich habitually used them, but everyone would have seen the electric banners on the front of theatres and music halls, and benefitted from the almost instant communication of news.

Audley End was not at the forefront of change. While some country houses installed electricity for lighting and gas for cooking, Mrs Crocombe's kitchen, despite being refitted after the fire of September 1881, remained very similar to that of the 1840s. There had been plans to install gas and, in the early 1870s, trenches had been dug and pipes ordered, but the plans were shelved at the last

FACING PAGE
The dining room
at Audley End set
as if dessert were
in progress.

Victorian Food and Kitchens | **141**

The kitchen with the roasting range lit. The mechanism above the fire is part of the smoke-jack (see p49).

minute. The house was lit with oil lamps and fuelled by coal, and although it did have central heating from the 1840s, this served only a selection of the ground-floor rooms, with the heat provided by a huge coal boiler in the basement.

The evolution of the British country-house kitchen was very slow, and a Victorian who happened upon a kitchen from 300 years before would not have felt ill at ease. By the 17th century, when women first started to work in professional kitchens, the basic pattern of a roasting range with spit, charcoal chafing stoves, and brick ovens was set. The next two hundred years saw a degree of technological change, including more efficient spits and the replacement of wood by coal for the main fuel. The brick ovens and chafing stoves were increasingly replaced with cast-iron ranges, such as those at Audley, from the late 18th century. Gas for cooking was increasingly popularised in the second half of the 19th century, but did not appear at Audley End.

Kitchens were focused on a large central table, which formed the main working space. Audley End still has its 19th-century table (with a modern top for the interpretation team to work on). They were lit from above with oil lamps or, from the early 19th century, gas, and finally, from the 1880s, electricity. Again, Audley lagged far behind, with oil still in use until the 1940s. Hot water might be provided by a boiler in the service wing, or at the back of the roasting range (as at Audley), or in some cases it still needed to be heated in large copper boilers and carried about by maids.

Large houses, those of dukes or members of the royal family, had all this and more. The kitchens at Windsor Castle had about 20 rooms, including one just for the steam-generating apparatus used for heating an enormous hot table in the centre of the main kitchen. They also employed over 45 people. But only the grandest houses had more than a handful of cooking staff. The roles were strictly hierarchical, with the cook at the top (a man, in the most prestigious houses), followed by an assistant (if the cook was male) or first kitchen maid, and ending with the scullery maid at the bottom. Big houses rarely employed girls straight from school (in 1880 it was compulsory to attend school only until the age of ten), for they were too young to have built up stamina or experience. Instead, scullery maids were usually about 15 to 17 years old. They could expect to be promoted after a year or two, often moving house to gain a better position. Life as a servant was very geographically mobile. Very few servants worked in large houses, which was a comparatively prestigious career path.

Hours were long. The scullery maid, for instance, was expected to rise before 6am to get the ranges up to temperature and would not go to bed until about 11pm. The work was very physical, and former maids recalled crying themselves to sleep at night through sheer fatigue. But a servant in a country house could also expect plenty of food – at least 1 lb (455 g) of meat a day, unlimited vegetables, and plenty of cheese and bread – and they were surrounded by other people. It was generally a much better life than that of servants who worked in smaller houses. Whether life as a servant was better than life working in a factory was down to individual priorities: a factory worker had nominal independence, they could live away from their place of work and could marry without having to leave their post; on the other hand a servant in a country house had accommodation and food provided, prospects of promotion, and transferable skills. In either case, options for women were limited. It was not until the very end of the Victorian period, with the boom in the urban service industry, that employment patterns really started to change.

Daisy Cranwell began life at Audley End in 1913 as a kitchen maid. She became cook in the 1920s.

THE DAILY MEAL PATTERN

It's easy to concentrate on the fact that Mrs Crocombe and her staff were cooking for the Braybrookes and forget the large number of other people that the kitchens needed to cater for. There were usually about 30–38 people to be fed on any one day, divided into three or four groups, each eating four meals a day.

The largest group of people were the servants. In 1881, when Mrs Crocombe was cook and Lord and Lady Braybrooke's daughter Augusta had married and left home (reducing the household), the indoor servants numbered 18–20, plus seasonal or daily extras.

The servants ate breakfast, dinner, tea and supper. Woe betide the house that underfed its staff. They would complain vociferously, and eventually leave. Audley End was able to get better staff than some, as it was well connected by rail and road, but the 1880s was full of talk of 'the servant problem'. Good servants knew their worth. They had agency, and used it. Their breakfast, tea and supper centred on ubiquitous bread and cheese, supplemented with cake. Leftovers and trimmings from the family's meals would also often find their way to the servants, unless they could be turned into other dishes, and one reason for the upper servants eating part of their dinner separately was so that they could get the choice pickings.

The family, meanwhile, had breakfast (usually a buffet), luncheon, tea and dinner. Again, dinner was the main meal, the one to which guests were most likely to be invited, and the most formal. The family would always change into evening wear for dinner, although they did

LEFT
A group of servants in the kitchen garden in the early 20th century. The then cook – Alice Taylor – is at the centre.

FACING PAGE
The main dining room at Audley End, where the family would eat when they had guests.

ABOVE
The nursery at
Audley End, where
the children would
have eaten their
meals.

RIGHT
Augusta Neville in
about 1870, when
about ten years old.
She and her
cousins Catherine
and Mary were
brought up at
Audley End
together.

not always eat in the large upstairs dining room, but also had a smaller, ground-floor family dining room which was nearer the kitchens. If they had guests, they would eat upstairs.

The number of people eating differed over the course of the year. When the family was in London, or renting a house elsewhere for a significant period of time, they took the cooking staff (or most of them), some housemaids, footmen and personal staff (valets and lady's maids). Laundry maids remained at Audley End, still processing laundry sent up by train from London. So, too, did the dairymaid (making cream and butter to be despatched to the capital) and the housekeeper, who served as head of the household in the family's absence. They all received board wages, additional payments on top of their normal salary to cover the cost of providing their own food and drink while the family were away. On census day 1881, most of the staff were at the Braybrookes' London house, in Upper Brook Street, including Mrs Crocombe and her kitchen maids.

The family often entertained, especially over the shooting season. Every upper-class visitor would bring their own maid or man with them, adding a mouth to be fed not only to the family dinner but also to the meals of the servants. They might also bring a driver or groom. Numbers eating in the servants' hall were also swelled during the long-standing 'house vs stables' cricket match in September (Charles Neville, Lord Braybrooke, was a keen cricketer, and a pitch had been laid out for him as a young man in 1842); for the servants' Christmas dinner on 26 December; and the servants' ball in mid January.

When children visited, the nursery would have been brought into use, and although children would have been accompanied by their own nursemaid, who often prepared their food in the nursery, the kitchens sometimes played a role. The Victorians were also extremely conscious of the role of food in caring for the sick, and sickroom food was given its own section in cookery books. If someone was a long-term invalid (the Victorian term), a separate sickroom nurse would have been employed to prepare specific meals away from the kitchen.

HOW DINNER WAS SERVED

Dining style in Britain during the Victorian era evolved from the 18th century à la Française service, to the Edwardian à la Russe. À la Française, which was still in use in some households until the second half of the 19th century, was a style in which a series of courses were presented on the table, with the dishes of each course presented simultaneously, arranged symmetrically and with a great deal of care as to their selection. Until the 1840s, it consisted of three courses: the first course was soups, fish and entrées, which were savoury fancy dishes designed to showcase the cook's skills; the second course was roast meats, game, vegetables and entremets (the sweet equivalent of the savoury entrées); and the final course was dessert, which always included fresh fruit and nuts, plus ices (ice creams) and sometimes sweet biscuits for dipping into wine. By the late 19th century savouries had also appeared along with dessert: highly savoury palate cleansers. If a separate cheese course was served, it came after the second course but before dessert. All the dishes for each course were arranged on the table, with diners helping themselves and others (carving would be done by the butler).

By the mid 19th century, a new way of serving was creeping in. À la Russe was a sequential way of serving, with food no longer on the table, but served from the side of each diner by footmen. Now, the courses were much more spread out, the various elements still essentially the same as previously, but served one after the other.

A table set in the old style, à la Française (top), and in the new, à la Russe (bottom), from Urbain Dubois' *The Household Cookery-Book* of 1871.

The new style was expensive, demanding new tableware (it gave rise to an explosion of specific implements, such as fish knives, fish forks and cake forks) and a footman for every two diners. All of this was regarded as dangerously nouveau riche by the old aristocracy, who clung to their 18th-century china and saw etiquette guides as very bad form indeed. Queen Victoria resisted the change until 1874, and never fully embraced the new style.

At Audley, we don't know how dinner was served but, based on our knowledge of the family, their habits and their antiquated kitchen fittings (as well as the old-fashioned recipes in Mrs Crocombe's recipe book), we have always taken the view that by 1881, by which time Avis was cook, they were serving in a sort of demi-Russe style – a transitional style between the old and new, wherein dishes were still put on the table simultaneously, but as five courses, rather than three. Thus, the Braybrookes would have served their soup and fish on the table together, for diners to choose between them, before they were replaced by four or more entrées. Next would be the roasts, game and vegetables, and, finally for the main meal, the sweet entremets. Dessert would be served before the ladies and gentlemen separated for a brief interlude, during which the men stayed in the dining room with port and brandy, while the ladies decamped to the drawing room to prepare tea, where all would reconvene later.

OTHER MEALS

Breakfast was served as a buffet, with hot food kept warm on plates filled with hot water or over spirit burners. There would have been a selection of hot dishes including porridge, devilled kidneys, bacon, eggs, sausages and hashes of game; cold dishes including potted meat, cold roast meat and smoked fish; fruit, both fresh and preserved; breads and fancy buns with jams, preserves and butter; and finally a choice of tea, coffee or chocolate with milk, cream and sugar. Some ladies preferred to have breakfast in bed, especially if they had had a late night.

Luncheon was still often à la Française in 1881, while afternoon tea was laid out on a sideboard or, especially if served outside, on small tables. The Tea House bridge at Audley End, designed by Robert Adam in 1782 in a Palladian (a neoclassical) style, has a pavilion at its centre, ideal for a spot of genteel tea-taking. Afternoon tea was a highly feminised, intimate meal, and the servants were dismissed, so that the ladies (and occasional gentleman) could enjoy themselves without being listened to.

Downstairs, meals were less formal, and often taken on the hoof. Breakfast, tea and supper could be rushed, and although there were given meal times, other duties took priority. For the kitchen staff, one person had to stay behind to keep an eye on any simmering pots, and all the house staff would have been keeping an ear out for bells ringing to summon them upstairs. The bell lobby at Audley End is just outside the servants' hall, furnished with a bench so that a footman could remain poised to respond.

The one proper sit-down meal in the servants' hall was dinner, which was the only hot meal. All the food would have been laid on the table, seating was in order of status, and where a waiter was needed, the role would have been fulfilled by the most junior member of the male staff: the steward's room boy. This was essential training for being let loose as a footman upstairs.

The alcove in the saloon at Audley End, set for tea.

THE NURSERY, THE SICKROOM AND THE POOR

ABOVE
Lady Braybrooke
and Augusta in
about 1867.

FACING PAGE
Meat jelly,
recommended to
Avis for feeding
the sick 'by
Dr Bradbury
of Cambridge'.

In addition to cooking for the family and the indoor servants, Mrs Crocombe and her team would have found themselves preparing food for various special interest groups.

When the Braybrookes' only child – their daughter, Augusta – was young enough to be permanently resident in the nursery, she had her own nurse, who would have prepared most of her meals and eaten with her. Her cousins, who lived with the family for some time with their widowed mother, dined with her too. When she was about five or six her nurse would have been replaced with a governess, who continued to eat with her in the nursery. Later, in her early teens, sometimes she would have dined with the family and, on those occasions, the governess would have eaten with the upper servants. It was only when she was 16 or 17, shortly before she was married, that she would habitually have dined with her parents. Had she been a boy, she would have been sent to boarding school at about 11 years old. Most upper-class girls at the time, however, were educated at home, as parents did not want to spend too much money on the education of girls, and also wanted to keep a close eye on them to ensure their eligibility on the marriage market.

By 1881, Augusta was married: to Richard Strutt, the second son of Lord Rayleigh, and a former party animal turned respectable entrepreneur. Having failed at his initial career choice, banking, Strutt set up the Terling Co-Operative Company, which was one of many such ventures aimed at improving the lives of the poor while also making a reasonable profit. He was able to retire on the profits aged 36, having married Augusta when he was 31 and she just 19. They had their only child, a son, in 1886 (he would die in the First World War), and their marriage seems to have been a very happy one. The nursery, empty after Augusta vacated it, would have been brought back into use when she visited with her young son, as well as being opened up for any other visiting children.

By the late 19th century, Augusta had sadly become a long-term invalid, possibly due to complications around the birth of her son. Now, when she visited, she would have fitted into another key area for specialist catering: the sickroom.

Most Victorian cookery books contain a section on cooking for the sick. 'Invalid cookery', as it was invariably known, was a vital branch of cookery, for, in an era before antibiotics and mass vaccination against such common diseases as measles, rubella, polio and mumps, illnesses which can now be prevented were rampant, and often had severe and long-lasting effects. The ethos behind invalid cookery was both to strengthen the body and, if the illness was short-lived, to aid recovery by tempting the palate to recover and, through that, encourage the body to follow.

Finally, there was another group of people dependent upon the country house: the local poor. Victorian society was still very reliant on individual charity and had not yet articulated into law the idea, central to later thinking, that the duty of a civilised society is to care for those who fall upon hardship. The first state-sponsored old-age pension scheme was still nearly 30 years off, and if Mrs Crocombe herself had fallen ill and been unable to work, she would have faced a hard future. The workhouse was never far away, especially for the urban poor. The rural poor were sometimes better off.

The area around a country house formed a tight community, with the local villagers reliant on the house for certain perks, such as skimmed milk from the dairy or permission to gather a certain amount of firewood (though every house was different in what it allowed). Equally, the house relied upon the local communities for casual labour. In addition, longer-serving servants might retire to the village when they could no longer work, while outdoor servants, such as gardeners, tended to marry and live in the villages. Country houses, with all their wealth, were seen as having a duty to their locality, something taken very seriously, especially by the women of the house, to whom charitable works had traditionally fallen.

Alms-giving, in the form of practical aid such as blankets, clothing and fuel, had long been a part of the role of the country house. Edible scraps from meals and off-cuts from the kitchens were taken out daily and distributed to those in need. At times of particular hardship, such as very cold winters or bad harvests, the kitchens might be asked to do more, providing food specifically for distribution to the local needy. Cookery books gave recipes for soups designed to be both cheap and nutritious. They were all intended to be made in large quantities and distributed to those in need.

A NURSERY MEAL

Children were usually cooked for by their nurse, but on occasion the kitchens may have provided for them. The Victorians believed children should not be fed strong food, lest it excite them, leading to behavioural problems. White meats and bland flavours were preferred, with a great deal of dairy and white bread, which were both considered easily digestible.

Pap was the most basic of nursery foods, ubiquitous from weaning through to young childhood. It was usually made with water, but could be made with milk. A typical recipe was one or two pieces of bread crust or two to three tablespoons of crushed rusk or unsweetened biscuit, simmered briefly in water, then puréed with a teaspoon of sugar. Queen Victoria was weaned onto bread and milk – simply boiling milk poured over pieces of white bread. Porridge was another alternative. All were usually eaten for breakfast.

A child's dinner was served early – about 1pm – and was generally a small amount of plain roast or boiled meat and a pudding. Avis has a recipe for a plain suet pudding of exactly the type served in nurseries: simply 8 oz (225 g/1¾ cups) suet; 8 oz (225 g/2½ cups) breadcrumbs; 4 oz (115 g/½ cup) sugar; and 2 small eggs all beaten into 4½ fl oz (125 ml/½ cup) milk, the zest of 1 lemon and ½ tsp baking powder. Boiled or steamed in a plain mould, this could have been pepped up with some dried fruit and even a little spice as the child grew older.

Supper was also sometimes served, depending on bedtime, and again was pap, bread and milk, or, as the child grew up, a small slice of cake or a biscuit.

A TRAY FOR THE SICKROOM

Alexis Soyer summed up the Victorian ideal for sickroom cookery, together, unfortunately, with its reality, when he wrote, 'nothing is more painful than to see any food ill-prepared for sick people, whose sense of taste is partially gone; everything ordered by the doctors should be cooked in the greatest perfection, especially as all they require is so very simple, and easily done, it is unpardonable to do it badly'. He was among many writers to suggest that the best foods for the sick were easily digestible, often easily chewed, and should be well-presented, so the eye excited the appetite. Speedy removal after eating was advised, so leftovers did not nauseate the patient.

Avis' manuscript contains several recipes suitable for the sick, one

of which (meat jelly) is marked as 'recommended by Dr Bradbury of Cambridge', and was presumably given to her by him specifically for the sickroom. Meat jelly was a favourite of many authors. Hers is not exactly exciting if you are not ill. It is simply 455 g/1 lb each of mutton, veal and fillet of beef, simmered without boiling for 8 hours, then strained and chilled to jellify. 'A teaspoonful occasionally' was the prescribed dose.

Brussels cream is another of her recipes which, while also suitable for a light luncheon or even a servants' dish, would not have been out of place in the sickroom. It's a cream blancmange made with ground rice to thicken it to the texture of bread sauce (or porridge), flavoured with lemon zest. There is no sugar, just a lump of butter to add texture. It could be moulded, but for the sickroom was probably served in a bowl or glass. Some doctors were keen to feed patients fortified wines, so it might be flavoured with Madeira or sherry.

It is important to hydrate when ill, so various drinks were suggested, from barley water to fruit waters, even toast water (literally water boiled with a piece of brown, but not burnt, toast, then strained, and cooled. It's surprisingly palatable). There was also lemonade, for which Mrs Crocombe wrote down several recipes of varying quality.

A SOUP FOR THE POOR

Whenever famine raised its head, soup kitchens were soon opened. This recipe comes from the chef and campaigner Alexis Soyer's *Charitable Cookery, or, the Poor Man's Regenerator* (1848). Soyer had spent time in Ireland, working with organisations trying to provide aid for the millions of Irish left starving during the potato famine of the 1840s. In 1847 he opened a soup kitchen in Dublin, which fed up to 5,000 people a day. Class differences were acutely showcased: the rich could pay 5s. to watch the spectacle of desperate people eating with spoons that were chained to both the bowls and the tables to prevent their theft.

Soak 11 oz (310 g/1½ cups) peas overnight in plenty of cold water. Drain. Peel and chop 1 large onion, 2 carrots, 2 sticks of celery. Dice 3 rashers of bacon and fry in 1 tbsp butter. Add the vegetables. Cook for a few minutes, then add the peas and 4 pt (2¼ litres/2 quarts) vegetable or meat stock. Bring to the boil and simmer for 45 minutes until the peas have 'split'. Add 2 sprigs of minced mint and salt and pepper to taste, and cook for a further 5 minutes.

Serve with bread (or quiet desperation).

OTHER FAMILY MEALS

KEDGEREE

Eliza Acton, *Modern Cookery for Private Families* (1845)

SERVES 4

2 eggs

140 ml/5 fl oz/⅔ cup cream

1 tbsp butter

340 g/12 oz/2 cups cooked
long grain rice

1 tsp cayenne pepper

½ tsp salt

340 g/12 oz/2 cups cooked flaky fish
(turbot is ideal, but cod or haddock
also work, as does salmon)

200 g/7 oz/about 20 cooked
prawns (shrimp)

pepper, to taste

chopped parsley leaves, to garnish

12 quails' eggs, hard-boiled for
1 minute 45 seconds, then sliced,
to garnish

....

RICE

*In the 1880s the rice called for in
recipes was often either Patna rice
or Carolina rice. Patna is long grain
(very long grain) and grown in India.
Carolina is also long grain but
American. You could also get Italian-
or French-grown rice of the risotto
(or short-grain) style, which was used
in puddings. For the true Victorian
experience here, use long grain rice,
but this also works with basmati.*

....

Kedgeree has Indian origins, in the form of *khichri*, originally a mixture of lentils, rice, onions and spices. It became anglicised with the addition of fish and the eventual dropping of the lentils. It is very similar to a lot of other now-global dishes, including the Malaysian and Indonesian nasi goreng, which also involves eggs, rice and very savoury flavours. Most cultures have some form of cooked carb with meat, fish or vegetables stirred into it (the British are very attached to their bubble and squeak, which is fried potatoes and cabbage). However, in its hybridisation of an Eastern dish with British ingredients, kedgeree is also typically British Victorian. Some people prefer to use smoked fish, especially Scottish haddock. However, the original uses unsmoked. You can add a little mustard powder or turmeric if you prefer the dish to be more yellow in colour.

Combine the eggs and cream in a bowl, mixing well. Heat a large heavy-based frying pan and melt the butter. Tip in the rice and spread it out. Add the cayenne pepper, salt and pepper, stir to heat through, then spread out again. Pour in the egg mix and cook very gently for 2–3 minutes until it just starts to coagulate.

Add the fish and prawns (keep a few back if you wish to use them for garnishing). Fold them in gently and keep the pan at a low heat for another few minutes, just heating the fish and prawns through. The mixture should be the consistency of thick cream – be careful not to overcook it.

Remove from the heat and serve onto hot plates, garnished with chopped parsley and sliced hard-boiled quails' eggs, plus a few reserved prawns, if you desire.

BRAIN CAKES

Georgiana Hill, *The Breakfast Book* (1865)

SERVES 6

6 lambs' brains

½ tbsp minced sage leaves

1 egg

45 g/1½ oz/½ cup breadcrumbs

pinch of cayenne pepper

salt, to taste

juice of ½ a lemon, to serve

buttered toast, to serve (optional)

pickles, to serve (optional)

TO COAT

55 g/2 oz/½ cup flour

1 egg, lightly beaten

55 g/2 oz/generous ½ cup breadcrumbs

200 ml/7 fl oz/scant 1 cup vegetable oil, for frying

For much of our history, cuts such as heads, hearts, kidneys and livers were just as prized as muscle meats. The vast majority of the Victorian population was involuntarily vegetarian – they simply could not afford meat – so the idea that part of an animal was less prestigious, or should be discarded, would have been unthinkable. Offal requires skill to cook well as, depending on the item, it may be stronger, tougher or more delicate than more common cuts. Brains are very rich, enjoyed for their creaminess and were often saved for the sick. This recipe comes from a breakfast book by Georgiana Hill, writer of a number of themed books, for which there was a vogue in the late Victorian era.

Soak the brains in iced water for 2 hours. Drain, then blanch for 1 minute in a pan of boiling water. Remove with a slotted spoon and drain in a colander. Trim off any excess sinew and veins.

Put the brains in a food processor with the sage and egg and blend. Stir in the breadcrumbs and season with salt and cayenne pepper. Leave in the fridge for 30 minutes so that the liquid can soak into the crumbs, and to allow the mixture to firm up enough to handle.

To coat, prepare 3 plates, the first with the flour, another with the egg and the last with breadcrumbs. Remove the brain mixture from the fridge and use a large tablespoon to help you form 6 cakes or patties, shaping them lightly with your hands.

Roll each cake in flour, then egg, then breadcrumbs, handling very carefully. (You may find a spatula helpful.) Heat the oil in a frying pan over a medium heat and fry the cakes until golden brown on both sides and cooked through.

Squeeze a little lemon juice over the cakes and serve piping hot. They are excellent with toast and butter, with pickles on the side, if you like.

POULET À LA SARTERE

Avis Crocombe, *unpublished manuscript* (no date)

SERVES 6

1 cold roasted chicken
(or parts thereof)

1 egg yolk

½ tsp mustard

140 ml/5 fl oz/⅔ cup neutral oil

1 tbsp white wine vinegar

1 tsp minced tarragon leaves

1 tsp minced chervil leaves, or parsley

1 tsp salad burnett leaves, or borage,
or finely chopped cucumber

salt and white pepper, to taste

herb leaves, edible flowers or sliced
cucumber, to garnish

Today, chicken is one of the cheapest and most readily available meats around. In the Victorian era, it was much more expensive and highly prized. Chickens were birds raised for eating, as opposed to fowl (for which separate recipes existed, see p53), which were birds raised for egg production and that were killed for meat only once they had stopped laying. Chickens were nevertheless older than the average bird today, as well as more muscular, with a better depth of flavour. It is very important to source a high-welfare bird for this recipe, preferably one which has been dry-hung, as they would have been in the past. This recipe highlights the range of herbs which would have been available to Mrs Crocombe from the Audley End kitchen garden. However, if you cannot obtain salad burnett, try borage or a little minced cucumber. Parsley can be used in lieu of the chervil.

Cut the chicken into bite-sized pieces and put them into a bowl.

Make the mayonnaise by whisking together the egg yolk, mustard and a pinch of salt. Continue to whisk, very gradually adding the oil in a thin stream, so that the mixture emulsifies, making a thick, yellowy mayonnaise. This is easy to do in a small food processor bowl, as it can take a little while by hand. If it splits, you might be able to recover it with a hasty teaspoon of iced water, but – sadly –generally it is ruined and you will need to start again. (Or use 150 ml/ 5 fl oz/²/₃ cup very good-quality ready-made fresh mayonnaise.)

Once you have made the mayonnaise, add the vinegar, still whisking (it will turn a bit paler). Stir in the herbs, season to taste with white pepper and gently mix it into the chicken.

Serve, garnished with herb leaves and edible flowers or cucumber.

ASPIC JELLY FOR BREAKFAST OR LUNCHEON

Avis Crocombe, *unpublished manuscript* (no date)

SERVES 4 (IN FOUR X 255 ML/
9 FL OZ/1 CUP MOULDS)

4 pigs' trotters

455 g/1 lb fat bacon, in a piece

1¼ litres/2 pt/1⅓ quarts beef stock

1 tbsp mushroom ketchup

3 leaves of gelatine (or 1 tbsp
powdered gelatine), soaked in
cold water (optional)

4 hard-boiled eggs

TO CLARIFY

2 eggs

1 slice of ham

This is one of those typically late Victorian recipes which generally appals modern eaters. It is an acquired taste, and very time-consuming to make. However, it also reflects Avis' reality and is representative of the kind of dishes enjoyed by those who could afford to employ a cook to spend days producing a single dish. By the time Avis wrote this into her book, tinned aspic was available, which could simply be reheated, and if necessary extra (packet) gelatine added to enhance the set. However, cooks such as Mrs Crocombe tended to reject such modern conveniences, arguing, not without reason, that they devalued the skills of the cook and never tasted as good as the proper stuff. You can also make this with calves' feet.

Put the trotters and bacon in a very large saucepan with the beef stock and mushroom ketchup. Top up with water if the stock does not cover them. Bring to the boil, skimming off any scum, and simmer for 3–4 hours, until the trotters are tender and the meat is falling off the bones.

Pull out the bones and discard them. This is a very fiddly task, so do the best you can (it's the kind of task best given to a scullery maid, really). You may find it wise to simply remove the meat from the main part of the trotter and not bother with the rather bony toes. Slice the cooked bacon into thin rashers.

Strain the hot liquid through a fine sieve. The Victorians would have clarified it, and it does yield a better result if you do.

To clarify, allow the stock to cool completely. Then whisk the eggs up, mince the ham and mix together. Add this to the cold stock and mix. Bring the pan very, very slowly to the boil without any further mixing. Once the pan is just boiling (do not allow it to boil too vigorously), remove from the heat.

The egg should form a 'raft' on the top of the liquid, dragging all the impurities with it. Carefully remove it with a slotted spoon and strain the liquid through a fine sieve or muslin.

The liquid (aspic), whether clarified or not, should jellify on its own (you can test this by putting a little bit on a cold saucer and putting it in the fridge for 15 minutes to see if it sets). Measure out 570 ml/ 1 pt/$2\frac{1}{3}$ cups. If in any doubt about the strength of the set, add the gelatine to the liquid, as it needs to set firm. (The rest of the liquid can be used as the basis for a soup or as stock.)

Put a little of the aspic in the bottom of each of the 4 moulds (muffin tins will work, or dariole moulds). Allow to set. Now slice the eggs and put a slice of egg on the aspic. Add a little more aspic and chill again to hold it in place.

Now fill the moulds in layers, with rashers of bacon and a little of the trotter meat interspersed with hard-boiled egg. You won't need all the meat or bacon; the rest can be made into another dish.

Chill the moulds for at least 6 hours before dipping the bases briefly into hot water and turning out.

A SECOND COURSE FOR TWO PERSONS [ANCHOVY AND OYSTER TOAST]

Avis Crocombe, *unpublished manuscript* (no date)

SERVES 6

20 oysters

250 ml/9 fl oz/1 cup double cream

4 chopped anchovies (canned is fine)

pinch of cayenne pepper

3 tbsp salted butter

6 slices of bread

....

HOW TO KEEP FOOD FRESH
*Keeping food fresh was as much of
a concern in the 19th century as it is
today. Houses such as Audley End had
regular – sometimes daily – deliveries
from suppliers. Food was stored in the
dry larder, wet larder (for fish) or cold
larder. Refrigerators existed in the 19th
century, but they were not electric nor
self-chilling. Instead, they were large
wooden boxes filled with ice, or ice
and salt.*

....

In Mrs Crocombe's manuscript, this is simply labelled as 'second course for two persons'. It's a low-key dish, but it packs quite a punch, thanks to the anchovies. Oysters were rising in price in the 19th century, having been relatively cheap in previous centuries. Over-fishing of native beds led to increasing scarcity in the 1870s and despite imports from Europe and, indeed, America, they never regained their status as a food for the masses. The Victorians enjoyed them both raw and cooked, and they were often included as an ingredient in other recipes, such as beefsteak pies, and sauce for cod (see p43).

Shuck the oysters and drain and discard their liquid. Put the oysters and cream in a saucepan and poach over a low heat until firm and plump. Blend in a food processor with the anchovies and cayenne until you have a smooth purée. Put into the fridge to chill.

Melt the butter and brush it on each side of the bread. Toast the bread under a hot grill (broiler) on both sides until golden brown.

Working fast, put a neat dollop of the oyster mixture onto each slice of toast and serve immediately.

SPONGE CAKE PUDDING

Avis Crocombe, *unpublished manuscript* (no date)

SERVES 6–8

FOR THE SPONGE

225 g/8 oz/generous 1 cup sugar

115 ml/4 fl oz/½ cup water

4 eggs, at room temperature

finely grated zest of 1 small lemon

170 g/6 oz/1⅓ cups flour

butter, for the tin

fresh fruit, to serve (optional)

candied peel, angelica or candied cherries, for decoration (optional)

FOR THE CUSTARD

570 ml/1 pt/2⅓ cups milk

1 egg, plus 7 egg yolks

85 g/3 oz/⅓ cup caster sugar

2 vanilla pods, split, or
1–2 tsp orange flower water

Another of Mrs Crocombe's recipes for using spare or leftover cake, this is slightly different to most sponge cake puddings of the time, which tended to be simple concoctions of layered sponge and flavoured custard. There were a number of other names for such puddings, the best known being cabinet pudding. The detail that the outer, darker part of the sponge cake should be alternated with the lighter inside is Avis' original recipe, and is typical of the thought which went into even simple-sounding dishes at the time. It is a recipe that can be almost infinitely varied, with the custard flavoured or coloured as desired, or with whole fruits added to it. The recipe for the sponge cake given here is another from Avis' book, but any other recipe will work. You can also make this as individual puddings.

Preheat the oven to 175°C/345°F.

Put the sugar and measured water into a small saucepan and heat until the sugar has dissolved. Simmer for 3 minutes. Meanwhile, whisk the eggs and lemon zest together until they are foamy. Pour the hot syrup onto the eggs in a slow and steady stream, whisking continuously. Continue to whisk until the mixture reaches room temperature. In modern terms, this is called a sabayon.

Sift the flour to make it as light and airy as possible. Gently fold it into the sabayon.

Line a 900 g/2 lb loaf tin with buttered baking parchment and transfer the batter to the tin. Bake in the preheated oven for about 45 minutes or until a skewer comes out clean. Cool in the tin for 10–15 minutes before transferring to a wire rack to cool completely.

➥➔

Make the custard by combining all the ingredients and your chosen flavouring in a bowl and whisking well.

Line the same loaf tin with more lightly buttered baking parchment and butter the sides well. This recipe works very well made in the same tin as the cake: then you know it will all fit together nicely.

Cut a piece of sponge cake about 1–1.5 cm/¼–½ inch thick to fit the base of the tin and place it there. Cut further slices, the same thickness, from the outside of the remaining cake to line the sides, alternating the crust of the cake facing outwards with the whiter interior to make wide stripes. (Any leftover cake can be used in a trifle, see p87.)

Pour in enough custard to cover the bottom, plus 1.5 cm/½ inch more, then chill for 30 minutes.

Preheat the oven to 180°C/350°F.

Fill a roasting tray with boiling water to come to halfway up the loaf tin. Remove the tin from the fridge and stand it in the tray. Bake for 5–10 minutes until the custard is just set, holding the base and sides firmly in place. Add the rest of the custard, cover the whole tray tightly with foil and return to the oven for about 90 minutes. The custard should be set, but still wobbly.

Allow to cool completely before turning out. Serve with fresh fruit, if you like.

For a fancier effect, as pictured, you can decorate the top of the pudding with shapes cut from candied peel, angelica or cherries. Flatten these out firmly and arrange them on the bottom of the lined tin or basin before you put in the first piece of cake.

....

LUMPS, BUGS AND BRAN

Most historic recipes will call for flour and sugar to be sifted before use. In some cases, such as for light sponge cakes, this ensures that the flour is airy and not compacted and helps the cake to rise. However, it was also important to sift dry goods because they were sometimes stored in conditions which led to lumps in sugar from moisture, or bugs in flour. Additionally, standard flour, if stoneground – as much of it still was in the 1880s – usually contained some bran. To make a light sponge, therefore, flour was sifted again in the kitchen.

....

CURRIED EGGS

Avis Crocombe, *unpublished manuscript* (no date)

SERVES 2

2 slices of good-quality bread

55 g/2 oz/¼ cup butter, plus
1 tbsp melted butter

4 eggs

4 tbsp double cream

1 tbsp mild curry powder

salt and pepper, to taste

minced parsley leaves, to garnish
(optional)

....

BREAKFAST LIKE A KING

*The idea that breakfast is the most
important meal of the day is relatively
new, spread by cereal manufacturers
taking advantage of the disruption to
eating habits during the Second World
War to promote their products. Until
the mid 19th century, most people had
a very light breakfast, generally based
on bread or a fruity bun. However, as
dinner got later, and lunch became
established at about 1pm, more
substantial breakfasts became
common. Even during Avis' time,
breakfasts were simple – porridge,
toast, and bacon and eggs. It was
only the rich – who had time to eat
multi-course breakfasts, as well as staff
to prepare them – who ate more.*

....

By the 1880s the grand country-house breakfast was in its heyday. Houses such as Audley End were not occupied all year round, as titled aristocrats needed to be in London when Parliament was sitting (they automatically sat in the House of Lords), and they often had several country seats. However, being in the country for the shooting season was almost obligatory. Participants – men and women – would leave the house after breakfast, sometimes not eating again until the light faded, which in the winter was at about 3.30pm, so large breakfasts were very useful. These were served buffet-style, with the various hot elements under cover or on spirit burners, and the family and their guests would help themselves. Most houses provided toast, buns, preserves, hot and cold meats, sausages, bacon, pies and eggs cooked in a wide variety of ways.

Toast the bread by grilling (broiling) both slices on one side, before turning them over, brushing with the 1 tbsp of melted butter and toasting the other side. Be careful that they brown, but don't burn.

Whisk the eggs lightly with 3 tbsp of the cream and the curry powder. Melt the remaining butter and add the egg mixture. Over a low heat, cook the eggs until they start to scramble, stirring and turning them regularly and gently so that they cook without becoming rubbery. When they are just cooked, remove from the heat, stir in the remaining 1 tbsp of cream, season with salt and pepper, and serve immediately with the toast, sprinkled with the parsley, if you like.

EGGS WITH CHEESE

Avis Crocombe, *unpublished manuscript* (no date)

SERVES 2–3

6 eggs

30 g/1 oz/¼ cup flour

2 tbsp butter

250 ml/8 fl oz/1 cup hot milk

60 g/2½ oz/generous ½ cup grated strong Cheddar cheese

1 tsp English mustard

1 tbsp breadcrumbs

pinch of cayenne pepper, plus more to garnish

salt

Eggs were popular not just for breakfast, but also for luncheon. Lunch was a relative newcomer, having made its appearance under a variety of names at the end of the 18th century. Until then, people ate breakfast, dinner and then supper in the late evening. However, since the Tudor era, dinner had been moving backwards in the day, from about 11am in the 1550s, to 2pm in 1700, to 5pm or 6pm by the 1780s. For the fashionable, it moved to 8pm in the early 19th century, and both luncheon and afternoon tea crept in to fill both time and peckish bellies. Lunch was often seen as a feminised meal, as men were likely to be working, or attending Parliament if they were titled. It was often made from recycled parts of previous meals, such as cold roast meat, which could be made into a curry or a soufflé, as well as easily prepared items such as these eggs with cheese.

Put the eggs in a saucepan of cold water and bring to the boil. Boil for 6 minutes, then cool under running water. Once cold, remove the shells and halve the eggs lengthways. Scoop the yolks into a bowl.

Make a roux by combining the flour and butter in a saucepan set over a medium heat, stirring to form a pale golden paste. Gradually add the hot milk, stirring well after each addition, to make a thick, creamy sauce. Add the cheese and stir until melted.

Add the mustard and breadcrumbs to the yolks, mashing them to combine. Add as much cheese sauce to the yolk mixture as you need to make a thick paste. Season with cayenne and a pinch of salt.

Put the egg yolk mixture into a piping bag fitted with a fluted nozzle and pipe into the hollows left in the cooked egg whites. Arrange on a platter and sprinkle the yolks with cayenne, to serve.

You can also simply mash the yolks with the grated cheese, spice and breadcrumbs, but this is rather less elegant.

CURRY

Maria Rundell, *A New System of Domestic Cookery* (1806)

SERVES 6

1 tbsp flour

3 tbsp mild curry powder

1 tsp chilli flakes (red pepper flakes)

800 g/1 lb 12 oz diced mutton
or lamb

3 tbsp vegetable oil or ghee

1 tbsp butter

3 onions, diced

4 garlic cloves, finely chopped

710 ml/1¼ pt/3 cups meat stock

1 small cauliflower

1 apple (Granny Smith, or similar
tart eating apple)

200 g/7 oz/1⅓ cups peas

1 small lemon

salt, to taste

455 g/1 lb/2 cups steamed rice,
to serve

quails' eggs, to garnish (optional)

....

CURRY

*The first mention of curry in English
dates to 1598, but the first recipe
wasn't published until 1747. The name
probably came from the Tamil* kari,
*filtered through the Portuguese and
then the English languages. It came to
mean anything spiced and stew-like.
The hybrid Anglo-Indian cuisine which
developed in 19th-century Britain
included kedgeree, chutneys and many
curries. Apples were used instead of
hard-to-obtain tamarind, pickled
cucumbers stood in for mangos, and
cream toned down the spice.*

....

Curries were tremendously popular in Victorian Britain.
The food of India had long been served in Britain, having been
introduced by officers and officials returning from the Raj (the
British Empire in India). The first curry house opened in 1810,
serving *khichri*, *chutnee* and *pulao* (later anglicised to kedgeree,
chutney and pilaf), mainly aimed at those who had lived in India
and missed its food. However, it was possible to buy ready-made
curry spice blends well before that. As they spread, British
curries changed until there was barely any resemblance to their
roots: the recipes were heavily anglicised, to suit both British
palates unused to hot spice, and the availability of ingredients
in Britain. By the 1880s, many curry recipes were essentially
versions of the older British 'hash': a means of using cold meat
from previous meals in an interesting way. Other recipes, such
as this, did use fresh meat.

Mix together the flour, curry powder, chilli flakes and a little salt.
Add the diced meat and stir well to coat. Heat a large, heavy-based
frying pan with the oil or ghee over a medium-high heat, then fry
the meat until it is browned all over. Set aside.

In a large saucepan, melt the butter. Add the onions and cook over
a low heat for 30–40 minutes until golden brown and soft. Add
the garlic, pour in the stock and return the meat. Stir thoroughly.
Simmer for 2 hours, until the meat is very tender.

Cut the cauliflower into small florets and peel and dice the apple.
Add to the curry. Cook for a further 5–6 minutes, then add the peas.
Taste, and adjust the salt if required. Finish with a squeeze of lemon.

Serve with steamed rice (Mrs Crocombe would have used Patna rice,
which is a long grain variety) and for a Victorian flourish, garnish
with halved quails' eggs (Mrs Crocombe would have used plovers'
eggs, but to do so is now illegal).

CAKES AND BISCUITS

MINCE PIES

Eliza Acton, *Modern Cookery for Private Families* (1845)

FOR THE MINCEMEAT

3 tbsp finely diced cooked beef
or tongue

55 g/2 oz/⅓ cup raisins

55 g/2 oz/⅓ cup peeled, cored and
minced apples

55 g/2 oz/scant ½ cup suet

85 g/3 oz/¾ cup currants

85 g/3 oz/⅓ cup sugar

2 tbsp chopped candied peel

½ lemon, boiled until tender,
then chopped

½ tsp ground nutmeg

½ tsp ground ginger

1 tbsp sherry or Madeira

1 tbsp brandy

salt

FOR THE PIES

about 375 g/13 oz puff pastry
(or sweet shortcrust pastry)

butter and flour, for the tins

No British Christmas would be complete without mincemeat tarts, but in the Victorian period, while associated with Christmas, they were eaten throughout the winter season. Mincemeat had late medieval origins and, as the name suggests, was based originally on meat. The first known recipes date to the end of the Tudor period, when the mix was about half to two thirds meat – generally beef, but also often mutton. There were also fish and egg versions, for religious fast days. The ratio of meat to fruit and suet gradually changed, until by the time Eliza Acton published her recipe, very little meat was left. Her original amounts make about 16 kg/35 lb of mincemeat, of which a mere 455 g/1 lb is beef. In modern recipes, only the suet is left as a reminder of the meat – and even that can be vegetarian.

Ensure all the solid ingredients are in pieces of roughly the same size. Mix all the ingredients in a large bowl with a pinch of salt, then store in sterilised jars (see p231).

To make mince pies, preheat the oven to 175°C/345°F. Roll out the pastry and use it to line 12–15 buttered and floured tartlet tins. Put 1 generous tsp (or more, depending on the size of the tins) of mincemeat into each and bake for 15–20 minutes until the pastry has puffed and turned golden brown and the filling is piping hot.

Serve hot or cold.

CHRISTMAS FOODS

Most Christmas recipes started life simply as food which was both of the winter season and suitable for feasts. Thus, the British Christmas invariably centres on a roast, which today is often turkey, but in the Victorian era was more likely to be beef. A great deal of

Christmas food is, like the mincemeat here, based around dried fruit, spices and alcohol, all of which were expensive when the recipes were developed in the late medieval and Tudor eras. They were also readily available in the depths of winter.

LEMON AID

The lemon is boiled both to take out some of the bitterness, and also to soften it enough to be easily chopped and added to the mincemeat.

QUEEN DROP BISCUITS

Avis Crocombe, *unpublished manuscript* (no date)

MAKES 18–20

225 g/8 oz/1 cup butter, softened, plus extra (optional) for the baking sheets

225 g/8 oz/1 cup caster sugar

4 eggs, at room temperature, lightly beaten

340 g/12 oz/2⅔ cups flour

225 g/8 oz/1½ cups currants

finely grated zest of 1 lemon

....

CURRANT AFFAIRS

Many of Mrs Crocombe's recipes call for currants. In this context they are a dried fruit, and not the fresh red, black or white currants that the Victorians also enjoyed. They are small, black and come from a red seedless grape (they are sold as Zante currants in the US). Raisins are larger and lighter in colour, and are dried white grapes. If you plan to soak the fruit, for example in brandy, to add flavour to cakes and biscuits, raisins are a better choice, as they take moisture more easily. Sultanas are also made from a variety of white grape, but dry to pale yellow. They are sweeter than either currants or raisins.

....

These easily made biscuits were one of the first recipes the team cooked from Avis' manuscript after Bob Stride donated it in 2009. They were an instant hit with all of the costumed interpreters, and have stayed on the list of dishes cooked regularly at Audley End ever since. The flavours are similar to those of the ubiquitous 18th-century queen cakes, which were little fruited sponges usually made in shaped tins. They are ideal for kitchen maids learning their trade (or for your own first steps into the world of Avis Crocombe).

Preheat the oven to 200°C/400°F.

Cream the butter and sugar together in a bowl until pale and fluffy. Add the eggs gradually, together with a little of the flour to stop the mixture curdling. Whisk after every addition.

Dust the currants with a little more flour (this stops them sinking into the mix) and fold them in with the lemon zest. Finally, sift the flour and add it to the mixture, folding it in carefully.

Line 2 baking sheets with buttered baking parchment or a silicon baking sheet and spoon or pipe the mixture onto the sheets. Leave enough room between each for the biscuits to spread out.

Bake for about 10 minutes, until lightly browned and cooked through, then carefully remove to a wire rack to cool.

POUND CAKE

Avis Crocombe, *unpublished manuscript* (no date)

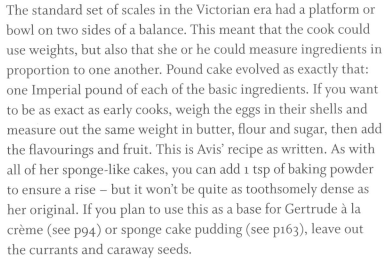

SERVES 6–8 (MAKES 1 X 15 CM/
6 INCH CAKE)

225 g/8 oz/1 cup butter, plus extra
for the tin

225 g/8 oz/1¾ cups flour, plus extra
for the tin

225 g/8 oz/1 cup caster sugar

4 eggs, lightly beaten

finely grated zest of 1 lemon

2 tsp orange flower water, or
a few drops of extract

1 tsp ground cinnamon

¼ tsp ground nutmeg

3 tbsp caraway seeds (optional)

100 g/3½ oz/¾ cup currants
(optional)

salt

The standard set of scales in the Victorian era had a platform or bowl on two sides of a balance. This meant that the cook could use weights, but also that she or he could measure ingredients in proportion to one another. Pound cake evolved as exactly that: one Imperial pound of each of the basic ingredients. If you want to be as exact as early cooks, weigh the eggs in their shells and measure out the same weight in butter, flour and sugar, then add the flavourings and fruit. This is Avis' recipe as written. As with all of her sponge-like cakes, you can add 1 tsp of baking powder to ensure a rise – but it won't be quite as toothsomely dense as her original. If you plan to use this as a base for Gertrude à la crème (see p94) or sponge cake pudding (see p163), leave out the currants and caraway seeds.

Preheat the oven to 180°C/350°F.

Butter and flour the cake tin, or a 900 g/2 lb loaf tin, and line the base with baking parchment. Cream the butter with the sugar until pale and fluffy. Gradually add the eggs, lemon zest and orange flower water, along with a little flour to stop the mixture curdling. Sift the rest of the flour and ground spices to add air.

Add a pinch of salt, the seeds and currants to the batter, then fold in the flour mixture. Beat on a low speed, if using a mixer, until the ingredients are combined, then spoon into the prepared tin.

Bake for about 55 minutes, or until a skewer comes out clean.

Allow to cool in the tin for 10–15 minutes before turning out and cooling on a wire rack.

Scales in the pastry room at Audley End.

ARROWROOT BISCUITS

Avis Crocombe, *unpublished manuscript* (no date)

MAKES 24

115 g/4 oz/½ cup butter

140 g/5 oz/⅔ cup caster sugar

85 g/3 oz/⅔ cup flour

85 g/3 oz/¾ cup arrowroot

2 eggs, lightly beaten

1 tsp orange flower water, or a few drops of extract

....

VICTORIAN OVENS

The range at Audley End, which was replaced following a kitchen fire in September 1881, has three ovens, heated by a system of pipes running around the range. One is intended for baking pastry and is heated from the bottom. Things burnt easily on the side nearest the fire, so usually ovens were fitted with a turnplate inside, which could be rotated regularly to ensure even cooking. Roasting was usually still done in front of the fire on a spit (see p49), but in smaller houses was increasingly done in the oven.

....

Arrowroot is a starch derived from various South American plants; it became very popular in the Victorian era both as a health food and as a thickening agent. Its great advantage is that it does not make sauces cloudy when used as a thickener, and it was often recommended in place of cornflour (corn starch) or *beurre manié* (cold butter and flour mixed together). This was probably deemed a healthy recipe in the 19th century, although the nutritional value of arrowroot has since been shown to be low. But it does give the biscuits a lovely flavour and texture.

Preheat the oven to 180°C/350°F.

Beat the butter and sugar together in a bowl until light and creamy. In a separate bowl, sift the flour and arrowroot together. Gradually beat the eggs into the butter mixture, adding 1 tsp or so of the flour mix every now and then to stop the batter curdling, and beating well after every addition.

Fold in the remaining flour mix and the orange flower water. Line 2 baking sheets with baking parchment. Drop the mixture onto the prepared sheets with a spoon, putting 6–8 biscuits on each tray. (You will have to bake these in batches.)

Bake for 15 minutes until just golden at the edges, then transfer to a wire rack to cool and crisp up. Repeat until they are all baked.

LEMON CAKES

Avis Crocombe, *unpublished manuscript* (no date)

MAKES 12

200 g/7 oz/scant 1 cup caster sugar

7 eggs, separated

finely grated zest and juice of 2 lemons

2 tsp rose water, or a few drops of rose extract

2 tsp icing sugar (confectioner's sugar)

¼ tsp cream of tartar (optional)

170 g/6 oz/1⅓ cups flour, sifted, plus extra for the moulds

butter, for the moulds

Avis' manuscript is not a balanced book, to say the least. It contains far more recipes for cake, biscuits and sweets than for anything else, and of these, more recipes for sponge-type confections than for any other type of mix. This is one among many recipes for a light, fatless sponge with delicate flavouring. The original recipe just uses well-whisked eggs as a raising agent, but we have given you the option of cream of tartar, just to guarantee a rise if you are not using a copper bowl. This trick works for all of the recipes in this book involving whisked eggs, or an egg white foam.

Preheat the oven to 180°C/350°F.

Whisk the caster sugar in a bowl with the egg yolks, lemon zest and juice, and rose water until light and fluffy.

Whisk the egg whites and icing sugar in a separate bowl. Adding the cream of tartar will help to stabilise the foam if you are not using a copper bowl. Carefully fold the sifted flour and meringue alternately into the yolk mix, ending with the last of the meringue.

Butter and flour 12 dariole moulds or small but deep muffin tins. Divide the mix between them, then give them a good tap on the work surface to remove any air.

Bake for 15–18 minutes or until a skewer comes out clean.

Invert the moulds onto a wire rack and allow to cool, before gently easing the cakes out.

WHITE CAKES [SHORTBREAD]

Avis Crocombe, *unpublished manuscript* (no date)

MAKES 18–20

285 g/10 oz/2¼ cups flour, plus extra for dusting

1 tsp ground cinnamon

170 g/6 oz/¾ cup salted butter, chopped

85 g/3 oz/⅓ cup caster sugar

1 egg, lightly beaten

This recipe is one among a number of variants on shortbread in Avis' manuscript. White cakes have various names, including Scotch cakes, and derive from 17th-century recipes, then often called short cakes. This version is delicately spiced with cinnamon and works well both as a light treat with a cup of tea, or with wine after dinner, which was how many biscuits were consumed in the Victorian era. For a decadent modern twist, the ends can be dipped in melted chocolate and then left to set.

Preheat the oven to 180°C/350°F.

Sift the flour and cinnamon into a bowl. Rub in the butter, then stir through the sugar. Add enough of the egg to make a stiff dough.

Roll the dough out on a flour-dusted surface to about 5 mm/¼ inch thick. Cut out rounds with a 6–8 cm/2½–3 inch cutter.

Line 1–2 baking sheets with baking parchment or a silicon mat and bake the shortbread cakes for 25–30 minutes until cooked in the centre, but not much browned.

Transfer carefully to a wire rack and allow to cool.

SCOTTISH JAUNTS

The Braybrookes sometimes rented a house in Scotland for the start of the shooting season. The 'Glorious Twelfth' was 12 August, when the law allowed the first grouse to be shot. The range of game eaten was large, and included some species, such as woodcock, blackcock, capercaillie and snipe, which are illegal to shoot (or highly problematic) today, as stocks are in sharp decline due to changing land management and a loss of habitat.

CAKE LORD BERNERS

Avis Crocombe, *unpublished manuscript* (no date)

SERVES 16 (MAKES 1 X 30 CM/
12 INCH CAKE)

170 g/6 oz/¾ cup butter, plus extra
for the tin

170 g/6 oz/¾ cup caster sugar

4 eggs, lightly beaten

225 g/8 oz/1¾ cups flour, sifted

115 g/4 oz/scant 1 cup sultanas

55 g/2 oz/½ cup mixed chopped peel

pinch of ground nutmeg

A really nice, solid cake recipe. It's uncertain whether Mrs Crocombe was passed this by one of her employers who got it directly from Lord Berners, or whether she got it from his cook. The Lord Berners involved was probably the 11th baron, Henry William Wilson, whose country seat was in Leicestershire, and who was president of the Royal Agricultural Society. Given Lord Braybrooke's interest in the Audley End herd of pedigree Jersey cows, they may well have socialised and shared their enthusiasm for farming. A later Lord Berners, the 14th baron, was famed for his eccentricity, and was (fairly) openly gay at a time when it was illegal to be so. For a modern twist, therefore, icing in rainbow colours would be entirely appropriate (not blue, as there wasn't a stable and food-safe blue until the 1930s).

Preheat the oven to 180°C/350°F.

Butter the cake tin and line the sides and base with a double layer of buttered baking parchment.

Cream the butter and sugar together until light and fluffy. Gradually add the eggs, together with a little of the flour to stop the batter from curdling.

Combine the remaining flour, dried fruit and spice together in a separate bowl. Fold this into the egg mixture. Transfer the cake batter to the prepared tin and give it a tap on the work surface to remove any air bubbles.

Bake for about 1 hour 15 minutes, or until a skewer comes out clean. If the top starts to colour too much during baking, cover it with foil.

Leave in the tin to cool, then turn onto a wire rack.

MOULDED GINGERBREAD

Maria Rundell, *A New System of Domestic Cookery* (1806)

MAKES 12–16 (DEPENDING ON THE SIZE OF THE MOULD OR CUTTER)

170 g/6 oz/½ cup black treacle

100 g/3½ oz/½ cup brown sugar

115 g/4 oz/½ cup butter

2 tsp ground ginger

1 tsp ground cinnamon

½ tsp ground coriander, or coriander seeds, if you prefer

½ tsp ground caraway, or caraway seeds, if you prefer

½ tsp ground mace

1 small egg, lightly beaten

300 g/10½ oz/2⅓ cups flour, sifted, plus extra for dusting

salt

....

FANCY MOULDS

If you do not have gingerbread moulds, you can buy wooden moulds, either new or vintage, or resin moulds. The latter are available both in modern designs and as replicas of antiques (search for 'springerle' moulds).

....

Gingerbread has its origins in the Middle Ages, when it was afforded immense prestige due to the quantity of expensive spice it contained. By the Victorian era, ginger had become one of the cheapest spices, and gingerbread was a firm favourite at fairs. This recipe is a Georgian one, from one of the most reliable and original texts of the period. The success of Maria Rundell's book helped to secure the financial stability of her publisher, John Murray, such that he could take the risk of publishing the fiction of one Jane Austen. This recipe uses a variety of spices, which combine to make a very complex gingerbread. Make sure you chill it very well after moulding, or the shape will blur.

Place the treacle, sugar and butter in a saucepan and warm through to melt the butter and dissolve the sugar. Add the ground spices (you can also leave the coriander and caraway seeds whole, if you plan to cut the gingerbread into shapes rather than mould it). Cook for 2 minutes, then remove from the heat and mix in the egg; you probably won't need all of it – start with about ¼ and only add more if you need to when you add the flour.

Add the flour and mix thoroughly to obtain a smooth, glossy paste. Wrap well in baking parchment or cling film (plastic wrap), or put it in a bowl covered with cling film and chill overnight.

The following day, take the moulds and brush them with a little flour. Remove a handful of dough from the mix and press it firmly into the mould. Carefully peel it out, trim if required, and place on a baking sheet lined with baking parchment or a silicon mat. Chill for at least 1 hour. Preheat the oven to 160°C/325°F.

Bake the gingerbread for about 25 minutes. It should not brown, but should be hardening on the edges. Remove from the oven and transfer very carefully to a wire rack. It will harden as it cools.

BROWN BREAD BISCUITS

Avis Crocombe, *unpublished manuscript* (no date); from William Jarrin, *The Italian Confectioner* (1820)

These are more like cakes to the modern British palate, but the terms biscuit and cake were rather interchangeable at the time. In Avis' manuscript this recipe is given without any method or attribution, but it comes from one of the most important confectionery manuals of the Victorian era. William Jarrin was an Italian-born confectioner who had worked at Gunter's, the best-known confectioner and caterer in London at the time. His book *The Italian Confectioner* was reprinted frequently until the 1860s and was a detailed look at both recipes and techniques – very much a professional book. The use of brown breadcrumbs here is not an instance of using up leftovers, for brown bread was rare upon the tables of the rich: Avis would have had to make (or buy) a loaf specially.

Preheat the oven to 170°C/340°F.

Whisk the yolk(s) with the sugar and lemon zest until light and fluffy. In a separate bowl, whisk the egg white(s) until they form stiff peaks. Fold the whites into the yolk mix. Finally, sift the flour to get some air into it, mix it with the breadcrumbs and fold them into the egg mixture.

Butter the cake moulds, which should be small and delicate, and preferably shaped in a suitably Victorian manner, and sprinkle the insides with sugar, rolling them around to coat and tapping out any excess. Spoon in the batter and stand the moulds on a baking tray.

Bake for about 12 minutes, until very lightly browned on top. Remove from the oven and cool on a wire rack.

....

HEALTHY BROWN BREAD
Brown bread was regarded for most of the past as decidedly inferior. It was not until the late 19th century, by which time white bread was affordable for the vast majority of people, that brown bread started to become – guardedly – acceptable. Companies such as Hovis and Allinson marketed their wares specifically on health grounds, pointing out that the removal of the wheatgerm in roller mills also destroyed much of the nutritional value of the loaf.

....

GINGERBREAD CAKE

Avis Crocombe, *unpublished manuscript* (no date)

SERVES 8–10 (MAKES 1 X 22 CM/
9 INCH CAKE, OR CAN BE BAKED
AS SMALL CAKES)

225 g/8 oz/1 cup butter, plus extra
for the tin

225 g/8 oz/generous 1 cup
brown sugar

3 tbsp ground ginger

2 eggs, lightly beaten

455 g/1 lb/1⅓ cups black treacle

455 g/1 lb/3½ cups flour

1 tsp bicarbonate of soda

115 ml/4 fl oz/½ cup warm milk,
plus extra if needed

icing sugar (confectioner's sugar),
to serve (optional)

Ginger was one of the cheaper spices in the past (along with black pepper) and was consequently much used. Cakes such as this developed in the 18th century when treacle became readily available as a cheap alternative to sugar. They are easy to make, and this one keeps for months, so it would have been ideal for the servants' hall. If you do happen to have any left, it makes an interesting alternative to sponge cake or breadcrumbs in some of the sweet puddings in this book. This is a real favourite at Audley End, and the team have cooked it regularly since the manuscript was donated in 2009. Many of them also cook it at home.

Preheat the oven to 180°C/350°F. Line the cake tin with well-buttered baking parchment.

Put the butter in a large bowl or mixer and beat it until it is pale and creamy. Now add the sugar and ginger and mix again.

Gradually add the eggs, continuing to mix vigorously. Reduce the mixer speed to medium, add the treacle, then fold in the flour.

Stir the bicarbonate of soda into the warm milk in a separate bowl until dissolved, then add this to the batter. (If you heat the milk in a jug you can then transfer it to an empty treacle tin, just to get the last scrapings of treacle out of the tin.) You are aiming for a thick, gloopy batter, so you may need to add a little more milk or water at this stage.

Pour the batter into the prepared tin and bake for 45–60 minutes, or until a skewer comes out clean. Once cooked, turn onto a metal rack to cool.

For a more elevated appearance, pop a paper doily on top and dust with icing sugar, before removing the doily to leave a rather delightful pattern.

SAFFRON BUNS

May Byron, *Pot-Luck* (1914)

MAKES 10–12

255 g/9 oz/2 cups flour

55 g/2 oz/¼ cup demerara sugar

1 egg, lightly beaten

4 tsp fresh (compressed) yeast, or 2 tsp dried yeast

85 ml/3 fl oz/⅓ cup milk, slightly warmed

neutral oil, for greasing

pinch each of ground cinnamon, cloves and mace

¼ tsp caraway seeds (optional)

finely grated zest of ½ lemon

2 tbsp butter, at room temperature

2 tbsp lard, at room temperature

pinch of saffron threads, soaked for 2 hours in 2 tsp warm milk

90 g/3 oz/generous ½ cup currants

salt

FOR THE GLAZE

1 egg

1 tbsp milk

Saffron has long been associated with the south-western counties of Cornwall and Devon, where Avis Crocombe was born and grew up. But in the 17th century it was also grown in Essex, in Walden, which became known as Saffron Walden. It was said that, at harvest time, the streets would be purple with the petals of the saffron crocus as they fluttered from the carts laden with discarded flowers. Saffron Walden is the nearest town to Audley End, bordering the estate on the east side. Many of the house's suppliers when Avis was cook were based there. Saffron, the food stuff, is not only very expensive, but also delicious. With their bright yellow colour, saffron buns were often associated with Easter in the past.

Make a basic enriched bread dough: combine the flour, sugar, a pinch of salt, the egg and yeast together with enough milk to make a soft – but not sticky – dough. Knead for 15–20 minutes and set aside in a warm place, covered with oiled cling film (plastic wrap), or in a bowl covered with a cloth, until it doubles in size (2–3 hours).

Remove the dough and flatten it out slightly. Put the spices, lemon zest, both fats, the saffron in its milk (which should now be yellow) and currants in the middle, fold it up and knead again, folding and squeezing so the new ingredients are well-incorporated (you can also just put everything in a food mixer fitted with a dough hook). Cover again and leave to double in size once more.

Preheat the oven to 180°C/350°F.

Lightly oil 2 baking sheets and shape the dough into 10–12 equal buns. Round them off and leave, covered in oiled cling film, to double in size (about 20 minutes). Mix the ingredients for the glaze in a small bowl with a pinch of salt and brush it over each bun. Bake for 15–20 minutes until golden brown.

These are best eaten on the day they are made, slathered with butter.

EASTER

For much of history Easter was a bigger festival than Christmas, with many foods associated with it. Chief among them in Britain in the 19th century were new season lamb, eggs (real and blancmange), and a number of fortified breads or cakes. Simnel cake, now associated with Easter, was, during Avis' time, more of a Mothering Sunday bake. Originally, Mothering Sunday was the day in Lent when people visited their home church. By Avis' time it was starting to gain its modern association with honouring mothers.

FRESH BREAD

Before the huge country-house breakfast of the mid 19th century, and for many even later, breakfast was centred on bread and baked goods. The rich liked their buns enriched with egg and filled with fruit and spice, and demanded them hot. Commercial bakers habitually worked through the early hours, ensuring there were hot buns ready for the shops and the street sellers, just as people were making their way to work. The classic Easter bun started life as a simple 'cross bun', becoming a 'hot cross bun' due to the demand to eat it still warm from the oven. The recipe for Bath buns on p191 works as the basis for a cross bun – just add more dried fruit and a little mixed spice (a sweet spice blend similar to pumpkin spice). Slash a cross in the top just before baking.

SAVOY CAKE

Avis Crocombe, *unpublished manuscript* (no date)

SERVES 8–10 (MAKES 1 X DEEP
21 CM/8 INCH CAKE)

butter, for the tin

340 g/12 oz/1½ cups caster sugar,
plus extra for the mould

5 eggs

1 tsp baking powder

225 g/8 oz/1¾ cups flour

2 tsp almond extract (or 55 g/2 oz/
⅔ cup very finely ground almonds)

2 tsp orange flower water, or a
few drops of extract

....
CAKE BANDS
*The original recipe calls for 'bands' to
be pinned around the top of the tin.
These were probably made of muslin,
and were dampened before pinning,
to slightly reduce the heat to the outer
edges of the cake (which tended to
cook more quickly than the centre) and
so encourage an even rise and stop the
cake peaking in the middle. You can
buy purpose-made cake bands today,
or make your own with several layers
of muslin folded over to give thick
strips of about 8 cm/3 inches wide.
Wet them, squeeze them out, and pin
or tie them around the top of the tin
before putting it in the oven.*
....

This is the first recipe in Mrs Crocombe's recipe book. She calls it a 'sponge cake', but fatless sponges were also known as Savoy cakes. It is one of two fatless sponges in the book. She also has more than 10 standard sponge cake mixes, used variously to make both small and large cakes and drop biscuits. Fatless sponges are lighter than standard sponge cakes, and were often used as the basis for other recipes, crossing over from cake to sweet very easily. They lent themselves to moulding and, by the late 18th century, it was possible to buy distinctive Savoy cake moulds with a flat top, which meant they would stand up easily in the oven. They could be served plain, or iced, especially after the development of royal icing and complicated piping techniques from the middle of the century onwards.

Preheat the oven to 180°C/350°F.

Start by buttering the mould or cake tin. Toss in some of the sugar and roll it around to coat the base and sides, tapping to remove any excess. (This will give it a crispy coating as well as helping the cake to come out of the mould.) Whisk the eggs until they are creamy. Add the sugar and continue to whisk until the mixture is very thick and pale. Separately sift the baking powder with the flour to aerate it. Add the flour to the egg mixture very gently, folding it in and trying to keep as much air in the mixture as possible. Midway through, add the almond extract and orange flower water.

Transfer the batter to the prepared mould or tin. Tap it gently on the worktop to remove any trapped air pockets and place in the oven for 30 minutes, or until a skewer comes out clean. Cool in the tin for another 30 minutes before demoulding.

You can either serve this plain, or pipe it with royal icing (made with egg white, and which you can make yourself or buy as a just-add-water prepared sugar mix).

CHRISTMAS CAKE

Charles Elmé Francatelli, *The Modern Cook* (1846)

SERVES 8–10
(MAKES 1 X 22 CM/9 INCH CAKE)

455 g/1 lb/2 cups butter, plus extra for the tin

340 g/12 oz/1⅔ cups sugar

455 g/1 lb/3½ cups flour, sifted

3 eggs, lightly beaten

340 g/12 oz/3 cups dried cherries, roughly chopped

455 g/1 lb/3 cups dried currants

455 g/1 lb/3 cups chopped candied peel

225 g/8 oz/2 cups ground almonds

finely grated zest of 2 oranges

275 ml/10 fl oz/1¼ cups brandy

1 tsp ground cinnamon

1 tsp ground ginger

½ tsp ground mace

½ tsp ground allspice

½ tsp salt

FOR THE ICING

1.15 kg/2½ lb marzipan (almond paste)

icing sugar (confectioner's sugar), for dusting

rice flour or cornflour (corn starch), for dusting

3 tbsp apricot jam, pushed through a sieve to remove lumps

1.15 kg/2½ lb royal icing (bought is fine), plus 225 g/8 oz for piping

food colouring, as desired (not blue)

Fruit cakes have a long and noble history, going back at least to the medieval era when richly spiced fruited breads were features of any celebration. During the 18th century the rich fruit cake as we know it in Britain today developed, complete with marzipan and royal icing. They were expensive to make, but could be kept for years. Until the late Victorian era they were usually made for Twelfth Night, but as the 19th century waned and Christmas celebrations became centred on Christmas day itself, they became known as Christmas cakes (though Queen Victoria had a Twelfth cake, for Twelfth Night, until the end of her life). This moist, delicious recipe is the one we used for the YouTube video. Avis included one in her book, probably intended for a servants' Christmas party – it starts with 50 eggs, is correspondingly huge and is one of the few revolting recipes she left to us.

Preheat the oven to 120°C/250°F. Cream the butter and sugar together and gradually add the flour and eggs, alternating between the two. Add all the fruit and nuts, the zest, the brandy, the spices and salt and beat very well.

Butter the cake tin and line it with baking parchment. Pour in the batter, then wrap the tin in 3–4 layers of brown paper, tying it round with string. Make a rough lid for the tin with more brown paper, folded to make 3–4 layers. Stand it on a tray (it tends to leak a little in baking). Bake for 6 hours, until a skewer comes out clean, the cake is golden and the kitchen smells like Christmas. Cool on a rack for half a day before decorating.

To decorate, first level the top of the cake if it is very domed. Make a long sausage of marzipan, use this to edge the top of the cake, then turn it upside down onto a cake board at least 38 cm/15 inches in diameter. Press down slightly so that the marzipan sticks the cake to

the board and use a palette knife to smooth it against the sides. Use more marzipan to fill in any large holes in the sides or top (ex-bottom) of the cake. Dust a work surface with a mixture of icing sugar and rice flour or cornflour and roll out a strip of the marzipan long and wide enough to cover the sides and about $^2/_3$ cm/¼ inch thick. Trim it to fit, leaving a slight overlap at the ends (you may find it helpful to make a template out of paper first). Roll out some more to cover the top.

Heat the apricot jam and brush it all over the sides and top of the cake. Sprinkle the strip of marzipan for the sides with the icing sugar mix and roll it up gently so that you can lift it into place. Unroll it to cover the sides. Where the edges meet, overlap them and slice away the top layer of this overlap with a neat vertical cut. Peel away and discard the top layer to leave a neat, straight join.

Put the marzipan for the top on the cake and trim any overlap, using a very sharp knife. Smooth both top and sides with a cake smoother and leave the cake to dry for at least a day.

Mix up the royal icing according to the instructions on the pack, if needed. When you reach soft-peak texture, you are ready to go. Using a palette knife, spread the icing on the top of the cake, working it well to remove the air bubbles. Scrape the excess off in a smooth movement. Dry for at least 3 hours, then cover the sides, again using a palette knife to apply and work the icing and a side scraper to take off the excess (it helps to use a turntable). Dry for another 3 hours. Repeat at least twice, allowing ample drying time, until you have a beautifully smooth and white cake. If it's not entirely smooth, try to make sure that any air bubbles or mistakes are in places where you can disguise them with cunning piping.

Dry the cake for at least a day before piping onto it using the remaining icing, coloured in whichever way you like and piped however you fancy.

BATH BUNS

Avis Crocombe, *unpublished manuscript* (no date)

MAKES 12 LARGE OR
24 SMALL BUNS

455 g/1 lb/3½ cups strong white
bread flour

2 tbsp fresh (compressed) yeast,
or 1 tbsp dried yeast

170 g/6 oz/¾ cup butter,
at room temperature

3½ tbsp milk

4 eggs, lightly beaten

140 g/5 oz/⅔ cup caster sugar

2 tsp salt

neutral oil, for greasing

115 g/4 oz/1⅓ cups candied
peel, chopped

2½ tbsp nibbed (pearl) sugar

2 tsp caraway seeds (optional)

butter and preserves, to serve

FOR THE GLAZE

2 tbsp milk

2 tbsp icing sugar
(confectioner's sugar)

Bath buns started life as Bath cakes, a yeasted, fruited bun, often served hot for breakfast. Jane Austen was a fan, ruefully but enthusiastically referring to 'disordering her stomach' with them in 1801. They were originally made with caraway comfits (sugar-coated caraway seeds sold in tins), but by the time Avis wrote down her recipe, comfits were very old-fashioned, and she left them out. Instead, the Victorians added dried fruit. Bath buns were on offer at the Great Exhibition in 1851, where nearly 950,000 buns were sold in just over 5 months. They do not keep well and are best eaten on the day you make them. They are good with butter and jam, but even better with a sharp cheese.

Mix the flour, yeast and butter in a large bowl, crumbing them with your fingers to a breadcrumb consistency. Warm the milk to blood-warm and add it to the flour mixture with the eggs, caster sugar and salt. Mix well in a mixer or by hand, before kneading, either with a dough hook attachment or again by hand, until the dough is silky and smooth and comes away from the sides of the bowl easily. Form into a ball and transfer to a lightly oiled bowl. Prove in a warm place for 30–60 minutes or until doubled in size, then knock back and leave for a further 5 minutes.

Add the chopped peel, half the sugar nibs and the caraway seeds, if using. Divide into 12 or 24 pieces of 115 g or 55 g (4 oz or 2 oz). Large buns are good for breakfast or supper; smaller are preferable for afternoon tea. Shape into rolls and place on an oiled baking tray. Cover with oiled cling film (plastic wrap) or baking parchment and leave to prove for 30 minutes or until they have doubled in size and become smooth. Preheat the oven to 220°C/425°F.

Just before baking, sprinkle the buns with the remaining sugar nibs. Bake for 15–20 minutes, until golden brown. Mix the milk and sugar together to form a glaze. Remove the buns from the oven and glaze immediately. Serve hot, with oodles of salty butter, or leave to cool and serve with a delicate pat of butter and optional preserves.

VICTORIA SANDWICHES

Anon, *Cassell's Dictionary of Cookery* (c.1875)

SERVES 6

115 g/4 oz/½ cup butter, plus extra for the tin

115 g/4 oz/½ cup caster sugar

115 g/4 oz/scant 1 cup flour

4 eggs, lightly beaten

1 tsp baking powder

70 g/2½ oz/¼ cup jam (jelly), such as strawberry or raspberry

icing sugar (confectioner's sugar), for dusting

....

VICTORIA AND HER SANDWICHES
There's no evidence that Queen Victoria regularly enjoyed Victoria sandwiches, or that they were invented in the royal kitchens. However, the queen did enjoy cakes, and in the 1880s the kitchens at Windsor would send regular parcels of teatime treats to her wherever she was staying. Her habits helped to popularise afternoon tea, as pictures of her taking tea when on holiday or in a tent on the lawn at Osborne House were published regularly in the Illustrated London News. *Formal afternoon tea was very much a phenomenon of the last quarter of the 19th century, when it was named and codified by etiquette writers, although as a concept it went back to the 18th century.*

....

One of many recipes named for Queen Victoria, this first appeared in Isabella Beeton's best-selling *The Book of Household Management* in 1861. Beeton's book was very skilfully written, with an empowering start – 'as with the commander of an army, so it is with the mistress of a house' – and a vast quantity of recipes. However, she didn't exactly promise original content, and the vast majority of her recipes were cobbled together from other books of the time, especially those of Eliza Acton. Beeton was highly aspirational, including advice on how to manage footmen, which was far above the level of most of her buyers. Cooks such as Mrs Crocombe would quickly have seen through her plagiarism, and the recipes were a bit below the level that Mrs Crocombe was cooking at. This version of Beeton's original is from *Cassell's Dictionary of Cookery*, a typically encyclopaedic later-Victorian book that is very popular with the team at Audley End, as it has recipes for almost everything conceivable.

Preheat the oven to 180°C/350°F.

Cream the butter and sugar until light and fluffy. Add a spoonful of flour to stop the mixture splitting, then beat in the eggs, whisking continuously. Mix in the rest of the flour and the baking powder.

Butter a rectangular cake tin (about 28 × 14 cm/11 × 5½ inches) and line it with lightly buttered baking parchment. Pour in the batter and bake for 35–40 minutes or until a skewer comes out clean. Allow to cool in the tin for 20 minutes before removing from the tin and cooling completely on a wire rack.

To serve, cut the cake in half horizontally with a serrated knife and spread the bottom layer with jam. Replace the top and cut the whole cake into 8 strips, to look like finger sandwiches. Dust them with icing sugar. Pile them up, two at a time, with each pair at right angles to the last, to form a lattice.

5

Mrs Crocombe and the Staff

by Annie Gray

BRINGING THE SERVANTS TO LIFE

When the service wing at Audley End House was renovated and reinterpreted in the spring of 2008, English Heritage decided to have a regular programme of costumed interpretation. I led the team of interpreters, usually playing the first kitchen maid, Mary Ann Bulmer. I was doing my PhD in food history at the time, and embraced the chance to use my research on the ground, while also learning a great deal about cooking Victorian food by simply doing it (clad, of course, in corsets and accurately reproduced gowns).

Most of the team had trained as actors, and few could cook. This was better than it sounds. I needed people who would accept Victorian ways of cooking and presenting finished dishes, without bringing too many modern preconceptions to the project. Our remit was to bring the kitchens to life, but within that we had a set of clear interpretative objectives: to show that country-house life encompassed many different social groups; give a voice to the traditionally voiceless; and play on a rich culinary heritage which had often been overshadowed by the notion that food in the past was all stodge and overcooked vegetables. Every dish that we cooked was chosen for its potential to enable us to start conversations with visitors as well as being representative of the era – and they all had to be easy enough that everyone could tackle them.

Later that year Kathy Hipperson started working at the site, declaring that she couldn't cook. She was (and is) a brilliant interpreter, and so a long habit started wherein she would simply field difficult culinary questions posed by visitors by 'asking my first kitchen maid – it's important she learns'. She not only played Mrs Crocombe, ageing up by wearing spectacles (Mrs Crocombe was 43 in 1881), but sometimes Sylvia Wise, the second kitchen maid, and Fanny Cowley, the dairymaid. There were ten key people who could each play at least three characters, and we swapped around regularly.

After a year in the kitchens (and the laundry and dairy), the team had a repertoire of about 20 recipes which everyone could cook, all backed up by research and all used as springboards to explore wider topics, such as the globalisation of cuisine, the physical labour of the era, Victorian views on health, and the ethics of industrial farming. But it was all based on secondary research, and we just had to accept that the voices and personalities of the real people we were portraying were unrecoverable. So, when Bob Stride approached us in 2009 with the manuscript book kept by the very cook we were interpreting, it was utterly amazing.

The book wasn't an autobiography, but it gave us an insight into Avis Crocombe's life. Previously, we'd based our portrayals of the servants we played on a mixture of things, from the memoirs left by other servants of the time, to close reading of contemporary diaries and fiction, to our own personalities, strengths and historical interests. Andrew Hann and his team at English Heritage informed our work through detailed genealogical work, which gave us the bare bones of the life stories of our characters, and helped us flesh out what we thought their motivations would have been. (When you find out that your character died in her early twenties, like the second kitchen maid, Sylvia Wise, it does tend to change the way in which you portray her.)

The manuscript recipe book didn't contain an essay on life at Audley End, or a description of the people within it, but could nevertheless be used to gain a sense of Avis as a working cook, how she wrote, what her education had been like, what books she had access to, and her changing employers. Though there were few dates, we could still see time passing, and food tastes changing. We could see to within a few pages when she started at Audley, and when she left. Best of all, the recipes within it confirmed the direction we'd taken with our own choice of dishes, and the kind of meals that we'd decided, based on other research, Avis would have been cooking.

This photograph was found with Avis Crocombe's manuscript, by her great, great step-nephew Bob Stride. It is thought to be of Avis and Benjamin Stride after their marriage in 1884.

AVIS CROCOMBE

Every interpreter played Mrs Crocombe slightly differently, bringing their own interests and experiences to the role. One was slightly scatty, one motherly, one a dedicated career woman, and another a devoted church-goer who despaired of her more worldly maids. Kathy's Mrs Crocombe was brisk, organised and a reassuring presence, though not one who put up with cheek. She was, perhaps, inclined to be kinder than she should have been, although a maid who presented a pastry disaster would certainly feel the sharp side of her tongue.

Kitchens were not, in reality, places for conversation, but Audley was full of chatter; public interaction was key to everything we did. Balancing historical accuracy with the need to convey information and impressions was crucial.

The same applied to constructing her character. As with all of the characters regularly portrayed at Audley, we have no idea what the real Avis was like. We have only the bare bones of her life, glimpsed through the census records and other official documents.

She was born in August 1837, in the tiny village of Martinhoe on the north coast of Devon, the daughter of Richard Crocombe and his second wife, Agnes. Richard had seven children (Mary, Agnes, John, Richard, Rebecca, Ann and Grace) with his first wife, Joan Squire. With Agnes he had seven more, the third of whom was Avis. The Crocombes were a long-established family and farmed 40 acres in and around the village. In 1841 there were seven children at home, including Avis, aged four. Others had already left home and, as was common at the time, helped out in providing a first step for their siblings as they entered the workplace. The school leaving age in the mid 19th century was about 10, and by 13 Avis was working for her brother John, who was 18 years older and farming 130 acres near Challacombe, about 9 miles from Martinhoe. She was a general servant, gaining experience in all areas.

Most servants in Victorian Britain remained generalist, and about three-quarters worked in small households with only one or two servants. Deciding to specialise and then work her way up within larger houses suggests that Avis was career-minded and dedicated. It's likely that after leaving her brother's service she worked for a member of the local gentry as a scullery maid, before seeking work through the servants' informal network or an agency to move on. She had the example of two of her sisters to follow: Rebecca, who was 14 years older, was a cook in a small household in Devon, while Grace, two years older, had worked as a kitchen maid in a much larger house, before leaving to get married in 1859. Another sister, Sarah, also worked in country houses as a cook, though she never quite reached the rank of a servant to titled aristocracy.

In 1861 and now 23, Avis had moved away from Devon and was working for John Robert Townshend, 3rd Viscount Sydney. A career politician, and member of the Liberal party, Townshend was Lord Chamberlain to the queen, a role without serious duties, but

nevertheless very senior. He ran a household commensurate with his status, which included Avis as kitchen maid, a scullery maid and a male cook, Alfred Fraden. Aristocrats rarely employed women as their chief cooks: they did not have the status of male chefs, especially the sought-after French chefs, who were invariably found heading the kitchens of the very wealthy.

These male chefs, French or not, were paid around double their female counterparts, commanding wages of about £100–£150 a year, depending on experience. A cook like Avis would be lucky to receive £60 a year, although the job came with additional perks, such as the right to sell rabbit skins (used by furriers for gloves and garments), bones (turned into fertiliser) and rags (which went for paper). Cooks and kitchen maids would also receive full board and lodging, and cooks could reasonably expect their own room. Maids would often share not only a room, but a bed.

Avis' next move was to a lower-status household, where a male cook was not a must and where she could obtain a promotion in rank and an increase in salary. By 1871 she was the cook–housekeeper at Langley Hall, near Loddon in Norfolk. Her new employers were Thomas and Catherine Proctor-Beauchamp. Thomas was a baronet, so still titled, but at the bottom of the scale. It was a large household, with three kitchen maids and three housemaids directly under Avis, and two footmen, two lady's maids, a nurse and a governess also present as indoor servants (the Proctor-Beauchamps had eight children). Avis now gained the honorific title of 'Mrs', despite being unmarried. It was felt that senior female

Charles Neville, 5th Baron Braybrooke in about 1870. Avis was employed by Lord Braybrooke by 1881.

servants with girls serving under them – the cook and housekeeper – should always be known as if they were married. The Proctor-Beauchamps would, like Viscount Sydney, have had a London house where they spent the 'season' (when Parliament was sitting and the social whirl in London was at its peak). It's likely that Avis networked her way into her next job for Lord and Lady Braybrooke through her London connections: Charles Neville, being a baron, also had a London house, at 42 Upper Brook Street, in a fashionable area of Mayfair.

The 1881 census was the one which English Heritage used when interpreting the Audley End service wing. Avis was now working as cook for

Charles Cornwallis Neville, the 5th Baron Braybrooke, and his wife, Florence. The Nevilles had one daughter, Augusta, who at 21 was already married and running her own household. The housekeeper's role at Audley End was a separate one, filled by Mrs Elizabeth Warwick. Avis had two kitchen maids: Mary Ann Bulmer, aged 25, from Yorkshire, and Sylvia Wise, a 21-year-old from Oxfordshire. There was also a scullery maid, Annie Chase, who was 17 and from Hampshire. Their lives would have been spent shuttling between Audley End, London, and rented houses taken on short-term leases. In the 1860s and 1870s, prior to Avis' employment, these had included Branksome Towers in Bournemouth (for the seaside) and Croftinloan House in Pitlochry (for the shooting season).

How or when Avis met Benjamin Stride is unclear. He was a widower and worked as a butler to the Throckmorton family of Coughton Court in Warwickshire. Probably, Avis and Benjamin met in London, as the Throckmortons' London house was in Davies Street, Berkeley Square, just round the corner from Upper Brook Street. In March 1884, when Avis and Benjamin married, she was 45 and he was 46. Benjamin already had three children from his first marriage: Mary Anne, a dressmaker, who at 19 was about to get married; Walter Benjamin, who would emigrate to New Zealand in 1894; and Anna Jane, aged 12. This was a marriage for love and pragmatism, and not to create a new family. Avis would have entered it knowing she not only could, but would have to, continue her career – they were both working class and it was unthinkable that she would stop working. But service in the kitchens was physically hard work and now she had the opportunity to leave service and become an independent worker.

The Strides, as Avis and Benjamin now were, married at the Church of St George, Hanover Square, right in the heart of aristocratic London, and therefore a traditional place for the marriages of the servants of the aristocracy. The couple took over a boarding house in Paddington, at 40 Cambridge Terrace, close to Hyde Park, where it's likely that Avis continued to cook, not only for her new family, but also for any guests desirous of board as well as lodging. The 1891 census shows that the Strides employed a domestic servant of their own: Avis had come full circle. A photograph of the time, passed down in the Stride family, may well be of Benjamin and Avis.

Avis and Benjamin continued to run the boarding house together until Benjamin's death in 1893. He left Avis an estate valued at £496 8s. 6d. (£63,000 in today's money) – eight times her likely annual salary at Audley End, which gave her the independence to continue in business. Now, Avis looked for assistance from her step-daughter, Anna Jane Stride, and they ran the boarding house together until at least 1920. Avis then retired to Bell Street, Marylebone, in north London, where she died in 1927 of chronic bronchitis. She was 89.

We don't know how Avis' recipe book came to Bob Stride's family, though it is likely that his grandfather, Daniel Stride, who was a retired police constable living in Chelsea, helped Anna Jane to settle Avis' affairs and came into possession of the book. After Daniel's wife died in 1932, he went to live with his eldest daughter, Elsie Stride, who ran a tobacconist's and sweet shop in Fulham. It was from his aunt Elsie that Bob inherited the recipe book.

It's rare that manuscript cookery books from this era survive outside the collections of the aristocracy themselves, and rarer still to know exactly who kept it, and how it survived. Through a happy twist of fate, this one came back to its home at Audley End, is back in use and is delighting a generation 150 years on.

SERVANTS' DISHES

SAVOURY ROLY POLY PUDDING (DEAD MAN'S LEG)

Based loosely on Alexis Soyer, *A Shilling Cookery for the People* (1854)

SERVES 6–8

FOR THE PASTRY

225 g/8 oz/1¾ cups flour, plus extra for dusting

85 g/3 oz/⅔ cup suet

½ tsp salt

about 115 ml/4 fl oz/½ cup water

200 g/7 oz bacon or ham, chopped

1 small onion, minced

200 g/7 oz/2¼ cups mushrooms, finely chopped

lard, for frying (optional)

Brilliantly cheap and infinitely versatile, this is the kind of dish that would have been served in the servants' hall at Audley End, and was also the kind of thing the servants would have grown up eating. It could be filled with anything – this one uses bacon and mushrooms, but sausagemeat also works, as do sweet fillings. Made with jam (jelly), it's known as a jam roly poly. Once made and wrapped, it could be put on to boil and left at the back of the range until done. Suet pastry is the easiest of all pastries: you don't need cold hands, and it takes a lot of punishment. Plus, it can be cooked in a lot of different ways – boiled, baked or fried.

Make the pastry by combining the flour, suet and salt in a large bowl with enough of the water to give a soft, springy – but not sticky – dough. Rest for 10 minutes before rolling out into a rectangle on a flour-dusted surface. You will need to measure its exact width against the pan you plan to cook it in, but 21 cm/8 inches should be about right. The length does not matter, but the pastry should be about 5 mm/¼ inch thick.

Spread the pastry with the bacon, onion and mushrooms, leaving a 2 cm/¾ inch gap at the sides and along the top edge. Roll up tightly from one of the short edges. Wet and flour a pudding cloth and wrap the pudding up tightly, but leave a pleat for the pudding to expand (you can also use baking parchment and foil). Tie the ends so that it looks like a giant boiled sweet in a wrapper with twisted ends.

Boil in simmering water for 2 hours, or steam on a rack over boiling water, with a lid on. When done, remove from the pan and gently take off the cloth.

You can eat it as it is, or leave to cool, chill well, slice, then fry the slices in hot lard.

....

DEAD LIMBS AND SHIRT SLEEVES

Yes, this really was known as dead man's leg (or sometimes arm). It looks like a water-logged or severed limb. It was also called shirt-sleeve pudding, possibly because it was often cooked in an old shirt sleeve.

....

GYPSIES' POTATO PIE

William Kitchiner, *The Cook's Oracle* (1817)

SERVES 6 (AS A MAIN COURSE)
OR 8 (AS A SIDE DISH)

455 g/1 lb waxy potatoes

1 onion

115 g/4 oz/½ cup salted butter,
plus extra for the dish

240 ml/13 fl oz/1 cup vegetable or
meat stock

about 320 g/11 oz puff pastry

1 egg

salt and pepper, to taste

Dating back to the early 19th century, this very plain pie is filling and cheap. It is best made with waxy potatoes that will keep their shape, but will work with a more fluffy variety if that is all you have. Plain though this pie is, it is nevertheless delicious. It is best served with gravy. Potatoes, which were introduced to Europe from South America in the 17th century, took about a century to become the staple food which they were across Europe by the Victorian era. The poor were absolutely reliant on them, as they were easy and reliable to grow and reasonably nutritious, as well as tasty. When potato blight struck in the 1840s, it led to mass starvation. Ireland was particularly hard hit – what became known as the Great Famine caused enormous suffering as well as a mass exodus, particularly to North America; it is estimated that about a million people died of starvation and disease.

Preheat the oven to 220°C/425°F.

Peel and thinly slice the potatoes and the onion. Butter a rimmed pie dish of about 25 × 15 cm (10 × 6 inches). Layer in the potatoes and onions, seasoning very well between layers. This dish relies upon the seasoning, so add as much pepper as you think you need, and then add some more. Pour over the stock.

Cut the butter into small pieces and dot it over the top. Roll out the puff pastry and cover the dish. Slash the top to make 2 cuts of about 3 cm/1 inch, or use a pastry funnel in the middle to let the steam out while cooking. Crimp the edges, or decorate with a pastry plait.

Mix the egg with a pinch of salt and 1 tsp of water to make an egg wash, and brush this all over the pie. Cook in the hot oven for 45 minutes until golden brown and puffed up.

SODA CAKE

Avis Crocombe, *unpublished manuscript* (no date)

SERVES 10–12 (MAKES 1 X 28 CM/
11 INCH SQUARE CAKE)

225 g/8 oz/1 cup butter, chopped,
plus extra for the tin

225 g/8 oz/1 cup caster sugar, plus
extra for the tin

455 g/1 lb/3½ cups flour

¼ tsp ground nutmeg

¼ tsp ground cinnamon

225 g/8 oz/1½ cups currants

255 ml/9 fl oz/1 cup milk

2 eggs

few drops of lemon extract, or the
finely grated zest of 1 lemon

1 tsp bicarbonate of soda

FOR THE SYRUP (OPTIONAL)

juice of 3 large lemons, or 2 oranges

100 g/3½ oz/½ cup sugar

A cheap, cheerful cake for servants' tea, this recipe is typical of the late 19th century. Artificial raising agents, such as baking powder, had started to be commercialised from the mid Victorian era onwards, but were largely rejected by cooks working in large houses as they tasted of soap and were a slippery slope to the deskilling of kitchen staff. However, their rise was inevitable, and eventually bicarbonate of soda came to be used specifically for its flavour, as well as for giving a good rise when mixed with something acidic, in this case milk. Elsewhere, especially in Ireland, where yeast could be in short supply or unaffordable, soda breads became popular, again using bicarbonate of soda. Eventually soda bread would become synonymous with Irish cuisine, especially for breakfast.

Preheat the oven to 180°C/350°F.

Butter the cake tin, then sprinkle in some sugar and roll the tin around to coat all the surfaces, tapping to remove excess.

Sift the flour, sugar and spices together. Rub the butter into the flour mix to form breadcrumbs. Mix in the currants. Whisk the milk and eggs together, combine with the flour mix and beat well.

Add the lemon extract or zest and the bicarbonate of soda and mix again. Pour into the prepared tin and bake for about 1 hour, or until a skewer comes out clean. Allow to cool for 10–15 minutes and then turn out of the tin and cool completely on a wire rack.

The cake is very plain, and could be elevated to a simple family cake with the addition of a lemon or orange syrup on the side, or drizzled over it. Make the syrup by combining the lemon or orange juice with the sugar and a little water in a saucepan and boiling until a syrup is obtained.

EVE'S PUDDING

Avis Crocombe, *unpublished manuscript* (no date)

SERVES 4–6 (FILLS A 570ML/
1 PT/2⅓ CUP PUDDING BASIN)

170 g/6 oz/roughly 2 apples

170 g/6 oz/2 cups breadcrumbs

170 g/6 oz/1 cup raisins, plus 1 tbsp

2 eggs, lightly beaten

1 tbsp brandy (optional)

100–140 ml/3½–5 fl oz/scant
½–⅔ cup milk

butter and flour, for the basin

wine sauce, to serve (see p105)

....

STAFF DUTIES

*There was a clear hierarchy: the cook
cooked for the family, planned menus
and ordered ingredients. She was
assisted by the first kitchen maid, who
worked on sauces, stocks and pastry.
The second kitchen maid cooked for
the servants. The scullery maid did all
the peeling, washing, gutting, plucking
and washing up of equipment. Fine
silver was washed and polished by
the butler, while family china and
glassware was looked after by the
housekeeper.*

....

Eve's pudding now is very different to the Eve's pudding written down by Avis Crocombe. Today, it usually has a base of apples – often Bramleys, the standard cooking apples of Britain, but which were not commercialised until the 1890s – topped with sponge cake. When recipes for it started occurring at the end of the 18th century, however, it was as a mixture of breadcrumbs, eggs and fruit, sometimes with suet as well. Many of the recipes in the manuscript seem to have later-18th- or early-19th-century origins and sometimes wording, which is a further indication that Avis was selecting fairly old-fashioned recipes for her book. This may well just be an indication that she was cooking for 'old money', the landed aristocracy, and not those who had made their fortune more recently in trade and banking, who may have preferred more modern cuisine.

Core, peel and grate the apples and mix together with all the ingredients except the brandy and milk. Then add the brandy, if using, and enough of the milk to form a stiff batter.

Butter the pudding basin and pour in the batter. Top with a wetted and floured pudding cloth, tied tightly around the basin, or use a disc of buttered baking parchment and a sheet of foil. Don't forget to leave a pleat, so that the pudding can expand.

Boil or steam for 3 hours. If boiling, the water should reach three-quarters of the way up the basin.

Turn out and serve with wine sauce and extra sugar in a sprinkler to the side. It is also good with custard.

ABOVE LEFT Service bells at Audley End.

RABBIT PUDDING

Mary Jewry, *Warne's Model Cookery and Housekeeping Book* (1868)

SERVES 6 (FILLS A 1¼ LITRE/
2 PT/1⅓ QUART PUDDING BASIN)

FOR THE PASTRY

455 g/1 lb/3½ cups flour

170 g/6 oz/1⅓ cups suet

½ tsp salt

170 ml/6 fl oz/¾ cup water

butter, for the basin

flour, for dusting

FOR THE FILLING

1 rabbit, boned

285 g/10 oz streaky bacon

1 tbsp flour

1 tbsp minced parsley leaves

leaves from 2 thyme sprigs

6–7 mushrooms, chopped, or
1 tbsp mushroom ketchup (optional)

2 tbsp white wine

170 ml/6 fl oz/¾ cup chicken stock

salt and pepper, to taste

Suet crust pastry was a basic of the Victorian kitchen. Easy to make and cook, and tasty, it was used for a huge variety of pies and puddings. The crust could enclose sweet or savoury fillings, which cooked gently within it over several hours. Meat puddings were a staple of the servants' hall, but today are almost forgotten – the sole survivor is steak and kidney pudding. You can use this basic recipe for almost any combination: veal and ham, beef and oyster, game and prune, mutton and parsnip, to name a few. Browning the meat is optional, but adds flavour. Mrs Crocombe would have used the bones for a plain stock afterwards.

Make the pastry by combining the flour, suet, salt and enough water to form a soft – but not sticky – pastry. Rest for 10 minutes. Butter the pudding basin. Reserve about a third of the pastry. Roll out the rest on a flour-dusted surface and use it to line the pudding basin, ensuring you have about a 2 cm/¾ inch overhang.

Chop the rabbit into bite-sized pieces. Dice the bacon. Mix, season and sprinkle over the flour and herbs. Mix in the mushrooms or mushroom ketchup, if using, and wine. Spoon into the basin. Add enough stock so you can see it just nearing the top of the filling, without overflowing. It should be level with the top of the basin.

Roll out the reserved pastry on a flour-dusted surface, wet the overhanging edges on the basin and stick the lid down firmly, pressing to seal. Trim to fit the basin, ensuring the seal is tight.

Wet and flour a pudding cloth and use it to cover the pudding, tying it round the top. You can, instead of a cloth, put a piece of buttered baking parchment on top of the pie and wrap foil around the whole dish. Leave a pleat in the cloth or foil so the pudding can expand.

Boil the pudding in simmering water (it should reach three-quarters of the way up the basin) or steam, for 1½ hours. Remove from the water, immediately remove the cloth or foil and cut a small hole in the top of the pastry to allow steam to escape. Serve in the basin.

A PLAIN WHITE LOAF

Eliza Acton, *The English Bread Book* (1857)

MAKES 1 LARGE (455 G/1 LB) LOAF

4 tsp fresh (compressed) yeast, or 2 tsp dried yeast

170 ml/6 fl oz/¾ cup milk

170 ml/6 fl oz/¾ cup water

455 g/1 lb/3½ cups strong white bread flour, plus extra (optional) for the cloth

2 tsp salt

neutral oil, for the tin

....

NOTE

Eliza Acton prefers using a sponge as a raising agent. A sponge is a mixture of the yeast and a little water and flour left overnight to develop flavour. You can replicate this by mixing the yeast here with half of the water and just enough of the flour to make a handleable dough and leaving it, covered, in a cool place overnight. Then add this mixture to the remaining ingredients and proceed as above. Acton also suggests removing a good handful of the final dough before shaping and baking and adding it to the next batch, to improve the flavour.

....

By the 1880s, few households in the south of England habitually baked all their daily bread. Even the queen ordered much of the bread used at the palaces from outside suppliers. But bread-making was still deemed a vital skill for working-class women, for, although there had been a great deal of improvement in the previous decades, much of the bread sold in England was still adulterated with inferior ingredients. For those at the bottom of society, bread really was 'the staff of life', by far the major part of their daily diet. Yet British bread was not well regarded. Eliza Acton opened her 1857 *The English Bread Book* with a lament on its 'want of genuineness, and the faulty mode as to its production'. Bread was always made with yeast in the Victorian era: sourdough was felt to reek of poverty and taste horrible.

Dissolve the fresh or dried yeast into the combined milk and water. Separately mix the dry ingredients. Add the liquid and mix together. Knead for 10–15 minutes to develop the gluten. Put into a bowl and cover with a lightly floured cloth or cling film (plastic wrap).

Leave to prove for 2 hours or until doubled in size, then knock back (press gently to remove the air), and leave for another 20 minutes.

Grease the loaf tin and shape the dough into an oval. Put it into the tin and leave to expand and fill the tin for another 30 minutes, or until once more doubled in size.

Preheat the oven to 220°C/425°F. Slash the top of the loaf lightly with a very sharp knife and bake for about 30 minutes until golden brown. Turn the loaf out of the tin and return it to the oven for 5–10 minutes, to brown the sides.

To test if it's cooked you can turn the loaf over and knock it gently on the bottom – it should sound hollow. Alternatively, and more reliably, it is done when the interior temperature reaches 94°C/201°F.

Cool on a wire rack.

BROWN MEAL CAKES [BISCUITS]

Avis Crocombe, *unpublished manuscript* (no date)

MAKES 15–20

225 g/8 oz/1¾ cups wholemeal flour, plus extra for dusting

3 tbsp bran

55 g/2 oz/¼ cup butter

1 tsp baking powder

2–3 tbsp milk

salt

Meal (or bran) was one of the lower grades of flour, and rarely used for bread. However, its nutty flavour and nutritional value made it ideal for a particular type of biscuit, namely those aimed at the health market. The term 'digestive biscuit', meaning a biscuit made with wholemeal flour, was first coined in the early Victorian period, usually accompanied by somewhat spurious health claims. By the time Avis wrote several recipes involving wholemeal flour into her book, the belief in the health benefits of wholemeal was well established. These are pleasant enough with tea, but better with butter and cheese – perfect for a servants' tea.

Preheat the oven to 200°C/400°F.

Mix the flour, bran, butter, baking powder and a pinch of salt to form crumbs. Add enough milk to form a manageable dough, fairly firm in texture.

Roll out on a lightly floured board and cut into rounds with an 8 cm/3 inch cutter. The dough should be 1.5–2 cm/½–¾ inch thick. Prick all over with a fork and bake for 10 minutes until firm to the touch and slightly browned. Remove carefully (they will be very crumbly) and cool on a wire rack.

....

BISCUITS

Biscuits in British English are sweet or savoury baked items (the name comes from the French bis cuit *or 'twice cooked'). They are usually crisp and dry. They can be like the American cookie (a word derived from the Dutch* koekje, *for a small cake) but tend to be plainer, smaller and less sweet. Biscuits are served with cheese (in which context they are sometimes called crackers), or with a cup of tea. (The permissibility of dunking is a whole other debate – Queen Victoria did it, so who are we to judge?)*

....

SPOTTED DICK

Alexis Soyer, *A Shilling Cookery for the People* (1854)

SERVES 8–10 (FILLS A 1¼ LITRE/ 2 PT/1⅓ QUART PUDDING BASIN)

225 g/8 oz/1¾ cups flour, plus extra for dusting

170 g/6 oz/1⅓ cups suet

170 g/6 oz/1 cup currants, plus 1 tbsp

3 tbsp sugar

pinch of ground cinnamon

1 egg

225 ml/8 fl oz/1 cup milk

butter, for the mould (optional)

salt

custard (see p113), to serve

Also known as plum bolster, after its shape (a bolster is a long, cylindrical pillow), spotted dick became a beloved English dish – helped by its school-playground-humour smutty name – in the mid 20th century. This version comes from Alexis Soyer (see p77), one of the 19th century's most flamboyant culinary figures. His books contain recipes that range from the solidly brilliant to the outrageously wacky, along with a set of recipes for the poor which, it must be admitted, have a whiff of the patronising about them. You can increase or change the dried fruit and spices here, or add a little jam (jelly). It is best with custard, but will work with cream, ice cream or even (rather more daringly modern) chocolate sauce.

Mix all the dry ingredients together and add a pinch of salt. Whisk the egg into half of the milk and pour this into the dry mix. Add enough of the remaining milk to make a soft dough.

Turn the dough onto a lightly floured surface and knead briefly.

Shape the dough into a sausage and wrap it in baking parchment and then foil, or use a wetted, floured pudding cloth, tying the ends so that it resembles a giant boiled sweet. Alternatively, you can use a pudding basin, in which case cover the top with a disc of buttered baking parchment and then a wetted, floured pudding cloth or foil, ensuring you leave a pleat to allow for expansion. If using a cloth, tie it firmly round the top of the basin.

Boil or steam for 2 hours. Turn out, remove the cloth and serve with custard.

AMBER PUDDING

Avis Crocombe, *unpublished manuscript* (no date)

SERVES 8–10 (FILLS A 1¼ LITRE/
2 PT/1⅓ QUART PUDDING BASIN)

butter, for the basin

570 g/1¼ lb/1½ cups marmalade
(see p231)

170 g/6 oz/1⅓ cups suet

115 g/4 oz/1⅓ cups fresh breadcrumbs

3 eggs, lightly beaten

wine sauce or custard, to serve
(see p105 and p113)

Amber pudding is so-called for its colour. The standard Victorian recipe was for an orange curd, made with butter, eggs, sugar and oranges, which was then baked in pastry. The result would be a translucent orange colour and absolutely delicious. Recipes for that type of pudding go back at least as far as the 17th century, and probably beyond. This version is equally delicious but more typical of the type of recipe favoured by mid-to-late Victorians. It is cheap to make, with easily obtainable ingredients, and requires very little attention once it is cooking. It would have sat at the back of the cast-iron range, simmering for several hours, while dishes for the family were prioritised. This recipe is not written in Avis' handwriting, and probably dates from the Edwardian era, or the 1920s, when she was running a boarding house in Marylebone.

Butter the pudding basin and line the base with a disc of buttered baking parchment. Mix all the ingredients, being careful not to overwork them in case the suet melts. Put the mixture into the pudding basin and smooth off the top. Cover with a disc of buttered baking parchment and then a pudding cloth or foil, ensuring that you leave a pleat in the middle to allow for any rise.

Place the basin in a pan of simmering water, which should come about three-quarters of the way up the basin. Top up the water periodically and do not let it boil dry. Put a lid on the pan and simmer for 3½ hours.

Serve hot, with custard if for a servants' meal, or wine sauce to elevate it a little.

MACARONI CHEESE

Henry Southgate, *Things a Lady Would Like to Know* (1874)

SERVES 2–3

1¼ litres/2 pt/1⅓ quarts water

570 ml/1 pt/2⅓ cups milk

225 g/8 oz/generous 2 cups macaroni

115 g/4 oz/½ cup butter, plus extra for the dish

170 g/6 oz/1½ cups grated Parmesan or other hard cheese

2–3 tbsp breadcrumbs

salt and pepper, to taste

....

MACARONIS AND MACARONI

In the 18th century a 'macaroni' was an extravagantly fashionable gentleman, one who imitated the tastes and fashions of the Europe he had travelled through during his Grand Tour – the finishing touch to the education of young men of the upper classes. The term quickly became pejorative, as high fashion grew ever sillier in the 1770s. Macaronis were characterised by their habit of wearing towering wigs, very tight hose and light, impractical patterned fabrics. All of these (apart from the hose) were also seen as feminine characteristics, and the widespread criticism of macaronis was tied up with unease over gender identity and notions of masculinity at a time of global war. The macaroni in the ditty 'Yankee Doodle Dandy' comes from this meaning – the titular character is not putting pasta on his hat.

....

Pasta has been combined with cheese since at least the medieval period, although the cheese was frequently soft cheese, and was flavoured with various spices. A recognisably modern version of macaroni cheese was being made by the 18th century, with Elizabeth Raffald, one of the best-known authors of the Georgian period, specifying Parmesan as the cheese. Her book *The Experienced English Housekeeper* (1769) was one among many English recipe books to be published in North America, then still under British rule, and American cookery books were quick to adopt her macaroni as a recipe. Macaroni had originally been a general term for any pasta, not just the hollow tubes known under that name today, and this recipe works with any shape or length you fancy using. That said, Henry Southgate's original recipe, which is the one we use here, calls for 'pipe macaroni', the advantage of which is that it crisps very nicely under the grill. You can easily vary it by adding bacon or sausages.

Preheat the oven to 200°C/400°F.

Bring the water and milk to the boil with a good handful of salt. When it boils, throw in the pasta and cook until it is just done (usually 6–7 minutes, but do check the packet). Drain.

Butter a shallow dish (about 21 cm/8 inches in diameter), and put in half the cooked macaroni. Dot this with a third of the butter and sprinkle with half the cheese. Season with pepper, to taste. Add another layer of macaroni, dot with another third of the butter and top with the breadcrumbs mixed with the rest of the cheese. Finally, melt the remaining butter and drizzle it over the top.

Bake for 15 minutes until the cheese is bubbling and golden. For a good crispy top, finish with 2–3 minutes under a hot grill (broiler).

THE HOUSEKEEEPER'S ROOM

BLACKCURRANT VINEGAR

Avis Crocombe, *unpublished manuscript* (no date)

MAKES 1¼ LITRES/2 PT/1⅓ QUARTS

455 g/1 lb/5 cups blackcurrants, fresh or frozen

570 ml/1 pt/2⅓ cups white wine vinegar

455 g/1 lb/2¼ cups sugar

....

THE HOUSEKEEPER OF AUDLEY END
Elizabeth Warwick, the housekeeper at Audley End, was 52 in 1881. Her background is unclear, but she was widowed young, by at least her early thirties, and had probably worked her way up from housemaid. She was clearly good, as well as experienced, as her previous employers included a military colonel with a household of five others and a separate cook, and Baroness Clementia Aveland of Grimsthorpe Castle in Lincolnshire. The baroness's household was substantial enough to include the relatively rare (and old-fashioned) roles of house steward and groom of the chamber. When Mrs Warwick retired she went to live in Audley End village, probably with a small pension from the Braybrookes to supplement her own savings. Like Mrs Crocombe, she was then able to employ her own servant, who, at 15, was probably in her first position.

....

Flavoured vinegars were very popular in the past and are making a gradual comeback today. Blackcurrant vinegar is excellent for culinary use, as it works well in both sweet dishes (particularly those with figs or other sweet fruit) and savoury mixtures (use it as you would balsamic). In the Victorian era it was also used as the basis of a drink, and a few tablespoons added to still or sparkling water makes a refreshing cordial. Blackcurrants are high in vitamin C and drinks such as this were given to children or the sick, to fortify them if they were not eating properly.

Put the blackcurrants in a bowl with the vinegar and bruise with a wooden spoon. Leave, covered, in the fridge for 2 days. Strain into a bowl, then push the currants through a sieve (or use a mouli). Keep the pulp, discarding the skins and pips in the sieve.

In a saucepan, heat the strained juice and pulp with the sugar, skimming as required. When the sugar has dissolved, decant into sterilised jars (see p231). Seal. Use within a year.

RHUBARB JAM

Avis Crocombe, *unpublished manuscript* (no date)

MAKES 4–6 JARS

1.15 kg/2½ lb rhubarb

850 g/1 lb 14 oz/4¼ cups brown sugar

140 ml/5 fl oz/⅔ cup water

finely grated zest and juice of 1 lemon

....

COPPER COOKING VESSELS

You will see serried ranks of copper pans in the Audley End kitchen. Highly conductive – so providing a good even heat – they are excellent to cook with. Copper was (and is) the choice of most professional cooks. Cooks took a high level of pride in the gleaming copper, which was polished by the scullery maid until it shone. For cooking (unlike for beating eggs, see p120), the copper was lined with tin, to prevent it leaching into acidic food. It was well known that too much copper could lead to nausea and vomiting and in extreme amounts would be fatal. The maid, therefore, would check for gaps in the internal tinning. If an untinned copper pan was not cleaned properly, acids from food could react with the copper to cause copper corrosion, or verdigris, which is readily soluble and poisonous. The usual pale green colour of unpolished copper is not verdigris, but simply the natural patina formed by copper's exposure to oxygen. Most copper pans were therefore tinned inside, except those used for sugar boiling and jam-making, as the sugar gets too hot for the lining. Today they are often lined with stainless steel.

....

Rhubarb has a very long history, but not as a culinary ingredient. It was first used as a purgative, both in its native Asia, from where it was imported in dried form, and in the Middle East and Europe by the ancient Greeks and Romans. In the 17th century, live plants were brought to Britain, but it was not until the 18th century that the stalks (now of a rather less digestively awkward variety) started to be used in sweet tarts. Consumption remained very low until a London plant breeder introduced the 'Victoria' cultivar, which is still widely grown. By the 1880s, rhubarb was being forced (grown in the dark to ensure pale, sweet stalks) on an industrial scale in an area known as the 'rhubarb triangle' in Yorkshire, from where a daily 'rhubarb express' train took fresh produce direct to the markets of London.

Cut the rhubarb into chunks. Put everything into a large saucepan. If using copper, make sure it is untinned (use a preserving pan).

Bring to the boil, stirring rapidly. Keep it boiling for 30–45 minutes until the mixture thickens and starts to form a jam. Check the set point, either by removing from the heat to perform the wrinkle test (see p231) or by using a probe thermometer (the set point is 105°C/221°F). If it is not at set point, keep boiling and checking until you get there.

Decant into sterilised jars (see p231), seal and keep for up to a year. Once open, refrigerate.

GINGER BEER

Avis Crocombe, *unpublished manuscript* (no date)

MAKES 4 LITRES/7 PT/4¼ QUARTS

4 litres/7 pt/4¼ quarts water

2–3 tbsp sugar

30 g/1 oz fresh ginger, chopped
and bruised

zest of 1 lemon, cut off without pith

1 slice of thick-cut bread

4 tsp fresh (compressed) yeast,
or 2 tsp dried yeast

....

WATER

*It is a tired myth that no-one drank
water in the past. Some water was,
indeed, polluted, and generally people
tried to avoid standpipes, which could
be fed by sources running through
graveyards or downstream of the local
tannery. However, most water was
perfectly healthy, whether it came from
freshwater wells, streams or rainwater
tanks. It was free, and was the major
drink of the majority of the population,
some of whom could barely afford
bread, let alone beer. Audley End, like
many country houses, had a cistern
on the roof to collect rainwater for
cooking, drinking and washing. It
directly fed a boiler at the back of the
roasting range, so was heated by the
cooking fire – a handy way to use a fire
which was already lit and very hot.*

....

There are a number of recipes for drinks in Avis' manuscript, most of which are for lemonade or ginger beer. This one is noteworthy for having a mention of Audley End, for underneath it is written a rare source: *'The Field' newspaper, copied from Lady B.Brook. A.E.* – the 'A.E.' standing for Audley End. First published in 1853 and still going today, *The Field* was devoted to field sports. Today it covers mainly shooting, hunting and fishing. This recipe is a little insipid for modern tastes, which tend towards a sweeter ginger beer, but it is a good representative of the Victorian era. By all means add a sweetener such as honey or sugar at the end, or give it a boost with a sweetish whisky.

Heat the measured water and sugar until the sugar dissolves. Add the ginger and lemon zest. Allow to cool to room temperature and decant into a food-grade bucket or a large bowl.

Toast the bread. Mix the yeast with a little warm water to form a thick paste and spread this on the toast. Add the toast to the ginger beer mixture. Cover and leave to stand at room temperature for 12–24 hours.

Strain the mixture through a fine sieve lined with kitchen paper or, better still, muslin or a jelly bag. Decant into clip-top jars or bottles, which will allow any gas to escape if it gets a bit lively.

Leave for at least 4 days and up to a few months.

GIN PUNCH

Based on references in the novels of Charles Dickens;
now an Audley End favourite

PER MUG

30 ml/1 fl oz gin

30 ml/1 fl oz ginger wine or brandy

2 slices of lemon

1 tsp brown sugar

1 tsp honey

generous pinch each of ground
cloves, cinnamon and nutmeg

hot water, to top up the mug

IF MAKING IN A PUNCH BOWL

1 bottle of gin

1 bottle of ginger wine or brandy

7–8 lemons, sliced

130 g/4½ oz/⅔ cup brown sugar

225 g/8 oz/⅔ cup honey

20 whole cloves

15 cinnamon sticks

1 tsp ground nutmeg

boiling water, to top up to taste

Punch was a ubiquitous party drink for the Victorians and recipe books of the time list a huge variety, from the cheap to the much more expensive. It was a drink designed for sharing, whether after dinner – when it could be mixed at the table in a male-only ritual generally ending in disarray – or at celebrations. This one is at the cheaper end of the scale, using gin, which was still only just losing its whiff of danger and desperation after being banned in the early 18th century, and ginger wine (or brandy). Good for a party, such as that held in the Audley End servants' hall after Christmas every year, it is also medicinal, or at least it might be. To make it, just mix all the ingredients together.

....

PUNCH

Punch seems to have originated in the British West Indies, where it was a drink based on rum, and mixed with citrus (either lemon or lime), sugar and water. The first references are from the 17th century, and by the 18th century it was very popular at parties or as an after-dinner drink. It was associated with men and contemporary illustrations often show groups of very drunken men carousing around a punch bowl. Later recipes vary the spirit and sometimes include the very British tea. By the 19th century, punch had become a catch-all word for a mixed drink, predating the more formal cocktails by some time.

....

ENGLISH CHUTNEE

Avis Crocombe, *unpublished manuscript* (no date)

MAKES 2–3 JARS

450 g/1 lb fairly sharp eating apples (roughly 4 apples)

1½ tbsp salt

115 g/4 oz/⅔ cup raisins

225 g/8 oz/1⅓ cups sultanas

455 g/1 lb/2¼ cups brown sugar

55g/2 oz/3 tbsp peeled and minced fresh ginger

2½ tsp minced garlic

1 tsp minced green chilli (roughly 1 serrano chilli)

1½ tbsp mustard seeds

570 ml/1 pt/2⅓ cups white wine vinegar

juice of 1 lemon

....

THE FOOTMEN'S COOK

Queen Victoria helped to give Indian cuisine a real boost when she decided to add a group of Indian footmen to her staff of personal attendants at her jubilee in 1887. Gorgeously clad in colourful silks and turbans, they stood out amongst the crowds which habitually surrounded her, and were often shown in portraits and sketches of her. Never scared to try new foods, she asked their cook to prepare an 'authentic' Indian dish for her, made with fresh spices ground between two stones, and cooked as they preferred. She liked it so much that she added a dish made by the Indian cook to her weekly menus for a while.

....

Chutney (or chutnee) was another Anglo-Indian recipe with roots in India, but filtered through the British experience. The name came from the Hindu *chatni*, which was a composite pickle, using sweetening agents, spice and vinegar to preserve and pickle mixed fruit and vegetables. Unlike jam or fruit cheese, or plain pickled vegetables and fruit, chutneys were complex and exciting, but also had texture. They kept well on long journeys and could be used to pep up plain meat or cold pies. The British adopted them enthusiastically, changing the ingredients to fit what was available and free-styling with gusto. Granny Smith apples – although not well known in Victorian England (they originated in Australia in the 1860s) – work well in this recipe.

Peel, core and cut the apples into small dice and sprinkle them with the salt. Leave to stand for 2 hours, then rinse and drain.

Place all the ingredients in a large saucepan and slowly bring to the boil. Reduce the heat to a simmer and stir intermittently to stop it sticking. The mixture should start to thicken after 30–40 minutes.

Decant the chutney into sterilised jars (see p231), seal and keep for at least a month before using. Keep in the fridge and use within three months once opened.

TO PRESERVE ORANGES AND PINEAPPLES

Avis Crocombe, *unpublished manuscript* (no date)

ORANGES

300 g/10½ oz/1½ cups sugar

285 ml/½ pt/1¼ cups water

12 oranges

70 ml/2½ fl oz/⅓ cup Cointreau or curaçao (optional)

PINEAPPLES

6 small pineapples

4½ litres/8 pt/4¾ quarts water

2kg/4 lb 6 oz/10 cups sugar

Citrus fruits and pineapples were the fruits of the day in the 16th and 17th centuries respectively. Both were exotic, delicious and hard to grow in Britain, although houses such as Audley End were cultivating both by the 1880s. These fruits, candied, are ideal for festive occasions such as Christmas, as they glisten like jewels in the flickering candlelight and firelight of a darkened dining room, and delight with their scent and taste. Fruits in syrup were served as part of a Tudor banquet, but would have been equally at home as a delicate dessert at Audley End in 1881.

For the oranges

Place the sugar and measured water into a saucepan and gently stir. Bring to the boil and simmer for 15 minutes to fully dissolve the sugar. Reduce until you have about 570 ml/1 pt/2⅓ cups of liquid (stock syrup). Keep hot.

Remove the peel and pith carefully from each orange. Place them all into a non-metallic container that can be sealed. Now add the liqueur, if using, to the stock syrup and pour it over the oranges to cover. Cover, label, then chill for at least 1 week before using.

For the pineapples

Cut the skins and tops from the pineapples. Place them into a large saucepan containing the measured water and set a circle of baking parchment on top, then bring to the boil. Cook until soft, then remove the pineapples and place onto a tray. Set aside.

Strain the cooking liquid. Measure out 4 litres/7 pt/4¼ quarts of it and return this to the saucepan with the sugar. Rapidly boil and reduce by a third. Once syrupy, pour over the pineapple in a very large, non-metallic container that can be sealed. You may not need all of the syrup.

Leave for 1 week in the fridge before cutting into cubes or slices.

....

WEIGHT WATCHING

One of the 5th Lord Braybrooke's peculiarities during Mrs Crocombe's tenure at the house was to weigh his guests before dinner. We still have one of his weighing books, which covers the period 1868–83, from which we can tell that on 22 November 1868, for instance, Lord Braybrooke weighed 10 st 2 lb 8 oz (64 kg 637 g) and Lady Braybrooke 7 st 10 lb 8 oz (49 kg 215 g). Their eight-year-old daughter, Augusta, who was present at this particular dinner with her cousins, weighed 3 st 4 lb (20 kg 860 g).

....

MARMALADE

Maria Rundell, *A New System of Domestic Cookery* (1806)

MAKES 4–6 JARS

12 oranges (Seville are best, but you can use eating oranges, which will give a sweeter result)

1.36 kg/3 lb/6¾ cups sugar

570 ml/1 pt/2⅓ cups water, plus more to cook the oranges

Avis' book contains three orange marmalades and one apricot marmalade. Marmalades developed in the Tudor era as expensive fruit and sugar concoctions which could be moulded or cut into shapes. For a long time, they were made with quinces, but in the 17th century oranges became popular. It took another 100 years for orange marmalade to stop being stiff enough to cut into blocks. Sugar became cheaper in the Victorian era and marmalade became associated with Scotland in the 18th century, perhaps because the Scots seem to have been instrumental in making it obligatory at the breakfast table.

Sterilise 4–6 heatproof tempered glass jars, by placing them in a low oven, preheated to about 140°C/275°F, for 15 minutes. Sterilise the lids in boiling water, if using lids.

Put the oranges in a large preserving pan with water to cover. Bring to the boil, cover with a lid or a disc of baking parchment and cook for 45 minutes. Remove 6 of the oranges and cook the remaining 6 for a further 15 minutes, until they are very soft.

With a very sharp knife, peel the first 6 oranges and cut the peel into short, thin strips. Set the peel aside. Quarter all the oranges, fishing out the pips and fibres. Place the peeled and unpeeled quarters in a blender or food processor and blend to a pulp. For very smooth marmalade, pass the pulp through a sieve or vegetable mouli. Put all the pips and fibres into a muslin bag (jelly bag) and tie up well.

Return the pulp to the clean preserving pan with the sugar, measured water and bag. Boil until it thickens and starts to cling to the spoon, about 15 minutes. Remove the bag. Add the reserved peel and boil for a further 5 minutes. Check it has reached setting point, either by doing the wrinkle test (does a drop placed on a chilled plate set and wrinkle if tilted?), or by using a jam thermometer (set point is 105°C/221°F). If it has not, keep boiling and checking until you get there. Spoon into the jars and seal immediately.

THE DAIRY

THE DAIRY

LORD BRAYBROOKE'S HERD

Lord Braybrooke kept a herd of pedigree Alderney (Jersey) cows. The estate's modern record-keeping system and scientific analysis of yields and methods of improvement won an award from the British Dairy Farmers' Association in 1882. We still have some of the registers which show not only that the yields were impressive, but that the cows had charmingly whimsical names, including Gossamer, Phiz, Glowworm, Primula, Spermlight and Squib.

It was unthinkable in Victorian Britain not to cook with butter, although lard and dripping were more common lower down the social scale. The kitchens got through anything from 9 to 13 kg (20–30 lb) of butter a week, plus cream, milk and other produce from the dairy.

Milk would be delivered to the dairy twice a day after the morning and evening milking sessions. It was put into settling pans to allow the cream to rise to the surface; the cream was then skimmed off. The skimmed milk that resulted was sometimes used in the kitchen or was sold to the local villagers. Being from cows with very-high-fat-content milk, it was not as anaemic as modern skimmed milk and was rather tastier, but still lacked the body necessary for many of Mrs Crocombe's recipes.

All the equipment required in the dairy was scalded for hygiene purposes, and, in the case of the wooden churn, soaked so that the wood would swell and seal any gaps. The cream was churned for anything from 45 minutes to more than 1 hour, depending on the weather conditions and the time of the year. The resultant lump of butter was then thoroughly rinsed and left to drain.

FACING PAGE
The dairy at Audley End, with its shallow bowls used for settling cream at the start of the butter-making process.

RIGHT
Lemon Leaf, one of Lord Braybrooke's pedigree Alderney cows.

THE DAIRYMAID AT AUDLEY END
*The dairymaid in 1881 was Fanny
(Frances) Cowley. She was 30 years old
and her position at Audley End was a
very responsible one, but with no good
prospects for career progression. In
1888 she married a carpenter and
joiner, James Tongue, who had already
fathered three children with her (so she
probably left Audley End in about 1883,
when her first child was born, or
perhaps before – she may have become
his housekeeper and fallen in love).
It is uncertain whether James was a
widower or divorced. They lived in
London and then Brighton. By the time
Fanny was 61 she had gone blind and
was cared for by one of her daughters,
but she lived another 20 years, dying
aged 83, two years after her husband.*

Once drained, the butter was worked repeatedly to get out the excess buttermilk, which would cause it to go rancid. In the winter, when the cows were in the barns and their milk lacked colour, the butter might be coloured with yellow dye extracted from carrots (by boiling) or marigold petals (which were soaked in a tiny bit of boiling water and then squeezed in a cloth to extract the colour). The buttermilk might go to the kitchen for use in ices or baking, or to be drunk in summer. It was also used in the laundry as a stain remover (it is particularly good for getting rid of ink).

At this stage, butter was usually salted. Unsalted ('sweet') butter went off quickly, so the majority of recipes used salted butter. It could also be flavoured, and popular choices included herbs such as watercress, parsley, thyme and savory (all of which were ideal as accompaniments to fish), or more punchy anchovies, crab or devilled mixtures containing mustard (which were good spread on toast as an after-dinner savoury). There were even sweetened butters, including 'fairy butter', which involved hard-boiled egg yolks, orange flower water and sugar. They were good standbys for making sandwiches, or quickly whipping up a sauce.

The dairy at Audley End was built in the 1760–80s, when Sir John Griffin Griffin was owner of Audley End. It originally had an entrance to Lady Griffin's private garden and may well have been intended as a 'hobby dairy', where Lady Griffin could indulge in the then-fashionable pastime of butter-making (always with a maid to get sweaty, of course). However, by 1881 the garden was gone and the dairy seems to have been responsible for providing all the butter used by the house, as well as selling any excess. That said, sometimes extra was needed, in which case it was bought in.

BUTTERMILK AND BUTTER

MAKES ABOUT 400 G/14 OZ
BUTTERMILK AND 600 G/
1 LB 5 OZ BUTTER

1¼ litres/2 pt/1⅓ quarts double
cream

at least 1¼ litres/2 pt/1⅓ quarts
iced water, for rinsing

1–2 tsp salt

To make butter at home, you can use a food mixer – unless you
have a handy butter churn. You can also drastically reduce the
amounts and use a jam (jelly) jar, shaken by hand.

Place the cream in the 'churn' and churn it for about 45 minutes
(or use a food mixer on medium-high speed). It will turn to whipped
cream, then granular whipped cream, and eventually it will separate
completely. Once it separates, keep churning for about 5 minutes.

Drain off the buttermilk and keep for other uses. Add half the iced
water and gently churn again to wash the butter. Drain and repeat
until the water runs clear. Drain, hanging the butter in a muslin
cloth, for at least 20 minutes.

Press the butter repeatedly with paddles to remove any further
buttermilk. Mix in the salt and store in the fridge until needed.
How long you can keep it depends very much on how well you have
removed the buttermilk.

The dairy room at Audley End.

6

Mrs Crocombe's Manuscript

by Annie Gray

This is Avis Crocombe's manuscript book as written. It was probably started in the late 1860s, when Avis was first appointed cook (or cook–housekeeper), and seems to have been kept until the Edwardian period or possibly a little later. Most of it is in her hand-writing, with a few entries uncertain and the last few pages definitely written by someone else.

The commentary is intended to give a bit of context to the recipes, many of which have been tested by our team of professional chefs. It is a mixture of cooking notes (if the recipe is not already included in the book as a modernised version), historical titbits and generally interesting facts.

If you plan to cook any of the recipes which we have not thoroughly tested, there are a few things to remember: firstly, eggs were smaller in the past. We recommend using two thirds of the amount of egg listed in the recipes, or using bantam or pullet eggs. Secondly, as per the notes in the front of this book, all butter is salted unless specified otherwise (unsalted butter was called sweet butter), and it is taken as read that you will adapt seasoning and ingredients to suit your personal taste. Do try to use high-quality bread, such as a yeasted sandwich loaf (not supermarket white sliced). Flour is plain, sugar is best as caster sugar, and all of the measurements she used are British Imperial (i.e. a pint is 20 fl oz – again, see the notes at the front of this book). Lastly, be warned, there are a few – but only a few – alarmingly nasty recipes here.

THE MANUSCRIPT	COMMENTARY

Avis Crocombs Receipt Book

Written in her handwriting, but note the difference in spelling: orthography was still not set and although the name was usually spelt with an 'e' (e.g. on official documents), Avis had only a basic education and seems to have spelt her own name without one. Her spelling can be idiosyncratic, to say the least.

Sponge Cake
recipe on p187

To 14 egg's 1 lb ½ sifted sugar, 1 lb of flour dried and sifted. Wisk the egg's till quite thick then add the sugar, mix it well together, add the flour, and a little orange flower water, a little volatile salts and bitter almonds, have ready your molds well butter'd and sugar'd. Pin band's round the Top and bake in an moderate oven

As this is a fatless sponge, it was also known as Savoy cake.

The bands refer to wet cloths which were fastened around the top and stopped the cake cooking too quickly round the outside, and so peaking in the middle. To replicate them, dampened butter muslin works. It is also possible to buy modern cake bands designed for the same purpose.

Volatile salts were also known as hartshorn or smelling salts – an ammonia solution, which could be created from the horns of the hart (deer) – which can be a challenge to get. It's also easy to end up with a soapy taste if you are not used to them, so use baking powder or another raising agent.

Pound Cake
recipe on p175

1 lb of flour, 1 lb powdered sugar, 1 lb butter, 8 eggs, cinnamon, nutmeg, a little orange flower water, essence of lemon, mix ½ with currants and ½ with seeds to your taste. Bake in a moderate oven

Arrowroot Biscuits
recipe on p176

3 oz of arrowroot, 3 do flour, 5 do sugar, 4 of butter and 2 egg's drop on the baking sheet. With a teaspoon and bake in a quick oven, add orange flower water

'do' means 'ditto', more usually written by Avis as Dº.

Our chefs were particularly keen on these biscuits dipped in chocolate.

Orange Marmalade
recipe on p231

3 doz ½ oranges, first grate the oranges, then half and quarter them, lay the peel in cold water for 24 hours, rub the pulp through a sieve, and boil the peel till quite soft, cut it in thin strips, and boil the pulp with a little grating, and 8 lbs of loaf sugar, for 20 minutes

To Preserve Oranges whole
recipe on p228

After you have cut off the peel. Anything you please. Lay them in water for a night afterwards boil them in a syrup as many times as you please

To Preserve Pine Apples
recipe on p228

Choose the firmest and trim them up boil them in water till quite soft, boil a good thick syrup and put them in for a little time every day until you think they are done. Slice as many as you please and do the same way

This may have American origins.

Soda Cake
recipe on p208

2 lbs of fine flour, 1 lb of sifted sugar, 4 egg's 1 lb of Butter, 1 pint of warm milk, 2 teaspoons full of milk soda, essence of lemon, nutmeg, cinnamon, 1 lb of currants bake an hour in a quick oven.

This is one of several soda cakes.

Lemon Cakes
recipe on p177

1 lb of sugar, ¾ lb of flour, 14 egg's, 2 tablespoonsful of rose water the raspings and juice of 4 lemons. Take your egg's which must be very fresh, and be particular in separating the whites from the yolks, for if you have any of the yolk with the white's, they will not beat up strong, and you will not be able to make this biscuit good without a very good white. To the yolks add the powder, sugar, the lemon raspings the juice, and the rose water beat this well together in a pan with a round bottom till it become's quite light this will require ½ an hour beating put your whites in a round bottom'd pan and wisk them till they will bear an egg which is quite strong enough, put your paste into the whites and mix it very light with a spoon, when well mixed take your flour and sift it and mix it in as lightly as possible. These biscuits are in general baked in small oval tins with 6 or 7 sheets of paper under them in a moderate heat. Butter the tins well as you will find it difficult to take out the biscuits, this is a very good biscuit if well made, take care to ice before you bake them, but very lightly, as the less they are iced the better so that they may be done equally all over.

Copied from William Jarrin, *The Italian Confectioner* (1820).

The phrase 'to bear an egg' was common in 17th- and 18th-century recipe books, so the recipe almost certainly had earlier origins.

Our chefs were surprised how moist these were, considering the lack of butter. As such, though, they do go stale fairly quickly, so eat them quickly (or use them for trifle).

Ginger Bread Cake recipe on p183	1 lb of flour, ½ lb of butter, ½ lb coarse sugar, 1 lb of treacle, ½ oz ginger a teaspoonful of carbonate of soda in a little warm milk. Work the butter in a basin then add the sugar and spice and 2 or 3 egg's, the treacle a little water and the flour by degrees. The milk and soda stir in just before you put in the oven	One of the real favourites at Audley End, done without fail most months. Absolutely superb.
Queen Cake's or Drops recipe on p174	1 lb ½ flour, 1 lb Butter, 1 lb sugar, 14 egg's, ¼ lb of Currants and the rasping's of 2 lemons. Melt your Butter to a cream, in a basin adding the powder sugar with the lemon rasping's and Stirring it for a quarter of an hour with 6 or 7 pieces of cane tied together in the form of a wisk till it become's quite light and white. Have your egg's ready broken in a basin and put in 3 or 4 at a time, allowing an interval of five minutes, and stirring your paste well every time you put in the egg's, when they are properly mixed, stir in your currants being first well washed and pick'd. Then add the flour sifted and keep stirring it for five minutes. These cakes about the size of ½ a crown, are baked in a hot oven with 6 sheets of paper under them.	Copied from William Jarrin, *The Italian Confectioner* (1820). An alternative and better Queen Drop recipe can be found on p245. The even earlier origins – probably 17th century – of this recipe are evident in the use of a twig whisk.
Sponge Biscuits	10 egg's, 1 lb of sugar, 6 oz of flour and raspings of 2 lemons. Keep the white and yolk's of your egg's separate, mixing the sugar and lemon with the yolks. Work them, adding potato, or corn flour. Fill the mold's which must be first butter'd, and then sift some sugar over the biscuits, like the cas'd[?] one's bake them in a moderate heat, and when they are of a fine colour, take them carefully from the molds, and set the glazed side downwards on a sieve that it may not fall	Copied from William Jarrin, *The Italian Confectioner* (1820).
Brown Bread Biscuits recipe on p182	1 lb of flour 1 lb or sugar 20 egg's, the rasping's of 4 lemon's and 6 oz of brown bread. MH[?]	Probably copied from William Jarrin, *The Italian Confectioner* (1820), but with the method left out. This is the original: **Brown-Bread Biscuits** 1lb. Sugar, 20 Eggs, the Raspings of 4 Lemons, 1 lb. Flour, and 6 oz. Brown Bread.

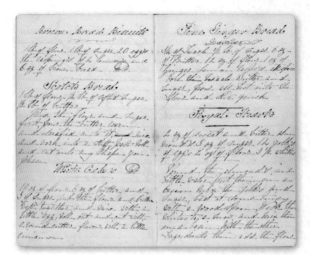

Take your eggs, separate the whites from the yolks, put the pounded sugar and lemon raspings with the yolks into a basin, and stir them with a wooden spoon till light and very white; then whisk up the whites of the eggs to a strong snow, put the paste to them, and mix it very lightly, and sift and mix your flour with the brown-bread, previously crummed. Bake these biscuits in small tins, such as hearts, ovals, and squares, with six sheets of paper under them, in a moderate heat.

This and White Cakes seem to be initialled 'MH'.

Scotch Bread	1lb of flour ¼lb of sifted sugar, ½lb of butter. Mix the flour and sugar first, pour the butter warm and clarified on to it, ~~and~~ mix and work into a stiff paste roll and cut into any shape you please	Shortbread, or a variant thereof.
White Cake's MH[?] recipe on p178	10 oz of flour, 6 oz of butter and 3 of sugar. Rub the flour and butter well together and mix with a little egg, roll out and with a round cutter, flavour with a little cinnamon	Another shortbread.
Fine Ginger Bread	¾ treacle ½ lb of sugar 6 oz of Butter, 12 oz of flour, 1 oz of Ginger Lemon raspe'd, all spice boil the treacle Butter and sugar, pour all hot into the flour and stir quick	This was pretty disastrous when tested – probably needs eggs. It's probably intended to be moulded gingerbread of the sort on p181.
Royal Heart's	2 oz of sweet and bitter almond's, 3 oz sugar, 14 yolk's of egg's, 2 oz of flour 3½ whites. Pound the almond's with little water put them in a basin mix the yolk's and sugar, beat it sometime with a wood spoon, wisk the whites to a snow, and mix them in a basin with the other ingredients then add the flour	A Royal Hearts recipe (without using two different types of almonds) appears in J. Thompson Gill's *The Complete Bread, Cake and Cracker Baker* (1881). The mix is used to fill buttered heart-shape tins.
Peppermint Water	4 dram's of essence of Peppert 1 dram of oil of do 2 lb of loaf sugar 1 Gal of boiling water, pour oil and essence on the sugar, then pour the boiling water, let it stand till cold	Medicinal; peppermint was used for all sorts of ailments.

Thin Hard Biscuits	1 lb of fine flour ½ pint of cream mixed well together into a stiff paste, beat well ½ an hour, roll out very thin and bake in a quick oven MH[?]	'MH' initials floating between this recipe and the next, Little Cakes.
Little Cake's	1 lb of flour, ¾ of sugar, ½ lb of Butter, 1 egg, the rind and juice of lemon, use the greater part of sugar to roll out instead of flour	More a biscuit than a cake, but the names were interchangeable.

Gateau de Pommes
recipe on p84

Boil together for fifteen minutes a pound of well refined Sugar and half a pint of water; then add a couple of pounds of nonsuches or any other finely flavoured Apples which can be boiled easily to a smooth pulp and the juice of a couple of small Lemons. Stew these gently until the mixture is perfectly free from lumps then boil it quickly keeping it stirred without quitting it until it forms a very thick and dry marmalade. A few minutes before it is done add the finely grated rinds of a couple of lemons. Afterwards when it leaves the bottom of the preserving pan visibly dry press it into moulds of tasteful form and either store it for winter use or if wanted for table serve it plain for dessert or ornament it with sprinkles of blanched almonds and pour a custard round it for a second-course dish, entremets.

Sugar 1 lb; water ½ pint: 15 minutes Nonsuches or other Apples 2 lb sugar juice 1 large or 2 small Lemons: 2 hours or more

Copied from Eliza Acton, *Modern Cookery for Private Families* (1845).

La Crème au Nesselrode
recipe on p92

Shell and blanch twenty-four fine Spanish Chestnuts and put them with three quarters of a pint of water into a small and delicately clean saucepan when they have simmered from six to eight minutes, add to them 2 oz of fine sugar and let them stew very gently until they are perfectly tender then drain them from the water, pound them while still warm to a smooth paste and press them through the back of a fine sieve while this is being done dissolve half an ounce of Isinglass in two or three spoons of water and put to it as much cream as will with the small quantity of water used make half a pint. Two ounces of sugar about the third of a pod of vanilla cut small and well rinsed and a strip or two of fresh Lemon rind pared extremely thin give these a minute to boil and then keep them quite hot by the mid of the fire until a strong flavour of the vanilla is obtained now mix gradually with the

This recipe is taken verbatim from Eliza Acton, *Modern Cookery for Private Families* (1845).

Chestnuts half a pint of rich unboiled cream strain the other half pint through a fine muslin and work the whole well together until it becomes very thick then this do it a couple of ounces of dried cherries cut into quarters and two of candied citron divided into very small dice press the mixture into a mould which has been rubbed with a particle of the finest salad oil and in a few hours it will be ready for Table. The cream should be sufficiently stiff when the fruit is added to prevent it sinking to the bottom and both kinds should be dry when they are used.

Chestnuts large 24; water ¾ Sugar 2 oz; Isinglass, ½ oz; water 3 to 4 tablespoonsful; cream nearly ½ pint; vanilla ⅓ of a pod; Lemon rind ¼ of a large: infuse 20 minutes in more unboiled cream ½ pint dried cherries 2 oz; Candied Citron

A Gertude a la Crême
recipe on p94

Slice a plain pound or Rice cake up as for Charlotte a la Parisienne and take a round out of the centre of each slice with a tin cutter before the preserve is laid on; replace the hole in its original form, ice the outside with a green or rose coloured icing at pleasure and dry it in a gentle oven; or decorate it instead with leaves of almond paste fastening them to it with white of egg. Just before it is sent to table fill it with well drained whipped cream flavoured as for Trifle or in any other way to the taste

Copied from Eliza Acton, *Modern Cookery for Private Families* (1845), where it appears as 'Gertrude à la Crème'. The term 'gertrude' must have crept (probably during the typesetting) as a mistake, instead of the French term *guirlande*, meaning 'garland'. Avis accordingly copied it down incorrectly, as 'A Gertude'. The recipe remains known as Gertrude to our brilliant team of chefs, who had a great deal of fun fixing leaves to the outside.

Charlotte a la Parisinne

This dish is sometimes called in England a Vienna Cake and it is known also we believe as a Gateau de Bordeaux. Cut horizontally into half inch slices a Savoy or Spong Cake and cover each slice with a different kind of preserve. Replace them in theire original form and spread equally over the cake an icing made with the whites of 3 eggs with four ounces of the finest sugar. Sift more sugar over it in every part and put it into a very gentle oven to dry the eggs should be wisked to snow before they are used. One kind of preserve instead of several can be used for this dish and a Rice Cake or pound may supply the place of the Sponge Biscuit.

The last in this section copied from Eliza Acton, *Modern Cookery for Private Families* (1845), though there is one more from her later on (Morella Cherries, p247).

Scotch Cake	2 lb of flour 1 lb of Butter 3 oz of sugar add a few seeds but be careful not to put any water to the flour but need flour and Butter to such a degree as you can easily form it into any size or shape you like	Another shortbread. The 'seeds' refer to caraway seeds, a popular flavouring, also valued for their digestive and breath-freshening qualities.
Elder Wine	To 10 parts of juice put 10 parts of water and 15 lb of sugar and ½ lb of Spice of all kinds	Dates to at least the 17th century.
Damson Cheese	Draw down the damson in a jar then pass the pulps and juice through a sieve to each lb of pulp put ½ lb of sugar boil over a quick fire until it will set	Jam-like. Jams have bits, jellies are drained through a jelly bag so that they are clear. This can be put in a mould, but was probably made in a flattish tin, to be cut into squares and wrapped in paper to be eaten when wanted.
Apricot Marmalade	Gather the sweet orange apricot peel them take out the stones put to each lb of fruit ¾ of a lb of Loaf Sugar boil over a quick fire until it will set blanch the [?..orlns] and put in while boiling	The missing word should be 'stones' or 'kernels', but it does not look like either. However, the meaning is clear (the stones add pectin and help it set).
Orange Wafers recipe on p138	2 dozen of oranges cut them in halfs save their rind and put in a large quantity of water to boil until quite tender then pound them in a mortar until quite fine pass it through a hare sieve with the juice and pulp to each pound add ¾ lb of sugar pounded mix it well them spread it on dishes to dry very thin as soon as it is little dry cut it in any shape you like put it on dishes and turn it frequently until quite dry wich will take some days	
Almonds Faggots recipe on p137	1 lb of sweet almonds cut them in long slices ½ of fine sifted sugar the whites of 4 eggs to mix them put your sugar into your bowl mix your eggs wisk to a strong froth put in your almonds till you can see them stand up drop them on wafer papers & bake them in a slow oven	William Jarrin, *The Italian Confectioner* (1820), has a recipe for these, but Avis' is not the same. However, Jarrin does provide guidance on presentation, suggesting the faggots should be piled in pyramids ('small heaps, as pointed as you can').
Mackronis recipe on p126	¾ lb of sweet almonds and a ¼ lb of Butter 1lb & ¼ of Loaf Sugar all pounded together and put through a sieve & then put back in the mortar again. Add six whites of eggs one and half potatoes boiled and mixed with it drop it on wafer paper about the size of a	'Macaroons' in modern parlance. Again, the name relates to macaroni cheese and macaroni men – see p218 for more.

walnut lay little fillets of almonds on the top bake in a slow oven

Another Way	with the same weight of sugar & the same of almonds five whites of eggs no potato and not put through a sieve put the fillets of almonds the same as above Bake in a slow oven	Our chefs found this rather a problematic recipe in comparison to the one above. It is more conventionally 'macaroon' but tends to spread into very thin biscuits.
Shrewsbury Biscuits	12 oz of Butter 12 oz of Sugar 1 lb of flour and 3 eggs well mixed together cut with a round cutter about the thickness of half a crown Bake in a Moderat oven	
Sponge Cake	8 eggs 1 lb of sugar with a cup of water boiled to a strong syrup 12 oz of flour rind of one Lemon Baked in a Moderate oven	
Sirrop for Ices	4lb of sugar to 2 lb of water	A basic syrup for making ice creams, water ices, etc. Most recipes use equal parts of sugar to water.
Queen Drop Biscuits recipe on p174	½ lb of Butter Beet to a cream ½ lb of sugar, 4 eggs ½ lb of Currants ¾ of a lb of flour a few drops of almond flavour drop them on paper	The almond essence is fine, but they are better with lemon zest as in the earlier recipe on p240.
Christmas Cakes	10lb of fruit 8 lb of flour 8 lb of Butter 2 lb of Candied peel about 50 eggs add a little treacle if agreeable Spice according to Taste	A fifth of this recipe fills a 40 cm/ 16 inch tin. It is very dry and rather unpleasant. Probably intended for the servants' hall, based on the quantities and general lack of richness.
Tea Cakes	3 lb of flour 1 lb of sugar ½ oz of caraway seeds ½ oz of [volatile] salts Steep the salts and sugar in one pint of Milk mix them together in the morning Bake in a hot oven	Biscuits, rather than cakes. Intended to serve with tea, hence the name. Good dunked.
Seed Drops	1 lb of flour 1 lb of sugar 1 lb of Butter 8 eggs & a few seeds Bake in a warm oven	Very similar to Queen Drop Biscuits, but not as nice.
Colchester Drops	1 lb10 oz of flour 1 lb10 oz of sugar 1 lb10 oz of Butter 8 eggs. Rub the mixture altogether till a thick cream then put plums on top and bake them in a slow oven on paper	Plums here can be any dried fruit.

Recipe	Ingredients/Method	Notes
Rice Cakes	½ lb of flour ½ lb of ground rice 1 lb of butter 1 lb of sugar the rind of 3 lemons grated work your Butter to a cream add your sugar breke your eggs in one at a time add your flour and rice Bake in a moderate oven	Compare to Rice Biscuits, below – cake and biscuit being used interchangeably.
Bath Buns recipe on p191	1 lb of flour 6 oz of Butter and 5 eggs 1 oz and a half of German yeast and a little milk let it lay ½ an hour then mix in 6 oz of white sugar broken small but not pounded ¼lb of citron mould them to the size wanted	German yeast is basically the stuff sold as 'fresh' yeast today (i.e. compressed yeast). The recipe takes much longer to prove than Avis' suggested half an hour, but she probably used the warming closet in front of the roasting range to boost the heat.
Ginger Bread	2 lb of flour 2 oz of ginger a little salt ½ oz of German yeast brewers yeast a tablespoonful 1pint of milk to rise until quite light then to be kneaded & set to rise until quite light make in one larg loaf or small ones as you like	Very old-fashioned with the yeast rise.
Rock Biscuits	1 lb of flour 6 oz of Butter 6 oz of sugar 4 eggs 12 Drops of essence of Lemon mix well together & put through a forcer Bake in a Moderate oven	'Forcer' refers to a biscuit piping device. A strong piping bag will do the trick.
Rice Biscuits	½ lb of rice ½ lb of flour ½ do sugar ½ of butter 2 eggs	See Rice Cakes above. These can be baked to form soft or hard biscuits.
Cake Lord Berners recipe on p179	¾lb of Butter ¾ lb of Sugar pounded beaten to a cream then add 8 eggs 2 at a time beat it 10 Minutes between each & add 1 lb if flour mix it in lightly ½ lb Sultanas ¼ lb mixed peel Cut in Dice 1 Nutmeg Grated bake in a moderate oven	
Rice Cake Mrs Godard	4 large eggs well beaten with a Breakfast Cup of pounded sugar and the rind of a Lemon then add 3 oz of Butter warmed and a large Breakfast Cup full of wheat & Rice flour, or equal quantity of each beat all well together put then in to Cups & Bake in a moderate oven.	These are lovely, crispy and good.
Souffle Lord Curzon recipe on p90	6 eggs divided the yolkes ½ lb pounded sugar beat yolkes and sugar together for 20 minutes then beat the whites up and mix it all together and bake it for 20 mtes [minutes] if one minute short or over	There was no Lord Curzon at the time Avis copied this recipe, but the likely person referred to is Alfred Nathaniel Holden Curzon, 8th

spoile it. Flavoured with Lemon or Orange these is grt [grated] with in beating the whites and yolkes together having the whites quite light before you put to the Yolks

Baronet and 4th Baron Scarsdale, whose family name was Curzon but whose title was Lord Scarsdale. The recipe was a flop in testing, so our chefs redeveloped it to work.

Black Currant Vinegar recipe on p221	Pick yr currants carefully, weigh them put them in a pan, pour vinegar upon them (1pint to every lb of currants). Bruise the currants let them stand two days, then strain off the liquor, and squeeze the currants thro a strainer. Add 1 lb of lump sugar to each pint of liquor put it over the fire in a stew pan stir it well till the sugar is melted let it simmer (not boil) for about 20 minutes skimming it thoroughly. When quite cold bottle it and seal the corkes.	Superb recipe. The vinegar can be drunk (mixed with water or soda water), used for dressings, or added to sweet and savoury sauces.
Ginger Nuts	Mix ¼lb of ginger with ½lb flour have ready melted ¼lb of Butter with ¼lb treacle & pour this onto the flour and ginger a little orange marmalade improves the flavour make it up into Cakes rather flat or round and Bake in a slow oven the more treacle will make them Softer	Whole recipe is scored out boldly.
Cream Cheese	Lay a wet napkin or cheese Strainer in a deep tart dish. Fill it to the top with very thick cream – let it stand till set. Mind to change the clothe twice a day always wetting it before you put it in the dish – it will be ready for the table in 3 or 4 days	
Dwarf Beens [Beans]	Make a pickle with Salt strong so as to bare up an egg and when cold through on the beens the must be gathered when dry ty them down very close	Possibly from Avis' time as cook–housekeeper at Langley Hall, as preserving was rather a housekeeper thing to do.
Brandy Morella Cherries	Let the Cherries be ripe freshly Gathered and finest that can be had cut off half the length of the stalk and drop them gently into clean dry quart Bottles with wide necks leaving in each sufficient space for four oz of pounded sugar fill them up entirely with the best french Brandy the fruits be sifted through with a neaedle Corke them Closeley	Copied from Eliza Acton, *Modern Cookery for Private Families* (1845). Acton adds to this 'the fruit will not shrivel if thus prepared. A few cherry, or apricot kernels, or a small portion of cinnamon, can be added when they are considered an improvement.'
Curing Hams	10lbs salt 3 oz treacle 3 oz pepper 6 Gil water Boil all together when quite cold put in the Ham. It should remain in for 7 weeks	Not something to be done at Audley, but it probably was done by Avis as a teenager at her brother's farm.

Raspberry Cakes	Take any quantity of fruit you please. Weigh and boil it when mashed. When the liquor is wasted add as much sugar as was equal in weight to the raw fruit. Mix it very well off the fire till the whole is dissolved then lay it on plates dry in the sun when the Top part dries cut it off into small cakes and turn them on a freash plate when dry put in Boxes with Layers of paper	A similar recipe, not completely verbatim but very close, appears in Elizabeth Hammond's *Modern Domestic Cookery* (1816) and also later – probably copied from Hammond – in John Edward Watson's *The Housewife's Directory* (1825), and others.
College Puddings	Take 2 spoonfuls of flour 3 eggs three quarts of a pint of new milk sugar and nutmeg to your taste put them in cups well Buttered currants may be added if approved of to be covered with wine sauce the cups must be only half filled. If you wish them rather richer take 3 spoonfuls of flour, 5 eggs leaving out the white of two and a pint of Milk.	Good; essentially a steamed sponge pudding. Do in dariole moulds or tall muffin tins.
Swiss Pudding recipe on p91	Take 2 oz of sugar, a Teaspoonful of water put these into a stew pan of a quart size and of such form as to make a mould, Boil this until it is Brought to a fine colour, Take the stew-pan from the fire and turn it about in every direction so as to make the sugar cover every part of the stew-pan Take the yolks of 8 eggs and the whites of 2 make a custard of them with a pint of unsweetened Milk. Put it into the stew-pan prepared as above, steam it one hour when it is nearly cold turn it out in a flat dish and take off all the brown syrup wich will come from it. Take a ¼lb of sugar rinds of 2 lemons and the juice of one a cupfull of water and one of sherry. Boil these in another stew-pan untill the ingredients have come to a thick syrup take out the lemon peel and pour it quickly over the pudding the last thing so that it may go to the Table with a fine Glaze	Essentially a crème caramel, and an easy one. Our chefs said it was both delicious and reasonably foolproof.
French Pan Cakes	½ pint of cream whipped untill thick the yolks and whites of 4 eggs beaten together – then mix wt the cream 12 tablespoonfuls of flour to be lightly whipped into the above this put onto 6 sheets well Buttered and Bake for a few minutes Place two together with fruits between	Not pancakes in the strictest sense, as these are more like sheet cakes and are served like the French mille-feuille. The mix is very delicate and hard to handle. Works fried as well as baked. For a true pancake, see recipe on p114, which is the recipe we worked with for the YouTube video.

Preserved Lettuce	Peel some young lettuce stalks stewed them in a weak salt & water for 12 hours then set them on the fire in cold spring water make them simmer not boil. Make a good syrup to ½ pint of water 2 lb sugar put as much Jamaica ginger when the syrup is put on to boil as you like boile the syrup dayley throw over the lettuce until the become feet for use	Compare to the recipe in Theodore Garrett's *The Encyclopaedia of Practical Cookery* (c.1891) – it's a different recipe, but the same principle. Preserved lettuce derives from the 17th-century French *gorge d'ange* (angel's throat), which was the candied core of the lettuce. Our chefs tested this and reported that it was pretty disastrous.
Soda Cake	2 lb fine flour, 1 do sifted sugar, 1 do butter, 4 eggs a little warm milk, 2 teaspoonfuls soda, 1 lb Currants	Yet another soda cake. Cheap, easy and cheerful.
~~**Brezelent[?] Cream**~~ **Lemon Sponge**	1 oz Isinglass ½ lb sugar 3 Gils of Water rind of a lemon put on the fire when all dissolved add 5 yolks of Eggs juice of 4 lemons or more if you think it requires it Rub one lemon on a syrup of sugar this all together put on the fire to set stirring it all het time when fairly cold whip two Whites of Eggs this well in and put in Your Mould	Recipe unchanged, just the title amended.
Eves Pudding recipe on p209	6 oz Bread Crumb 6 Do fruit 6 D° Raisins & six of Apples chop the Apples & Raisins to gether rather fine 3 eggs a little Milk boil 3 hours serve with melted butter with a little Brandy	D° is ditto.
Arrowroot Souffle Pudding	2 Table Spoonfuls of Arrowroot ½ pint of Milk a small piece of Butter sugar to taste 4 yolks of Eggs whip the whites Garnish with Dried Cherries or sultanas Arrowroot and Brandy sauce	Needs the garnish.
Cream Cakes	2 oz Butter 2 oz flour 2 of white Sugar one Egg beat all well together Line the Tartlet tins with paste put a small quantity of jam in each and cover it with the mixture	
To make Tomata Sauce recipe on p78	Take them when ripe bake them in a oven till the are tender skin and rub them through a sieve to every pound of Pulp put one quart of Chili Vinegar, one ounce of Garlick one Do Shallots half an ounce of Salt ½ D° of Ground White Pepper. Boil the whole till it is tender, pass it through a sieve, then add to every pound the juice of three Lemons boil it again till it looks smooth and the thickness of Cream. Let it stand till cold and then Bottle it.	Copied from Richard Dolby's *The Cook's Dictionary* (1830). D° is ditto.

Ginger Bread Biscuits	1lb flour ¾ Do Treacle ¼ D° Course Sugar ¼ D° Butter little Spice ¼oz Ginger	D° is ditto.
To Preserve Oranges or Lemons	Cut a hole in the stalk first the size of a shilling and with a small blunt knife scrape out the Pulp quite clear without cutting the rind. tie each separately in muslin and lay them in Spring Water changing the water twice a day in the last boil them until they become tender on a slow fire observe that there is a enough at first to allow for wasting as the must be covered to the last to every 1 lb of fruit sugar 2 oz double refined sugar and one pint of water boil the two halves together with the juice of the oranges to a syrup and clarify then strain well and let it stand to be cold the boil the fruit in the syrup for one hour if not clear do this daily until they are done Pare and core some Green Pippins and boil in water till it tastes strong of them do not break them only gently press them with the back of a spoon strain the water through a Jelly Bag till quite clear then to every fruit put a 1 lb of Double refined sugar then put and juice of a lemon and boil to a strong syrup drain off the syrup from the fruit and tendering each orange with the hole upwards the pan pour the Apple over it the bits cut out must go through	Copied from Richard Dolby's *The Cook's Dictionary* (1830).
Lemon Cheese Cakes recipe on p120	Grate the rind of two lemons in 1 lb loaf sugar Break in small Pieces ¼ fresh Butter 6 yolks of Eggs 4 Whites juice of 3 Lemons put all in a stew-pan. Stir on the fire till the sugar is dissolved. Stand at the side till it begins to thicken like Honey a Teaspoon full of Grated Biscuit will make a Dish this mixture will keep any time tied down in jars	
Brown Meal Cakes recipe on p215	1 lb of Brown Meal add a quarter of Butter a little salt two Teaspoons baking Powder mixed with cold Milk Rather dry roll the Paste rather thick cut with a Tin Biscuit Cutter bake in a very Quick oven 10 minutes	
Buns	1 lb Butter flour ¼ Butter ¼ sugar ¼ currants one Egg two teaspoonfuls Baking Powder mix with cold Milk Bake in a Quick oven.	

St Clair Puddings

1 oz Gelatine put it to soak in a basin in ½ pint cold milk for ½ an hour Boil I pint of Milk and add it gradually to the Gelatine and 3 yolks of Eggs sugar and flavour to taste put on the fire keep stirring till it begins to thicken but not allow to Boil strain through a fine sieve or strainer just before it is cold add a little whipped Cream will be a great improvement pour in small moulds or cups with a little jelly at the bottom or without set in a cold place

A set custard – one of a number in the manuscript.

Arrowroot Biscuits

3 oz of Arrowroot 3 of flour 5 of sugar 4of butter 2 eggs flavour to the taste work the sugar and butter first then add the root & eggs lastly the flour drop onto the baking sheet with a teaspoon in a quick oven by adding a little more flour convert in to a Paste roll out and cut with a cutter by doing this you may have two Kinds under one Trouble

Note the practical advice at the bottom!

Orange Marmalade
recipe on p231

12 oranges slice 6 and boil quickly with 6 pints of water until you can mash them with a wooden spoon pass through a Jelly Bag to each pint allow 1 lb sugar the remaining 6 boil so you can pierce with the head of a pin to each 3 lb sugar one pint of water out the sugar in the pan add the chips boil altogether- syrup Boil until it clings to the spoon add the chips boil altogether until you think it is done
1870 8 Doz oranges

To Roast a Swan

Take 3 lb of beef beat fine in a Mortar Season with pepper salt mace nutmeg onion will heighten flavour. Put it into the swan tie it up tight with a small piece of Tape that the gravy & other things may not escape A meat paste rather stiff should be laid on the breast and some whited brown paper should cover the rest 15 minutes at least ere the swan you take down pull the paste off that the breast may get brown

This and the gravy recipe on p252 are taken from the instructions habitually sent out with swans from Norwich. Written as a rhyme in the original, Mrs Crocombe has tweaked it, but it is clearly the same basic text. In the 1870s she worked about 9 miles from Norwich, but this may be coincidence, as Norwich swan breeders advertised that they could send their swans wherever needed. The rhyme is quoted in a number of contemporary sources, including Alexis Soyer's *The Gastronomic Regenerator* (1846) and Henry Coleman Folkard's *The Wild-Fowler* (1859).

Here is the original:

To Roast a Swan.

Take three pounds of beef, beat fine
in a mortar:
Put it into the swan—that is, when
you've caught her.
Some pepper, salt, mace, some nutmeg,
an onion,
Will heighten the flavour, in Gourmand's
opinion.
Then tie it up tight with a small piece of
tape,
That the gravy and other things may not
escape.
A meat paste, rather stiff, should be laid
on the breast,
And some whited-brown paper should
cover the rest.
Fifteen minutes, at least, ere the Swan
you take down,
Pull the paste off the bird, that the
breast may get brown.

The Gravy

To a gravy of beef good and string you'll be right if you add ½ pint Port wine pour this through the swan then serve the whole up with some hot Currant Jelly

Original instructions for the gravy:

To a gravy of beef, good and strong,
I opine
You'll be right if you add half-a-pint
of port-wine;
Pour this through the Swan – yes, quite
through the belly;
Then serve the whole up with some hot
currant-jelly.
N.B. The swan must not be skinned.

Orange Wafers

Take 4 dozen of the thickest seville oranges squeeze out the juice take out the cores and boil the peels in about 3qt of water till tender. Take them out and dry them of the water. Chop them very fine then put them in a mortar with exactly their weight in sugar pound two hours. Spread on tins with a long knife dry them before the fire slowly they must be cut before they are quire dry in any shape and kept in a tin box.

Pouding de Pommes a la Frangipane	Peel and core 12 apples, slice them into a deep Dish over which shake some powder sugar then spread it over with apricot or other jam and very thin slices of fresh Butter over that take an oz of arrowroot and mix with it a pint of cream sweeten to taste stir it over the fire till it begins to thicken boil then lay it over the Apples and Bake it in a moderate oven. If the Arrowroot should be too thick add a little milk so that it will just pour out of the Stewpan	Copied not quite verbatim from Richard Dolby's *The Cook's Dictionary* (1830), in which he calls it Apples à la Frangipane: **Apples à la Frangipane** *Peel and core a dozen apples, slice them into a deep dish, over which shake some powder sugar, thinly spread it over with apricot jam, and very thin slices of fresh butter over that mix an ounce of potatoe flour with a pint of cream, a small bit of butter, and sugar to sweeten it; stir it over the fire till it begins to boil, then lay it over the apples, and bake in a moderate oven.*
Chutnee	4llb of either toms Apples Peaches or Rhubarb after the skins and stones have been removed ½ oz of Cayenne 2 of Garlic Ginger Salt 2 lb of Crystallised Brown sugar 2 of Sultanas chopped 2 qt of Vinegar simmer the fruit in 1 qt vinegar until pulpy mix all the other ingredients together simmer for 10 minutes in the other vinegar mix both together & Bottle it for use the longer it is left the better it becomes	
Brown Bread Pudding recipe on p116	½ lb breadcrumb ¼ of butter mix Peel sugar to tast a little black jack 3 eggs keep the whites separate and whip light a little wine or Brandy Serve with Wine or Brandy Sauce	American origins – note use of term 'black jack'.
Orange Marmalade	1 Doz Oranges sliced ½ boiled in water till soft enough to mash with a spoon pass through a Jelly Bag to every pint 1 lb sugar grate & boil the other ½ whole till soft enough to pierce with a Pin head strain on a sieve cut them in qrt take out the pulp cut in strips to every 1 lb one of sugar ½ pint of Water boil all together Reduce to a strong syrup add the Chips boil although til you think it is done try on a plate Put the pulp through a tammy add enough to make 6lb from what was passed through the Jelly Bag ¾ sugar to each ill boil well together over a quick fire till it clings to the spoon	This is the third recipe for orange marmalade! See p231.

Ginger Beer	12 Gallon of water 1 lb stone ½ lisbon sugar the whites of 12 eggs well beaten mix all well together put it on the fire when near boiling skim it when it does boil add 12 oz best Ginger a little bruised when it has boiled ½ an hour pour it on 14 lemons which must have been peeled very thing and cut into thin slices when it is about the heat of new milk pour it in the Cask with the rind of the lemons only a larg spoonful of new yeast ½ oz of Isinglass bung it close when it has been 3 weeks or a month in cask bottle it cork it well and it will be ready to bring in 3 weeks	Makes a nice beer, not very fizzy or sweet.
Cream Cheese	Take a small Wooden Box What holds 1 pint or 1½ of Cream Lay a Cloth in it & pour that quantity of cream into it seal it well from the air or any earth that might get in & lay the box for 24 or more 48 hours when the cream will become solid	Untested!
Rhubarb Jam recipe on p222	¾ brown sugar to 1 of fruit to every 10 lb of fruit 4 Lemons juice and rind cut fine	Lovely.
Orange Jelly	To every lb of bitter oranges put a quart of water. Grate a little of the rind of the oranges. Cut them in small slices and put them on to boil till the water is half boiled in. Then strain it through a Jelly Bag. To every pint of juice, 1¼ sugar. Boil it till it jellies. The largest of the seeds to be left out as they make it rather strong	Not a jelly jelly (in the British sense of a wobbly pudding), but a jam jelly.
Almond & Potatoe Pudding recipe on p80	Blanch a ¼lb sweet almonds & boil in ½ pint new milk for 20 minutes then pound them to a soft paste dissolve in the milk ¼lb butter and 6 oz cold mealy potatoes roasted or steamed to a fine powder grate the rind and strain the juice of a larg lemon grate the six part of a nutmeg beat 5 freash eggs yolks and whites separately mix these ingredients altogether adding the whites of the eggs last beat for ¼ of an hour or longer butter a tin mould bake in a quick oven for 40 minutes turn out carefully and serve at once the top may be strewed over with sweet almonds chopped to the size of Split Peas. May 20. 1875	Copied verbatim from Anne Eliza Griffiths' *Cre-Fydd's Family Fare* (1864). 
Beignets a la Royale recipe on p131	¼ lb parmesan cheese 4 yolks of eggs ½ pint milk cayenne & salt about a spoonful of made mustard & a tablespoonful of good white stock a little cream or pat	A tricky recipe, which needed a lot of work. However, the simple expedient of not warming the milk fixed it –

of butter put on the milk cheese to warm the pass through a hair sieve then mix all the other ingredients together butter some timbales moulds & steam them 20 minutes when cold cut them rather thick egg & bread crum them fry in boiling fat strew cheese over them

otherwise the whole thing splits. Our chefs also adjusted the egg amount.

Luncheon Cake

1 lb Sultanas 1 flour ¼lb moist sugar 1¼ butter to be rubbed into the flour 2 oz candied Peel – a Teaspoonful of Carbonate Soda dissolved in ½ a pint of new Milk lukewarm & 1 Egg to be put into the oven immediately

This is typical of the era. Luncheon cake was the generic name used for a soda-raised cake, usually done as a tray bake.

Soup Maigre
recipe on p31

To make Potage au purée de navets take 8 or 10 Turnips two heads white celery & two larg Onions, mince them small put ¼lb fresh Butter in a clean Stewpan let the whole stew very quickly until tender have ready some Broth wich is made from some fresh Bones moisten the puree with a sufficiency of this liquid & rub the whole through a Tammy add cream & Season to palate warm in a bain au Maire or else it will curdle.

'Bain au maire' is Avis' dreadful spelling of bain-marie.

Salt Beef (Pressed)

To a piece of Brisket of Beef 10 or 12 lb weight Take 1 lb of butter ½ moist sugar a little salt-peter the size of an Egg Rub the Beef well with it. Let it remain in the pickle for a fortnight – Boil it very slow for 5 Hours take out the Bones and put it between 2 Dishes with a heavy weight on it

---

Poulet à la Sartere
recipe on p159

Audley End
Cut up a cold fowl (boiled or roast) sauce yolk 1 egg, a spoonful of mustard, a little tarragon, chervil & burnett, chopped very fine, season with pepper & salt mix it well in a bason with a little oil & vinegar until it becomes thick

'Audley End' is noted above.
The sauce is basically mayonnaise.

Fig Pudding
recipe on p101

Take equal quantities of figs bread crumbs, suet & sugar. Mince all up fine together season with cinnamon, nutmeg & a little brandy put in a pinch of C. soda butter a mould and boil it for 3 hours or more according to Size

'C. soda' is carbonate of soda.

Pickle for Tongue

2 lb Saltpetre – 2 D° Salt 2 D° Brown Sugar – 9 days in Pickle is enough – in summer more salt is required – the Tongue should hang till tender before it is put with Pickle

D° is ditto.

Rabbit Soup recipe on p29	2 killed fresh stewed well with 3 onions and 2 sticks of celery in 2 quarts of water then pick all the meat from the bones pound it well in the mortar and rub it through a tammy. Make it quite hot for dinner but take particular care it is not allowed to boil when quite hot to send to table put some cream and the yolks of 2 eggs to 2 full quarts soup 2 spoonfuls of cream is sufficient NB half the above for a small party if for company 2 Chicken instead of Rabbits make an excellent soup, if with veal a Knuckle is required.	This works with any meat.
Breast of Mutton recipe on p57	Boil the mutton for 3 ½ hours if quite tender take out all the bones & lay it between 2 Plates with a weight put on the upper one – then rub a very little butter on it with yolks of Eggs & bread Crumbs & broil it Plain gravy or brown sauce with Chopped Capers in the dish	
Mutton Cutlets recipe on p55	Take a rack of mutton, cut the Cutlets thick, lay them in a Stewpan with 2 onions a little pepper & about a pint of stock stew them very gently for an hour or an hour & ½ till quite tender – when done put them on a dish & another over then with a weight to press when quite cold pare them nicely & put them again into a Stew pan with a spoonful or two of Stock & a little glaze turn the Cutlets tow or 3 times & Serve very hot.	Neck cutlets are best, as they take slow cooking, but it can be done with beef or veal as well.
Aspic Jelly for Brk or Luncheon recipe on p160	A set of larg pigs feet & lard stewed till quite tender & bones taken out Have ready a rich scoured jelly well flavoured with mushroom Catshup put it to the feet & lard & warm them up, pour into a mould, putting in layers of hard boiled Eggs cut into slices, turn out & serve	'Brk' is breakfast.
For 2nd Course for 2 Persons recipe on p162	Bruise 2 anchovies in a mortar 20 oysters chopped fine and mixed with the anchovies & heated with 2 teaspoonsful of cream stirring all the time, Spread on hot Toast	This would also work as an after-dinner savoury.
Marionade of Chicken recipe on p53	Lemon Peel or lemon juice, few allspice or few cloves & 2 or 3 bay leaves put into a basin of water in this soak for 4 or 5 hours the divided joints or pieces of chicken. When taken out sprinkle them with salt and pepper, dip them into a batter of the consistency of thick cream & fry them a pale brown	Our chefs loved this, and called it VFC (Victorian Fried Chicken).

Curried Eggs
recipe on p166

Take 2 eggs To tablespoonsful of cream beat them together adding a teaspoonful of curry powder and a little salt. Melt a piece of butter in a pan put in the eggs and keep stirring til the are soft. Serve on a piece of hot buttered toast. 2 minutes sufficient to cook this dish

Particularly good with goose eggs.

Fillet of Beef Parisian
recipe on p66

Cut a piece of the Fillet crossways including some fat the thickness of an inch, beat it slightly flat with a chopper, set on a Gridiron, put it on a very sharp fresh fire turn it 2 or 3 times, when ½ done season with ¼ of a teaspoonful of salt ¼ that of Pepper put on a hot plate rub over with one ounce Maitre dhotel butter served up with fried Potatoes

Eggs with Cheese
recipe on p169

Boil eggs hard, halve them and take out the yolks. Mix the yolks well with a little grated cheese salt and nutmeg mustard & a very little Crumbs of Bread. Put this again into the white part of your eggs and serve it with white or brown sauce or toast – this may be done without the Grated Cheese

These can be done as Avis suggests, but in testing we preferred to add a bechamel sauce, which makes a smoother and more modern (for the 1880s) result.

Buttered Eggs

~~Cut in slices & stewed with white~~
Put 2 oz of Butter in a stew pan Break 3 eggs stir it with a knife till done then spread it on toasted Bread

Each word of the first line of text is crossed out.

A simple, effective recipe for scrambled eggs. As ever with eggs, cook very slowly on a very low heat to avoid rubberiness.

Hard Boiled Eggs

Boil 3 or 4 hard cut in halves and ½ Teaspoonful of Harveys 1 Teaspoonful of Cinnamon a little Thyme Parsley Chervil and Tarragon Added to a little good stock & poured over

Essentially hard-boiled eggs with a sauce. Harveys was similar to Worcester Sauce: a spiced condiment sold in bottles.

To Stew Truffles

After having thoroughly washed the Truffles let them simmer gently for 6 or 7 hours, or longer if they feel hard in some Good broth, ½ a Bottle of sherry then small carrot & one onion. Cut in pieces, a good bunch of Parsley with some Thyme & bay leaves tied up with it. just before serving the Truffles they must be taken from the liquor & put into a clean stew pan with ½ a Glass of sherry and placed over a very slow fire. The stewpan being covered till they have absorbed the brine they must then be served very hot Fresh Butter should be handed round with them the above may

Truffles were a luxury then as now, and the inclusion of this recipe is a reminder than Avis Crocombe cooked for the aristocracy. However, it's as economical as such a recipe can be, with the advice that the liquor can be reused.

appear rather too expensive way of dressing Truffles but the liquor will serve for any number of time you may want to dress the Truffles, and be improved every time it is served – of course the quantity required must be kept up occasionally adding a small quantity of broth & a glass of wine now & then the Truffles that may be left should always be kept in the Liquor

Windsor Sandwiches recipe on p127	¼ lb tongue – ¼ lb parmesan 1 oz of butter and a little Cayenne, pound all together and pass it through a sieve. Cut the bread to fancy and then put the preparation between. Dip them in Butter and parmesan and fry them a light brown	
Spong Cake Pudding recipe on p163	Cut your Spong Cakes in slices long ways Butter your mould and stick the slices of Spong Cake round it placing the slices the brown and white part alternately round it. Then make a good custard and pour it in the middle of the mould and steam it 1 hour Wine sauce round it	Note that this method (of sticking the slices of cake to the mould with butter) gets round the difficulty of stopping the cake floating upwards when filling the mould with custard.
Custard Pudding (very good) recipe on p100	1 oz isinglass to stew with ½ pint cream till it is dissolved – then take the yolk of 7 eggs well beat, then put in a pint & ½ of cream. Put it over the fire to boil. Stir it till it gets thick, then strain it through a silk sieve, also strain the isinglass and put them altogether. Sweeten to taste, put in a little orange flower water & some Brandy, put it into a shape & do not turn it out until it goes to table. The tins must be put in cold water for a moment before the puddings are put on the Dish, put some Wine Sauce or Currant Jelly round the Dish	This is, indeed, very good.
Brussels Cream	To a Table Spoonful & half of Ground rice add Cream to fill a moderate sized Mould Rub the peel of a lemon on some sugar, add a lump of Butter the size of an Egg, put it on the fire to boil stirring it continuously, let it boil 5 Minutes Add a ¼ of an oz of clarified Isinglass sweeten to taste Put the whole in a Mould on Ice & when cold & served up, pour a little Melted Currant Jelly around the dish – the rice must not be thicker than Bread Sauce	Essentially a blancmange. It could also be served for luncheon or as a servants' dish.

Birkenhead Pudding	6 oz bread Crumbs – 6 do beef suet finely Chopped, 6 oz moist Sugar, the rind & juice of ½ a lemon one Tablespoonful of Brandy one of Cream one small pat of Orange marmalade Chopped fine Mix all well together & boil 4 hour	Jam suet pudding. Ideal for servants. Elevated by the brandy in this context. It would also work for luncheon or supper, or as an upper servants' dish.
Madeira Pudding	Line a dish with puff paste cover the bottom with Apricot jam ½ an inch thick put 4 yolks Eggs with pounded Sugar then add a Teacup of good Cream – or milk & 2 Glasses of Sherry pour this into the Dish & bake a light colour & serve it hot	'or milk' written in pencil
Suet Pudding recipe on p154	½ lb suet ½ do bread crumbs ¼lb sugar rind of 1 lemon grated. 2 eggs. A tea cup full of milk beaten up with the eggs ½ Teaspoonfull Baking Powder. Wine Sauce	
Cheese Seftons recipe on p129	½ lb of Cheshire Cheese grated 2 handsful of flour a pinch of Cayenne pepper. Mix this with ¼lb butter & rub it into a stiff paste, roll it into narrow strips & put into a very moderate oven for a few minutes. Not to be Brown.	There were many recipes for Seftons – all probably based on Louis-Eustache Ude's original, 'Ramequins à la Sefton', which appears in the 1829 edition of *The French Cook*. The recipe was named for his employer at the time, the Earl of Sefton.

There were many recipes for Seftons – all probably based on Louis-Eustache Ude's original, 'Ramequins à la Sefton', which appears in the 1829 edition of *The French Cook*. The recipe was named for his employer at the time, the Earl of Sefton.

Later versions appear in Alexis Soyer's *The Modern Housewife* (1849), which has several variants of the recipe, as does Eliza Acton's *Modern Cookery for Private Families* (1845). Isabella Beeton's *The Book of Household Management* (1861) and Charles Senn's *The New Century Cookery Book* (1901) also have versions.

All are based on puff pastry with cheese layered into it: the presentation with roundels also occurs in several of the above (as well as Margaret Fairclough's *The Ideal Cookery Book* of 1911).

Another variant can be found in Anne Eliza Griffiths' *Cre-Fydd's Family Fare* (1864), which we know Mrs Crocombe consulted for at least one other recipe. They are called cheese

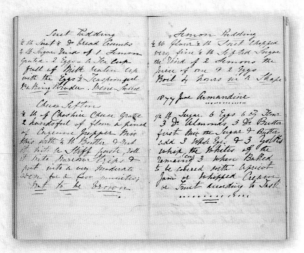

biscuits and are a straight mix, no puff pastry.

As an alternative to the puff version, our chefs tested a basic cheese straw and reported that it was delicious. Mix 55 g/2 oz/½ cup flour, 115 g/4 oz/1 cup Cheshire cheese, a pinch of salt, 55 g/2 oz/¼ cup butter, a pinch of cayenne, 1 egg yolk and 1 tsp water into a stiff paste, roll out thinly and chill for at least an hour. Cut into straws and chill again for 20 minutes before baking for 10 minutes at 170°C/340°F.

Lemon Pudding	½ lb flour ½ lb suet chopped very fine ½ lb sifted sugar the rind of 2 lemons the juice of one & 2 eggs. Boil 4 hours in a shape	Lovely.
1877 June Armandine	½ lb Sugar 6 Eggs 6 oz flour 3 do almonds 3 do butter. First mix the Sugar & Butter add 3 whole eggs & 3 yolks whip the whites of the remaining 3 when Baked to be covered with Apricot Jam or Whipped Cream or Fruit according to Taste	Rather a fancy way to present a sponge: ideal for an aristocratic sweet.
Rice Cakes	½ lb Flour ½ Rice ½ Sugar 1 Teaspoonful Baking Powder 1 or 2 Eggs & little warm milk ¼ lb Butter. Essence of lemon	
Cake Pudding	3 oz Butter 6 loaf Sugar 5 flour 4 Eggs well beaten let all this be well mixed & then put them into cups Twenty minutes will bake them. Serve with Sauce	Yet another variant on the theme of sponge cake, this is a steamed sponge, made in individual moulds. The numbers refer to ounces, and the sauce could be Wine Sauce or any other sweet sauce.
Castle Puddings recipe on p103	Equal weight of eggs, flour, white sugar & butter flavoured with a little lemon baked in coffee cups or small Pudding Moulds great care should be taken that they are sufficiently done a very little more than ¼ lb of each of these ingredients will make 5 Puddings – the Eggs should be weighed in the shell the puddings are served with a little pounded loaf sugar over each wine sauce in a boat	

Madeira Pudding	Line a Dish with Puff Paste cover the bottom with Apricot jam ½ a inch thick Put 4 yolks of Eggs with pounded sugar then add a Teacup of good Cream & 2 Glasses of Sherry our this into the Dish & Bake a light colour serve hot	This is exactly the same as the previous recipe for Madeira Pudding on p259.
Buttered Eggs	Put 2 oz Butter in a Stew Pan Break 3 Eggs Stir it with a knife till done then spread in on Toasted Bread	This is exactly the same as the previous recipe for Buttered Eggs on p257.
To Cure a Tongue	Rub in well 1 ½ oz Salt petre let it remain 4 hours – then clean the Tongue from the Salt petre & Rub in well together 1 lb Com. Salt ½ moist Sugar at them and aft 5 days it will be fit to dress. Boil very Slowly	Fairly standard recipe for a cure. Most tongues would have come ready-cured from the butcher, as they tend to today.
Biscuit Pudding	weigh 3 or 4 Eggs – the same weight of flour, Loaf Sugar, & Butter Mix the Sugar & Butter well together Bake them in Tea Cups ¾ of an hour in a moderate over & serve them with Wine Sc.	An absolutely standard sponge cake recipe, with all the ingredients in proportion to the eggs. Note the use of tea cups to bake in – a lovely example of the devolution of high-end material culture throughout the country house. Compare to Cake Pudding on p260. 'Wine Sc' is wine sauce.
Apples & Cream in a Mould recipe on p97	1 oz Isinglass dissolved in ½ pint of water strain it add a pint of Lump sugar & the peel of 1 lemon with a little Noyeau if agreeable to flavour it. Then the Apples as for a Charlotte but let them cool. Put the Cream into the mould & a small Quantity of Apples at a time or the later will break the cream, for the[y] should be in the midst of the mould remain so when Dished up	Noyeau refers to Crème de Noyaux, which is an almond liqueur. 
Gateau de Pommes recipe on p84	1 ½ lb lump sugar put into 1 pint of water. Let it boil until it is sugar again – add 2 lb apples pared and cored a peel of a large lemon, boil altogether till quite stiff then put into a mould & turned out when cold with a thick custard round it	The second recipe for gâteau de pommes (apple cheese).
Mock Brawn	Take the Head feet, & ears of a Pig & salt them a week then boil them till the bones come out. When quite hot break it well up into a stew Pan and Pick all the bones out let it remain in the stewpan till cold & then turn it out a proportion of Cow Heel if you have it is an Improvement	Originally brawn was pork shoulder brined, poached and sliced. By the 19th century it was more often the brawn which is common in Britain today: head meat which had been boiled and, usually, put into a basin with a little of

the boiling liquid and pressed beneath a weighted dish. This sort of brawn looks like a course terrine. The use of 'mock' here suggests it is a 17th- or 18th-century recipe, when both types of brawn co-existed.

Pudding à la Victoria recipe on p83	4 oz Citron 4 preserved Cherries 9 of Green Gages split 3 of fresh butter ½ Jordan Almonds 2 tablespoonfuls of moist sugar 4 penny Spong Cakes soaked in milk 2 Eggs & a small quantity nutmeg Lemon Peel & juice the Citron to be cut in small pieces Almonds split to be made in a plain mould lined with the ingredients and part mixed to be steamed 2 Hours and served with sauce of equal parts of thin Arrow-root & Red Currant Jelly.	The numbers, up until Jordan almonds, refer to ounces.
Sultana Pudding	½ lb Sultanas ½ Suet Chopped fine a teacupful Bread Crumbs 2 eggs well beaten a teacupful of Milk a little Ginger & nutmeg half a wineglassful of Brandy boil 3 hours	Another suet pudding; fairly plain but tasty.
Croquettes de Parmesan	4 oz parmesan cheese 2 Do butter 1 yolk egg a little cream pound altogether whip the white on one larg Egg	
Croustard au Parmesan recipe on p134	Cut some Slices of Bread with a Round Cutter fry them in Butter add the same ingredients as Above	
Boston Cream	Ten pints of water, 3 lb loaf Sugar, put into a pan and boil, then pour into a bowl and stand till quite cold, then add ¼lb Tartaric Acid two teaspoonfuls of Essence of Lemon and the whites of three eggs beaten to a froth, Bottle and it will keep for months, – Drink a small quantity of carbonate of Soda, half a glass of the Cream, and fill up with water	Possibly medicinal.
Meat Jelly	Lean Beef (fillet) Veal, & Mutton each 1 lb Cut up small & put into a Saucepan w water simmer (but do not let it boil) by the Side of the fire for 8 hours strain the liquid (from a small Quantity of tasteless fibre that remains) let it Jellyify into a Soft mass A Teaspoonful occasionally Recommended by Dr Bradbury of Cambridge	Medicinal, clearly, and intended for the sick or elderly. See p155.

Ginger Beer recipe on p223	1¼ Lump Sugar ¾ oz Ginger well pounded, the peel of 1 Lemon cut very thin put them into a Pitcher then add eleven pints of boiling water, stir the whole then cover it up – when cooled till only milk warm put 2 Spoonfuls of Yeast on a piece of Toast hot from the fire add the juice of the lemon – let it work for twelve hours strain thro a muslin & bottle it – it will be fit to drink in 4 days "The Field" Newspaper. Copied from Lady B. Brook. A.E	A rare mention of Audley End. We once forgot a batch of this for a year and then sent the interpreter playing the gardener off with a couple of bottles. He drank both and promptly fell asleep under a tree. The visitors thought it was part of the show.
Ramakins recipe on p125	2 oz old cheese, 2 Do stale bread each grated very fine, 3 Eggs well beaten Sufficient cream to mix into a thick batter, 2 Teaspoonsfuls of Mustard, a little salt & Cayenne pepper fill the papers ¾ full a few minutes will bake them	Note the use of papers. Ramekins as dishes to hold food are first recorded in the *OED* in 1895.
For a Fondue	Grate ½ lb Cheshire Cheese Add 4 eggs well beaten a Teacupful of Cream & 1 oz milked butter 2 Teaspoonfuls of bread Crumbs bake it one hour	Less of a fondue in the modern sense than a cheese custard.
Orange Cream	The juice of 4 Oranges yolk of 4 Eggs beat very well, sweeten to taste, set it on a gentle fire stirring it one way till it is a thick Cream	Orange curd by another name. Good on toast or as a tart filling.
[untitled]	1 ½ Oz Salts 1 oz Cream of Tartar 1 slice of Lemon, pour one pint of hot water over the lemon let them stand for one hour then dissolve the Salts and Cream of Tartar	Possibly medicinal, or a very tart lemonade. Quite revolting.
Dec – 1889 **Lady Abbess Puddings**	Take of pounded sweet Almonds ¼ lb moisten them with cream oz orange flower water pound these to a stiff mass in a mortar fill 12 small tartlets tins with the mixture bake in a moderate oven until baked a light brown colour have ready some whipped cream cover them thickly with it place a dried cherry in the centre of each Pudding	This recipe is called Lady Abbess Puffs in Eliza Acton's *Modern Cookery for Private Families* (1845), *Cassell's Dictionary of Cookery* and Maria Rundell's *A New System of Domestic Cookery* (1806). Cassell's has a pudding but it is different. This recipe and the one below are in a different hand – it is not known whose.

Dec 1889 **Swiss** ~~Puddings~~ **Baskets** recipe on p103	Take 6 castle puddings & scoop out the centre of each one a little then roll them on a plate with red currant jelly spread upon it have ready some finely chopped pistachios then lightly sprinkle some over each pudding fill the centre of each basket with whipped cream and place a narrow strip of angelica across to form a handle to the basket and place a crystallised cherry on the centre of each one or a strawberry	The same hand as the recipe above.
English **Chutnee** recipe on p227	4 lbs sour apples after being peeled & cored, 1lb raisins, 2lbs sultanas, 4 lbs moist sugar, ½lb green ginger 4 oz salt, 2 oz garlic, ¾oz chilies fresh & green or ¼oz dry, 4 oz mustard seed, 2 bottles of vinegar, juice of half a lemon. Cut the apples rather small sprinkle salt on them, let them stand one night then strain off the water & boil them in a bottle of Vinegar put by till cold, boil the sugar into a thin syrup, pound the chilies & ginger very fine mince up the other things very fine & mix all together put into the sun daily for a month.	From here to Chocolate Pudding the handwriting has changed again; it is neither that of the previous two pages, nor of Mrs C. It may be the hand of her step-daughter.
Ginger beer	8 quarts of water, 2 lemons, 2 lbs of loaf sugar, 2 oz of whole ginger, 1 oz cream of tartar, the whole of one egg, tablespoonful of yeast. Slice the lemons, bruise the ginger, add the sugar on which pour the water boiling, when nearly cold add cream of tartar whole egg & the yeast. Well stir & let stand for 12 hours then skim, strain & bottle. It is ready for drinking in 24 hours.	The same hand as above.

Amber
Pudding
recipe on p217
	1 pot of orange marmalade, 6 oz of suet, 4 ozs bread crumbs, 3 eggs & boil for 3½ hours.

		The same hand as above.
		   A completely different recipe to the standard amber pudding, which is an orange curd baked in pastry (compare Dolby, Rundell and others).
		   One of the chefs' favourites in testing – they said the fantastic, sharp flavour really belied the basic nature of the recipe.

Friars omelet	8 oz of large apples, 2 oz fresh butter, sugar to taste & some bread crumbs. Boil the apples to a pulp, stir in the butter & add the founded sugar when cold add in egg well beaten up, then butter the bottom of a deep	The same hand as above.

baking dish & strew the bread crumbs so as to stick over the bottom & sides, put in the mixture & strew bread crumbs plentifully over the tops put it into a moderate over & when baked turn it out and put powdered sugar over it.

Meringue of any kind of fruit recipe on p113	Thick custard at the bottom, fruit next, custard again and then fruit again & another layer of custard & the whipped whites of egg & sugar together on the top. Bake a short time until golden brown	The same hand as above.
Chocolate Pudding recipe on p89	½ lb chocolate, 5 oz breadcrumbs, ¼lb caster sugar, ½ pint milk, 4 eggs & 5 oz butter. Put the chocolate, milk, crumbs & butter in a stewpan to thicken. When quite thick put into a basin, Divide the yolks from the whites & cook the yolks well up with the sugar & add to the other ingredients. Then well whip the whites & add. Mix all slightly pour into a mould and steam one hour. Serve very hot with cream in a jug. It is very nice cut in slices & eaten cold as well as hot	The same hand as above. Very similar to the recipe in Eliza Walker Kirk's *Tried Favourites Cookery Book* (1900).
Colettes D Oeufs	4 hard Boiled Eggs Cut in Squares ½ pint Bechamel Sauce, with raw yolks of Eggs a little Tongue Truffle mushrooms little Cayenne pepper & salt when cold flour egg & breadcrumb & frying fat serve with fresh parsley.	Back to Mrs Crocombe's handwriting and fluid grammar, this is clearly a recipe for cutlets of eggs, or egg cutlets, with the title in French. Like that of so many cooks, her French is phonetic. The mixture is used to make small cutlet-shapes. Dip each into flour then egg then breadcrumbs and fry.
Cheese Favourites	Put a teacupful of water into a saucepan, add 1 oz of Butter let it boil up put 2½ oz of flour into it stir it till Quite smooth little C/pepper & Salt break 1 Egg mix thoroughly add 1 more egg mix smooth 1 oz Grated Parmesan Cheese when all are well mixed take a Collander hold it over frypan of hot lard & fry & serve Hot.	A lovely way to make curly cheesy mini-doughnuts. Wear protective sleeves.
Pyramids au Parmesan	Put a little aspic jelly in the bottom of some timbale moulds allow it to set before putting in the Cheese mixture ½ Pint custard 2 yolks of Eggs 1 oz cheese pepper & Salt to taste half an Ounce Gelatine to set	These should, clearly, be done in small pyramid moulds. Intended as an after-dinner savoury. Note use of aspic, now freely available ready-made

Custard pour the mixture in in the moulds when Cold turn out garnish with chopped aspic a spray of tarragon on each one

in a tin. Earlier recipes call for calf's foot jelly. Time has moved on!

Yorkshire Cake

One egg, its weight in flour, butter, ground rice and sugar. One teaspoonful of baking powder and a very little milk: mix all together spread over 2 dessert plates well buttered and bake from 10 to 15 minutes when finished slip them off the plates spread preserve upon one and press the second cake gently on the top then sprinkle with caster sugar.

This is written in the third new hand in the book – Mrs Crocombe's handwriting does not appear again. As with the previous two different hands, this belongs to an unknown other: possibly Edwardian, but more likely 1920s or 1930s.

Wine Sauce
recipe on p105

1 gill of water
2 tablespoons of Apricot Jam
1 ounce of Caster Sugar
squeeze of lemon
a glass of sherry or claret

American Ice

1 pint of new milk
½ oz Gelatine
2 oz Caster sugar
2 new laid eggs

American Ice Cont
Soak the gelatine in milk for ½ an hour put it on to boil keeping it stirred all the time, add sugar, separate the whites from the yolks beat yolks & add to milk, boil up again then add the whites which have been beaten into thick froth, add little vanilla to taste beat up well together put in mould.

This recipe, and the one above, are laid out as we would expect a modern recipe to be – with a clear list of ingredients followed by, in this case, the method.

This is not an ice. It is a plain mousse. Do not leave out the vanilla – but other flavourings also work.

Egg Savoury (cold)

Boil 2 eggs for 10 minutes
Leave till cold in a bowl of water
Shell & cut length ways in halves. Take out the yolks, pound the yolks in a mortar with a small piece of Butter a tiny piece of minced cold (lean) bacon, finely chopped parsley, & a little pepper & salt. Fill the whites with this mixture & serve with a little green round.–
   Salad or water cress does.

[some pages following cut out, followed by blank pages]

This is a much older recipe than that above, and is probably Victorian in origin. Compare it to the earlier Curried Eggs on p257.

Cheese Fritters

¼ of... ...
2 ...ful of flour
a pinch of Cayenne pepper
+ ... butter

Make first a paste, + then rub
the ... above into the paste
... of making a puff paste
using a moderate heat, ...
for a very short time. Do not
oven.

BIBLIOGRAPHY AND GENERAL READING

Cookery books

*denotes a book we know was used by Avis Crocombe

Anon (c.1875, and later editions), *Cassell's Dictionary of Cookery*

Acton, Eliza (1845, and later editions until 1918), *The English Bread Book*

*Acton, Eliza (1864, and later editions), *Modern Cookery for Private Families*

Beeton, Isabella (1861, and numerous later editions), *The Book of Household Management*

Bishop, Frederick (1852, and later editions), *The Illustrated London Cookery Book*

Byron, May (1914, and later editions), *Pot-Luck*

*Dolby, Richard (1830, and later editions), *The Cook's Dictionary*

Fairclough, Margaret Alice (1911), *The Ideal Cookery Book*

Farmer, Fannie (1918 rev. edn), *Boston Cooking School Cook Book*

Folkard, Henry Coleman (1859), *The Wild-Fowler*

Francatelli, Charles Elmé (1846, and later editions), *The Modern Cook*

Garrett, Theodore (ed.) (c.1891), *The Encyclopaedia of Practical Cookery*

Gill, J. Thompson (1881), *The Complete Bread, Cake and Cracker Baker*

Gouffé, Jules (trans. Alphonse Gouffé) (1867), *The Royal Cookery Book*

*Griffiths, Anne Eliza (1864, and later editions), *Cre-Fydd's Family Fare*

Hammond, Elizabeth (1816), *Modern Domestic Cookery*

*Jarrin, William (1820, and later editions), *The Italian Confectioner*

Jewry, Mary (1868, and later editions), *Warne's Model Cookery and Housekeeping Book*

Kirk, Eliza Walker (1900), *Tried Favourites Cookery Book*

Kitchiner, William (1817, and later editions), *The Cook's Oracle*

Marshall, Agnes (1885, and later editions), *The Book of Ices*

Raffald, Elizabeth (1769), *The Experienced English Housekeeper*

Rundell, Maria (1806, and later editions until about 1911), *A New System of Domestic Cookery*

Senn, Charles Herman (1901, and later editions), *The New Century Cookery Book*

Southgate, Henry (1874, and later editions), *Things a Lady Would Like to Know*

Soyer, Alexis (1846), *The Gastronomic Regenerator*

Soyer, Alexis (1848, and later editions), *Charitable Cookery, or, the Poor Man's Regenerator*

Soyer, Alexis (1849, and later editions), *The Modern Housewife*

Soyer, Alexis (1854, and later editions), *A Shilling Cookery for the People*

Ude, Louis-Eustache (1813, and later editions), *The French Cook*

Watson, John Edward (1825), *The Housewife's Directory*

General reading

Girouard, Mark (1985), *The Victorian Country House*

Gray, Annie (2017), *The Greedy Queen: Eating with Victoria*

Horn, Pamela (2015), *Ladies of the Manor*

Palmer, Marilyn and West, Ian (2016), *Technology in the Country House*

Pennell, Sara (2016), *The Birth of the English Kitchen, 1650–1850*

Sambrook, Pamela (2002), *The Country House Servant*

Sambrook, Pamela and Brears, Peter (2010), *The Country House Kitchen 1650–1900*

Stobart, Jon and Hann, Andrew (2016), *The Country House: Material Culture and Consumption*

Plus, for something a little different, the magnificent *The Victorian Kitchen* and *The Victorian Kitchen Garden*, two series produced by the BBC in the late 1980s and never bettered.

ACKNOWLEDGEMENTS

Annie Gray would like to thank Kathy Hipperson and the many women who have played Avis and her kitchen maids, putting in many hours on recipes and bearing with me when I nicked all their props; Andrew Hann for being my partner in crime since that memorable phone call in 2009; Bethany Fisher for researching sources; at English Heritage, Gareth Clifford, the mastermind behind the videos, and Dominique Bouchard; Jonny Walton, who filmed the videos, and the cast: Lucy Charles (as Fanny Cowley), Tracy Russell (as Elizabeth Warwick), Benjamin Lawrence (as Edgar Ashman) and Kiel O'Shea (as James Vert). Thanks to Sophie Wright, food stylist extraordinaire; and the crack chef team of Miranda Godfrey and Ian Sutton aided by Li Ting Hsu. Thanks also to Westminster Kingsway College for kind use of facilities. Personal thanks to Matt Howling for putting up with me writing yet another book when I said I was taking a break, and to Richard Gray and Jess Smith for scraping me off the floor when the need for cup measurements finally sent me over the edge.

Andrew Hann would like to thank Jan Summerfield, Bryony Reid, Shelley Garland, Phillipa Mapes and the rest of the English Heritage team who helped make the service-wing project such a success back in 2008.

Both Annie and Andrew would like to proffer huge thanks to Katherine Davey, editor extraordinaire, for sterling work in the face of endless cup measurements, obscure fart gags and all of the minutiae of life in the Victorian country house. Finally, we would both like, of course, to thank Bob Stride for generously donating the recipe book to English Heritage, opening up a window into the past for us and our visitors.

INDEX

Page numbers in *italics* refer to illustrations.

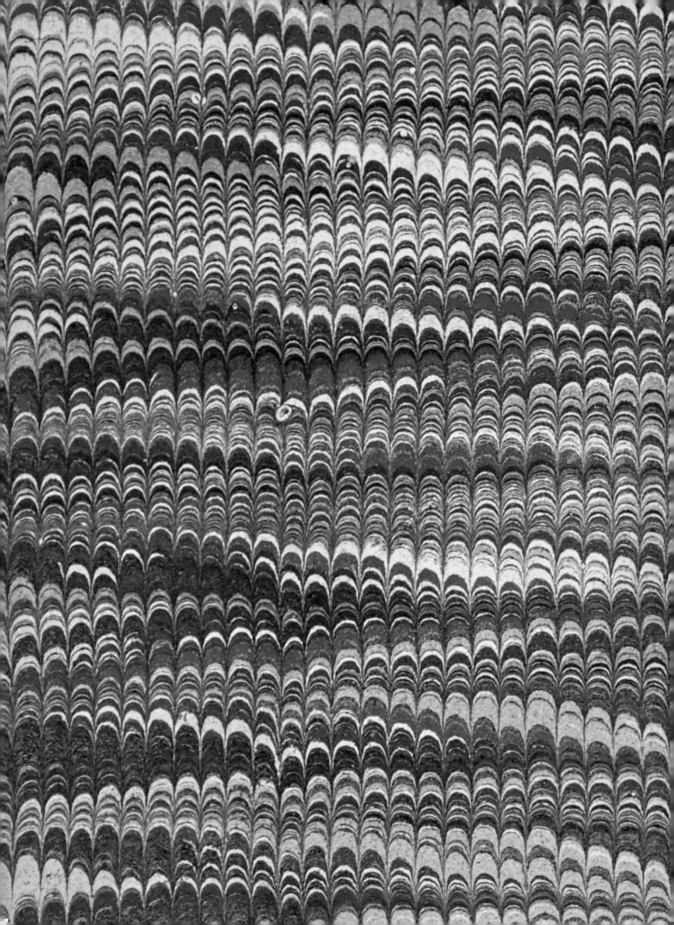